PLACE IN RETURN BOX to remove this checkout from your record.
TO AVOID FINES return on or before date due.
MAY BE RECALLED with earlier due date if requested.

DATE DUE	DATE DUE	DATE DUE
MAR 1 6 2010		

2/05 p:/CIRC/DateDue.indd-p.1

D1264034

People of the Dream

People of the Dream

MULTIRACIAL CONGREGATIONS
IN THE UNITED STATES

Michael O. Emerson with Rodney M. Woo

PRINCETON UNIVERSITY PRESS
PRINCETON AND OXFORD

Copyright © 2006 by Princeton University Press
Published by Princeton University Press, 41 William Street,
Princeton, New Jersey 08540
In the United Kingdom: Princeton University Press, 3 Market Place,
Woodstock, Oxfordshire OX20 1SY

All Rights Reserved

Library of Congress Cataloging-in-Publication Data

Emerson, Michael O., 1965–
People of the dream : multiracial congregations in the United States / Michael O.
Emerson with Rodney M. Woo.
p. cm.
Includes bibliographical references and index.
ISBN-13: 978-0-691-12451-3 (alk. paper)
ISBN-10: 0-691-12451-5 (alk. paper)
1. Race relations—Religious aspects—Case studies. 2. Religious institutions—
United States—Case studies.   3. United States—Race relations—Case studies.
I. Woo, Rodney M., 1962–   II. Title.

BL2525 E47 2005
277.3′083′089—dc22   2005049941

British Library Cataloging-in-Publication Data is available

This book has been composed in
Printed on acid-free paper. ∞
pup.princeton.edu

Printed in the United States of America

10 9 8 7 6 5 4 3 2 1

To Ace, Juice, Principessa, and Snowflake —
always you will be my buds.
—M.O.E

To my father and my mother, who instilled inside of me
a passion for all races to be in the same community
of believers, and to my wife and sons, who
have shared this journey with me.
—R.M.W.

Table of Contents

Acknowledgments

No BOOK is written alone. My greatest fear is forgetting someone who contributed, and to those of you who I fail to name here, I apologize.

I began this study knowing next to nothing about multiracial congregations. I read the few books I could find on the topic, and then called the author of two of those early books, Charles Foster of Emory University. He was kind enough to talk to me about what he had learned in his study of three multiracial congregations in Atlanta, and made important suggestions for my study. As I outlined what we needed to know about multiracial congregations, I knew it was going to be a large study that must have a national focus. It was going to cost money and take time.

After talking to a number of friends and colleagues about the idea, including Christian Smith, Johan Sikkink, and Greg Keith, I wrote a letter to the Lilly Endowment with my idea for a national study of multiracial congregations, to see if they might be interested in funding such a study. I was a junior faculty member at the time, had yet to publish a book, and had never directed my own large-scale research project. But Chris Coble, Craig Dykstra, and others at Lilly had interest in the topic, and invited me to write a full-scale proposal for funding.

In writing the full proposal, a key need was to find coresearchers. The project was too big for one person. I read a book called *Beyond Black and White*, by George Yancey, and thought that Yancey was a sociologist who seemed to have the training and interests necessary to be part of this study. I took a risk and called him. We had never met and he had never heard of me. But after listening to what I was proposing, he said the timing was perfect. He was thinking of doing a similar, smaller scale study in Milwaukee. He agreed to join me. I am most thankful that he did. He made contributions I could not have. My sincerest thanks to him for joining me in this research and working tirelessly on it. I gained a new friend and colleague.

We needed a third person to join us. Steve Warner, in addition to being a top scholar in the field, is known as someone who is well connected and willing to help younger scholars. Though he did not know me, I called him asking if he could recommend anyone to serve as a coinvestigator on the project. He took the time to talk with me about what sort of person I was looking for, and then recommended Karen Chai Kim, a graduate student at Harvard finishing her dissertation on Korean Buddhist and Christian congregations. She turned out to be a perfect recommendation, and for his recommendation, his encouragement, support, and top-notch research, I thank Steve Warner.

I called Karen, told her about the project, and asked if she would consider joining the research team. After giving it some thought, she accepted. Her views as a well-trained ethnographer, and as an immigrant and Asian American, gave perspectives to the project otherwise not possible. She too worked tirelessly, and made many sacrifices so the research could be completed. The project also benefited from her seemingly endless network of friends and acquaintances. I am grateful to have found in her not only a fine colleague on the project, but as with George, a lifetime friend.

This book could not have been written and the project from which it derives could not have been conducted without the handsome support of the Lilly Endowment, and the help of Chris Coble and Craig Dykstra. They took a chance on this grant. I hope it has been worth it.

Thank you to the many people in the many congregations that participated in this project. Thank you for taking time to share your thoughts and feelings about your lives. A special thank you to the people of Wilcrest. Thanks for living your lives. Thank you to the staff at Wilcrest. And a colossal thank you to Rodney and Sasha Woo. Clearly this book would not be what it is without your years of help and effort. All the best!

Thank you to the aging scholars. You know who you are. I also thank, in alphabetical order, Nancy Ammerman, Eduardo Bonilla-Silva, Sharon Bzostek, Esther Chang, Mark Chaves, Brad Christerson, Dan Dehanas, Curtiss DeYoung, Helen Rose Ebaugh, Korie (spell it right!) Edwards, Tim Essenberg, Sally Faubel, Roger Finke, Tyrone Forman, Bob Groux, David Hartman, Scottye Holloway, Jim Hurd, Leo Gabriel, Charles Gallagher, Rachel Tolbert Kimbro, Amanda Lewis, Valerie Lewis, Karen McKinney, Pedro Moyo, Roy Patterson, Jen'nan Read, Paul Read, Mark Regnerus, Judy Rodriguez, Wade Clark Roof, Sarai Sanchez, Harley Schreck, Perry and Joyce Thinesen, and Darwin Zitzloff (I actually don't know Darwin well at all, but we went to the same high school, and because I began this list with the letter A, I thought it would be nice to end it with the letter Z).

The final year of writing this book was an unusual one. My family and I moved from Rice to Notre Dame and back to Rice. Thanks to both institutions for their support of this work. At Rice I thank Bob Stein and everyone in the sociology department, including the postdocs I have worked with—Jen'nan Read, Michael Aguilera, and Elaine Howard Ecklund. Special thanks to Chandler Davidson, Elizabeth Long, and Bill Martin. At Notre Dame I thank Mark Roche, Dan

Myers, Maureen Hallinan, David Hachen, Johan Sikkink, Rory Mc-Veigh, and the students of the graduate seminar in race and ethnicity.

Donna Ring helped shape this book without even knowing it. She invited me to teach a Pew Summer Graduate Seminar on race and religion, which forced me to think more deeply about the issues. She also has engaged me in a number of discussions and pointed out sources of which I was not aware. Thanks also to the graduate seminar students, who worked hard and were willing to debate ideas. Many of them are going to have fine academic careers. I gave a number of talks and presentations of portions of this book's material while writing it, and thank all the participants of these sessions who asked astute questions and made helpful suggestions.

I am most appreciative of Bernadette Escamilla's contributions. She formatted this book, searched for sources, faxed materials, ordered books, and did many other detail tasks necessary to complete the work.

A special thanks to Fred Appel, who made this a much better book by forcing me to think and write better. He is skilled at his profession. Jodi Beder did an extraordinary job copyediting this book, and deserves a special thank you. Christian Smith, Valerie Lewis, Ed Blum, and two anonymous reviewers read and commented on the all or the majority of this manuscript. I am most appreciative of their efforts. They helped improved the book. Of course, any weaknesses and controversial positions are mine.

Thank you to Winfred and Stephanie Neely, Earnest Gray, Aaron Johnson, Keith and Janice Parnell, and all the fine people of Living Hope. You nourished our souls during the final months of writing this book. We thought we would be with you much longer than we were, but we are grateful for our time together. Thank you for accepting us.

Family is where it is at. Mom, Dad, Ann, Rick, Karin, Abby, Maria, Uncle Dick and Aunt Barb, and the others of the extended Ferreras, Puglisis, and Emersons, and mom- and dad-in-law and the Severson clan (twenty-some nieces and nephews and counting). Most importantly, to Joni and the dudes and dudettes — eternally grateful that we share life and love together.   M.O.E., Chicago, IL

There would be no Wilcrest story apart from the staff and members of Wilcrest. My thanks go to the members of Wilcrest, who took an enormous risk to call a 29-year-old pastor named Woo, to lead an all-white congregation in decline on its journey to become a multiracial congregation. We have labored together, cried together, laughed together, and dreamed together. The church not only walked with me, but provided time and resources to enable me to write what was being lived out on a daily basis. I also want to thank our entire staff, but especially Monty Jones, our worship leader, who has been stretched beyond his wildest imagination. Finally, I want to thank my wife, Sasha, who believed in me and the dream when no one else did. Without her pouring her encouragement into me and into the church, especially during some of blue times, I am not sure if this dream would ever have become a living reality.   R.M.W., Houston, TX

People of the Dream

As I DRIVE westward from the center of Houston down Bellaire Boulevard, I cannot but help notice the transitions. Passing through a white neighborhood that gives way to a predominately Latino neighborhood, I am presented with yet another change. The names of businesses, the street signs, even the requisite "First Month Free" banners on the apartment complexes are in Mandarin Chinese and Vietnamese lettering. Houston's new Asiatown announces itself in large and small ways. In the typical Houston sprawling fashion, this Asiatown stretches for miles in a bewildering series of strip malls and stand-alone buildings, many in varying Asian architectural styles.

Now, ten miles out from the center of the city, I pull up to a stoplight and wait to turn left onto Wilcrest Avenue, just a block away from the original location of Wilcrest Baptist Church, one of the congregations I have been studying for a research project. The stoplight is taking interminably long to change to green. I notice the children waiting to cross the street, the people entering the restaurants and shops, and, just off of the main streets, others sitting outside on their front steps. Every major racial group is represented at this intersection. Many are immigrants from Mexico, Cuba, Haiti, Vietnam, or Nigeria, while others, especially the blacks, whites and some Latinos, are multi-generation Americans. The neighborhood is not pretty. Many houses have mildew on them, the paint long since faded; the streets and sidewalks need repaving. It has seen better days, though there is new development — especially a few blocks down, where the shiny Hong Kong Mall stands proudly. This is a working-class neighborhood, its residents too busy making a living to spend much time beautifying it. But the area buzzes with activity and hopes for better lives to come just around the corner.

During the 1960s, a tumultuous time when America profoundly changed and Wilcrest Baptist was founded, this neighborhood looked very different. In 1968, the year of Martin Luther King's assassination, this location was not part of Houston as it is today, but was Alief, a burgeoning suburb swelling with young middle-class white families moving into their recently built homes. As residents living here during these early days reported to me, one could hear the hum of newness, excitement, youth, and optimism throughout this community of Alief.

Increasing the draw of Alief's newness and the affordability of the homes was the feeling of some, especially young white families with children, that they were being pushed out of Houston. Desegregation in the Houston schools had not yet occurred to any significant degree, but the Federal government had recently ordered the district to desegrate. In the next few years, big changes were in store for Houston schools. In the mid-1960s, Houston witnessed riots, racial conflict, and a rising murder rate, pushing it up to the nation's fourth highest murder rate. With the changes in immigration resulting from the 1965 Immigration Act, a growing number of Hispanic and Asian immigrants were arriving in the city. The unsettled times and many whites' attitudes toward racial minorities were more than enough to push large numbers of young white families outward toward suburban areas like Alief. In addition, newly arriving white families, moving to Houston at a rapid rate, flowed to these outlying areas. The Houston metropolitan area was growing fast, and Alief reflected that growth.

Back in Houston proper, some of the members of Sharpstown Baptist Church recognized the population trends and cast their eyes westward toward Alief, an area ripe for a new Baptist church. After some discussion, Sharpstown helped purchase land in Alief for the new church, and agreed to sponsor the fledging congregation, starting by sending a few families from Sharpstown. While the building was under construction, an interim pastor served the congregation. In 1970, Wilcrest had its official beginning with its first full-time pastor, Reverend Ed Welsh. Drawing on the rapid growth of the neighborhood, Wilcrest Church itself grew at a rapid rate. By 1974, Wilcrest added a second service to accommodate all of its members. The congregation also began planning for a new, larger building for worship and for religious education classrooms.

In 1979, wanting more time to tend to a needy son, Pastor Welsh resigned. He was replaced by the Reverend James Windom in 1980. As Alief continued to boom—the population quadrupled between 1970 and 1985—Pastor Windom oversaw continued growth in the church. Times were good at Wilcrest.

However, changes were in store. Though resisted by many in the area, Houston progressively annexed Alief. No longer an outlying suburb, Alief was now only one neighborhood among many in the massive city of Houston. Then, in 1986, the oil bust hit Houston like a meteor storm. Jobs vanished, and many people, in need of work, moved on. The neighborhood in which the church was situated saw great declines in its population. Wilcrest's attendance dramatically declined.

In the late 1980s, the Houston economy began to recover, and people began moving to Alief again. But these were different sorts of people. The neighborhood, merely a few years previous nearly all white, was by 1990 nearly 80 percent non-white, a mix of African Americans, Hispanics, and Asians. Despite the recovery of the Houston economy and population, no such improvement occurred at Wilcrest. By 1990, the church's membership and attendance had declined to less than 200, down from more than 500 during its peak.

Eager for new members, the pastor had teams of members go door to door to invite people to the church. But, according to the members I interviewed, something about the process was puzzling. Every time they gathered to invite new people to the church, the pastor sent them a few miles west of their present neighborhood, to the newly developing suburbs. He was consciously choosing the strategy of passing over the racially and economically changing neighborhood surrounding the church and instead was sending the members to outer neighborhoods, populated by people of the same race and class as Wilcrest members. It took a while for the members to realize what was happening. When they did, they had mixed reactions.

The strategy, it turns out, was and is a popular one. It even has a name — the homogenous units principle. Church growth books have been written advocating the concept that bringing in people highly similar with regard to characteristics like race is the fastest way to grow congregations, that congregations using the principle run more efficiently, and that people in homogenous congregations find them more fulfilling.

Pastor Windom took this principle seriously. At a church leaders' meeting one Sunday afternoon in 1990, he presented his strategy for the congregation's ministry. He recommended that they sell their current building and property, and move to one of the neighborhoods where he had been sending people to knock on doors. He was so serious about this proposal that he had already identified a potential new site and building. He asked for the church leaders to approve this plan.

In the minds of the church leaders (called deacons in this congregation), this was a momentous decision. They called a special meeting to discuss the pastor's proposal. Some, the strongest supporters of the pastor believed they should move, as the pastor recommended. After all, they were a white church, and whites were heading further west, out of Alief. As a church, these were the people they could best serve, helping to instill faith via a culture in which whites felt at home. To stay true to their mission, they should follow the people. More pragmatically, if they were to survive as a church, surely they would have to move. They could sell their building to one of the many non-white congregations seeking a home. But a few other deacons felt that they were meant to stay in their present neighborhood, regardless of who lived there. Such a decision might mean remaining a small congregation or it might mean trying to attract white families from outside the neighborhood. But most assuredly it also meant seeking to attract the people of the immediate neighborhood.

With great earnestness, the deacons discussed and prayed. The decision these church leaders' were about to make—to go or to stay—would have tremendous ramifications for the future of the congregation, and they knew it. They called for a written vote. After tallying up the results, one of the leaders stood up to announce the results. "Allow me to have your attention please. The votes have been cast. We have made a decision. . . ."

CHAPTER ONE ▪ Dreams

Michael O. Emerson and Edward J. Blum

THIS BOOK is an in-depth study of contemporary multiracial religious congregations. Its goal is to both understand religious life in the United States, and learn something about the future of race relations in the United States. "Sunday morning is the most segregated hour of the week." This quip, or some version of it, is said so often that it seems many people have become numb to it. I have never been able to verify who first said it. Some say Martin Luther King; others attribute it to people much before his time. The saying's meaning—that people are most racially segregated during the time of their religious gathering—is taken as such common knowledge that people usually do not give it much thought.

Despite a world in which racial separation in religious congregations is the norm, some congregations are racially mixed. I thought it would be fascinating to study these congregations, which are rare enough that for many people they are exotic. It seemed to me that by understanding such multiracial gatherings of religious people, we could understand much larger issues at the core of living in this complex and ever-changing place called the United States. This nation, like others, is growing increasingly diverse, both racially and ethnically. Much debate swirls around topics related to this growing diversity, such as the appropriate model for race relations and cultural continuity, and how new immigrant groups will fare relative to racial and ethnic groups already in the United States. Part of this debate is about the role of religious congregations for immigrant groups and group survival. Will they worship in ethnic congregations or in other types of congregations? How about their children? What will this mean for race relations?

Religious congregations are a specific type of organization—a private, volunteer organization—and together these organizations constitute a specific type of institution—what we may call a *mediating institution* between the small private worlds of individuals and families and the large public worlds, such as politics, the educational sys-

Edward J. Blum, a historian of race and religion in the United States, coauthored this chapter.

tem, and the economy. For these reasons and for reasons discussed in the next section, studying multiracial congregations provides an opportunity to better understand larger issues of race, religion, and American identity through organizations and institutions.

We have so many questions that need answering. How do racially mixed congregations come to be? How common are they? Who attends these congregations? How did their members get there? What are their experiences like? What contributions to and detractions from improved race relations and equality, if any, do these congregations make? Do these congregations tell us anything about the changing nature of race and ethnicity, or about religion?

In the chapters to come, based on extensive research, I seek answers to all of these questions. I find that multiracial congregations are atypical, more racially diverse than their neighborhoods, places of racial change, and filled with people who seem to flow across racial categories and divisions. They are filled with a different sort of American. As I explain later in the book, I call them "Sixth Americans," and they may be harbingers of what is to come in U.S. race relations. I also find that multiracial congregations entail risks—such as the misuse of power to squelch cultural practices and, in some cases, to maintain inequality—and payoffs—such as providing supportive places for cultures to be practiced and taught to a variety of people and, in some cases, to reduce inequality. Whether one thinks multiracial congregations are a "good thing" rests in part on how one evaluates these risks and payoffs.

WHY CONGREGATIONS?

If we want to fully understand race relations in the United States, we must understand the role of religion.[1] If we want to understand religion in the United States, we must understand its core organizational form—the religious congregation. I use the term "religious congregation" to mean any regular gathering of people for religious purposes who come together to worship, have an official name, have a formal structure that conveys a purpose and identity, are open to all ages, and have no restraints on how long people may stay. A gathering of college students on campus every Friday night for worship is not a congregation, then, because, among other reasons, it is only open to students of the college, and its members must leave when they graduate. Congregations are typically associated with a place where the

[1] Emerson and Smith, *Divided by Faith* (2000).

congregating occurs, but this place — a mosque, temple, church building, synagogue, or any other place of worship — can change as the congregation's size or resources change. There are over 300,000 congregations in the United States, making them the most common and widespread institution in the nation.[2] They are more common than all McDonald's, Wendy's, Subways, Burger Kings, and Pizza Huts, combined. (In an interesting twist on this fact, when a McDonald's closed a couple of blocks from my home, a Pentecostal congregation bought it. Now instead of serving one-minute hamburgers, the still-McDonald's-looking building serves up fervent three-hour worship services.)

The majority of Americans will regularly participate in or visit a congregation in any given year. In a fifteen-nation study, the United States scored highest in religious membership (55 percent), and had membership rates twenty or more percentage points higher than every other nation in the study except Northern Ireland.[3] To varying degrees, more than one hundred million Americans are involved in religious congregations.

Congregations are the places where Americans most often go to seek the meaning of life, to worship, to find direction, and to receive social support. Major life events happen within these groups. Religious congregations are where very many newborns are officially recognized and welcomed into the human community, where Americans most often get married, and where people most often gather to say goodbye to deceased loved ones and friends.

But the role of congregations goes far beyond these essential functions. Clergy and congregations are the number one place Americans turn to when they have serious problems, more than the government or human and health service professionals.[4] Professor Ram Cnaan of the University of Pennsylvania School of Social Work found in his extensive study of congregations that they serve as one of the most critical safety nets for the nation's poor, with three-quarters of congregations having some mechanism for assisting people in economic need.[5] In fact, in this same study, Cnaan and his colleagues found that congregations provide service in more than 200 areas, including recreational and educational programs, summer day camps for children and youth, scholarships for students, visitation of the elderly

---

[2] Cnaan et al., *The Invisible Caring Hand: American Congregations and the Provision of Welfare* (2002).

[3] Curtiss, Grabb, and Baer, "Voluntary Association Membership in Fifteen Countries" (1992).

[4] Cnaan et al. 2002; Veroff, Douvan, and Kulka, *Mental Health in America* (1981).

[5] Cnaan et al. 2002.

and sick, counseling services, housing construction and repair, neighborhood redevelopment, clothing closets, food pantries, international relief, supporting neighborhood associations, credit unions, community bazaars and fairs, health clinics, and language training.[6] Furthermore, in the United States more volunteering occurs in and through religious congregations than anywhere else.[7]

In one of the most important works in the study of religious congregations, scholar R. Stephen Warner convincingly argued that congregations are the center of religious life in the United States, and that even religions that are not traditionally congregationally based, such as Buddhism, become so as they adapt to U.S. life.[8] The last phrase—"as they adapt to U.S. life"—is key to this book. Religious congregations have always occupied a central role in immigrant adaptation and support, the production of culture (music, for example), social network formation, and the production of norms and worldviews. In an impressive study of what congregations do, sociologist Nancy Ammerman shows that most congregations are linked into seven main national networks—Mainline Protestant, Conservative Protestant, African American Protestant, Catholic and Orthodox, Jewish, Sectarian, and Other.[9] These traditions exist as almost independent worlds, producing their own educational materials, musical styles and songs, conferences, scripture translations, and worldviews. As Robert Wuthnow argued, in addition to race, these traditions, rather than denominations per se, structure the main religious dividing lines.[10]

Religious congregations are vital to understanding U.S. life and certainly U.S. race relations. If we want to understand the future of race relations, one place we must look is inside the multiracial congregations. For while the role of racially segregated congregations in race relations has been made transparent, no large-scale study of racially mixed congregations has until now been undertaken. One

[6] See chapter 4 of Cnaan et al. 2002. Also see Chaves 2004; Cnaan 1997; Grettenberger and Hovmand 1997; Hodgkinson and Weitzman 1993; Silverman 2000. In his impressive national study of congregations, Chaves (2004, chapter 3) shows that while congregations are involved in social service and in a significant number of areas, the average congregation's social service work typically is limited to short-term, emergency aid of food, shelter, and clothing. When congregations are more extensively involved, it is usually in partnership with secular and government agencies.

[7] Nancy Ammerman, *Pillars of Faith* (2005); Robert Wuthnow, *Learning to Care* (1995); Wuthnow and Evans (eds.), *The Quiet Hand of God* (2002).

[8] R. Stephen Warner. "The Place of the Congregation in American Religious Configuration" (1994).

[9] Ammerman 2005, chapter 1.

[10] Robert Wuthnow, *The Restructuring of American Religion* (1988).

can find books that study a single multiracial congregation, comparative studies that look at three or six or even thirty or more multiracial congregations, practical how-to books, and theological books about multiracial congregations.[11] These are important works to be sure, but all of these studies rely on personal observation and reflection, or on nonrandom samples of a few congregations, or on qualitative data only, or are not systematically analyzed from a social scientific perspective. This study differs in that it uses both quantitative and qualitative data from a random sample of congregations—both multiracial and uniracial—and a random sample of people in congregations, plus in-depth study and interviews. Using these methods and data allow us to outline the contours of multiracial congregations, place them in the context of all religious congregations, and understand, at least minimally, their role in race relations and racial (in)equality. Yet, before embarking on a contemporary study of multiracial congregations, we first must understand the historical context. Have multiracial congregations existed in the past?

HISTORICAL OVERVIEW

In 2003, Bishop Fred A. Caldwell, pastor of Shreveport, Louisiana's Greenwood Acres Full Gospel Baptist Church, a large African American congregation, put forth a unique proposal. He was offering to *pay* non-blacks to attend his church. Adamant that his church should not be segregated, Bishop Caldwell said that for at least one month he would pay non-blacks five dollars per hour to attend the multiple-hour Sunday morning service, and ten dollars an hour to attend the church's Thursday night service. And he would pay this money out of his own pocket. Bishop Caldwell told the Associated Press, "This idea is born of God. God wants a rainbow in his church." He said the inspiration came to him during a sermon. "The most segregated hour in America is Sunday morning at 11 o'clock. The Lord is tired of it, and I'm certainly tired of it. This is not right."[12]

This story was first reported in the local Shreveport newspaper, but was soon picked up by papers across the country. The day the story

[11] For example, see Ammerman and Farnsley 1997; Anderson 2004 Becker 1998; Christersen, Edwards, and Emerson 2005; Davis 1980; Fong 1996; Foster 1997; Foster and Brelsford 1996; Gratton 1989; Jenkins 2003; Kujawa-Holbrook 2002; Law 1993, 2000, 2002; Marti 2005; Ortiz 1996; Parker 2005; Peart 2000; Pocock and Henriques 2002; Rhodes 1998.

[12] From the online article, "At Long Last, Going to Church Finally Pays," by John Boston (2003).

appeared in *USA Today*, ten people sent me on-line links to the article, many with an e-mail subject heading like, "You've got to see this!" The story was soon the talk on radio airwaves and television outlets, both locally and nationally. Internet chat rooms were talking about it, and people were debating it at the proverbial water cooler.

Pay people to attend worship services? To many, paying people to worship seemed outrageous. Others thought the idea was brilliant, highlighting the racial segregation in houses of worship across the nation. Still others thought the bishop should not focus on the race of the people who attended his church, but merely minister to whoever attended. They found his "religious affirmative action" deeply troubling. Discussion spread beyond this simple offer to pay people to attend one church, and turned to whether the racial makeup of congregations matters. Shortly after this story hit the national news, I was a guest on a two-hour radio call-in show in Baltimore. The show's hosts opened by discussing Bishop Caldwell's offer to pay non-blacks to come to his church, and featured the more general topic of congregational segregation and multiracial congregations. The issue touched a hot button among the listeners. The hosts kept commenting that their lines were lit up, jammed full. I could hear and feel that the callers were passionate about this topic.

When the first "post-pay-to-attend-offer" Sunday service was held, reporters were eager to see the results. The headlines told the story: "Few Take Pastor Up on Offer," said one headline. A year after the offer, though, some effect could be seen. According to a report in one magazine, about two dozen whites were attending the congregation, and five whites had become members.[13]

Bishop Caldwell's quest to create a multiracial congregation amid the strong norm of church segregation is part of a long history in American religious practice and life. Caldwell was accurate in identifying Sunday morning as a time when people of different races rarely joined together. But worship time has never been completely segregated. From the seventeenth century, when scores of British colonists first trekked into North America, to the beginning of the twenty-first century, some whites and blacks have worshiped alongside one another.[14] Historically, racially mixed churches have often been marked by profound racial discrimination, as black men and women either were forced by their white masters to attend church

[13] Olson, Ted. 2004.

[14] Throughout this book, "whites" and "blacks" mean non-Hispanic whites and blacks. Hispanics/Latinos can be of any racial group, according to the present U.S. government definition, but in this work they are treated as a separate racial group.

with them during slavery or were separated from whites in balconies or back rows. Even after the abolition of slavery and the legalization of racial segregation, however, some whites and blacks continued to challenge racism and prejudice by joining together in churches and religious organizations.

When the first wave of British settlers and African servants arrived in the New World, there was little church interaction between them. Very few of the British colonists attended church services regularly, while even fewer of the Africans were Christians. The vast majority of imported Africans either maintained their traditional tribal faiths or maintained the Muslim beliefs to which they had previously converted in Africa. Because of prior missionary activity, a few were Catholics.[15] The first Great Awakening during the middle of the eighteenth century, however, drastically altered this pattern by bringing blacks and whites together in a religious context. Evangelical preachers such as John Wesley and George Whitefield highlighted the individual's relationship to God, proclaiming that each individual is tainted with sin and each has the opportunity to experience new birth in Christ. Whitefield, who led massive revivals along the Eastern seaboard and became a national celebrity, maintained that since whites and blacks were equally mired in sin, they were both "naturally capable of the same improvement." John Wesley assured one elderly slave that in heaven, she would "want nothing, and have whatever you can desire. No one will beat or hurt you there. You will never be sick. You will never be sorry any more, nor afraid of anything." To these evangelicals, one's place in the kingdom of man bore no relation to one's place in the kingdom of God—rich or poor, white or black, master or slave, all would be equal in Heaven.[16]

The egalitarian implications of evangelical teachings were not lost on many slaves. John Wesley and George Whitefield marveled at the numbers of African Americans who flocked to hear them preach. Poet Phillis Wheatley, a New England slave who had converted to Protestant Christianity, acknowledged the ways in which African Americans heard a racially radical message in Whitefield's teachings. In a poem to honor the evangelist, she imagined Whitefield as specifically calling to African descendents:

---

[15] Jon Butler, *Awash in the Sea of Faith: Christianizing the American People* (1990); Sylvia R. Frey and Betty Wood, *Come Shouting to Zion: African American Protestantism in the American South and British Caribbean to 1830* (1998); Christine Leigh Heyrman, *Southern Cross: The Beginnings of the Bible Belt* (1997).

[16] Albert J. Raboteau, *Slave Religion: The "Invisible Institution" in the Antebellum South* (1978); Frey and Wood 1998, chapter 4.

> Take him, ye Africans, he longs for you,
> Impartial Saviour is his title due:
> Wash'd in the fountain of redeeming blood,
> You shall be sons, and kings, and priests to God.

To Wheatley and other African Americans, evangelical Protestantism taught that an "Impartial Saviour" represented a God who called all of his followers to be "sons, and kings, and priests."[17]

The number of African American members of Protestant denominations rose impressively in the wake of the revivals. (The number of black Catholics was minute during this time.) In 1786, there were slightly fewer than 2,000 African American members of Methodist churches, equaling about 10 percent of the total Methodist membership. More than 12,000 African Americans had enlisted in Methodist churches by 1797, comprising about 25 percent of the denomination's total membership. A similar pattern existed in the Baptist churches. By 1793, blacks made up about one quarter of Baptist congregations.[18]

After the American colonists won their independence from Great Britain, the revolutionary ideology that all men were created equal, coupled with a reduced need for slaves, led the northern states to gradually abolish slavery in their states. This helped create a substantial group of free African Americans, many of whom continued to attend churches with whites. In the South, whites, slaves, and a small number of free blacks also participated in religious communities together. In both regions, however, some whites chafed at worshiping alongside African Americans. In Philadelphia in the 1790s, for instance, free African Americans who worshipped at St. George's Methodist Church found themselves mistreated by white leaders. Richard Allen, a free black Methodist minister, vividly remembered the encounter where whites forcefully sought to move the black congregants:

> [T]he elder said, "Let us pray." And we had not been long upon our knees before I heard considerable scuffling and low talking. I raised my head up and saw one of the trustees, H—— M——, having hold of the Rev. Absalom Jones, pulling him up off his knees, and saying "You must get up—you must not kneel here." Mr. Jones said, "Wait until prayer is over, and I will get up and trouble you no more." With that he beckoned to one of the other trustees, Mr. L—— S—— to come to his assistance. He came, and went to William White to pull him up. By this time prayer was over, and

[17] Phillis Wheatley, "Elegiac Poem, on the Death of That Celebrated Divine, and Eminent Servant of Jesus Christ, the Reverend and Learned George Whitefield (1770).
[18] Raboteau 1978, p. 131.

we all went out of the church in a body, and they were no more plagued with us in the church.

Led by Allen and Absalom Jones, these African Americans proceeded to establish their own independent churches and to create two new denominations, the African Methodist Episcopal Church and the African Methodist Episcopal Zion Church.[19]

Although these all-black denominations grew in size and strength during the early nineteenth century, and although whites often forced African Americans who remained in mixed congregations to occupy separate areas, many blacks and whites continued to worship together. In the South, not only were multiracial churches places where blacks and whites interacted, but they also provided judicial systems where all members could bring suits for inappropriate behavior against one another. There were clear hierarchies among congregational members, though, and African Americans did not have as many rights as whites. Whites and blacks who worshiped together also seemed to hear quite different messages. Southern white clergy generally stressed obedience and faithfulness during sermons and Sunday school lessons for their African American congregants. Many southern blacks, however, found biblical tales of liberation far more compelling. One black maid clearly understood Christianity as a faith of freedom when she told her mistress, *"God never made us to be slaves for white people."* [20]

Still, racism saturated interracial religious interaction in both the South and the North. As a slave in Maryland, Frederick Douglass attended church services and revivals with his white masters and overseers, and he participated in household devotions as well. Douglass found that the whites who displayed their Christianity most in public were the same individuals who sought to thwart African American expressions of faith. It was Douglass's "Christian master" who repeatedly stopped him from teaching a Sunday school class for other slaves. Yet even when Douglass fled to Boston, he could not escape racial prejudice in the churches. What he encountered in interracial northern congregations appalled him. In one church that he attended, the black members were only allowed to take communion after the white congregants had taken the sacrament and had been dismissed. "[T]he result was most humiliating," Douglass recalled. He left this church never to return. "I went *out*, and have never been in that church since, although I honestly went there with a view to

[19] Rt. Rev. Richard Allen, *The Life Experience and Gospel Labors of the Rt. Rev. Richard Allen* (1983), p. 25.

[20] Donald G. Mathews, *Religion in the Old South* (1977), p. 221.

joining that body. I found it impossible to respect the religious profession of any who were under the dominion of this wicked prejudice, and I could not, therefore, feel that in joining them, I was joining a Christian church, at all."[21]

Had Douglass attended Catholic Mass, he would have found similar practices. It was not uncommon for free persons of color to have to wait to make their devotions until whites had completed theirs and for slaves to have to wait until free persons of color finished before making their devotions.[22]

Black congregations in the North and secret religious meetings held by southern slaves became important settings in which African Americans worshiped freely and crafted their own interpretations of Christianity. After observing racial discrimination in several other mixed churches, Douglass decided to join, in his words, "a small body of colored Methodists, known as the Zion Methodists. Favored with the affection and confidence of the members of this humble communion, I was soon made a class-leader and a local preacher among them. Many seasons of peace and joy I experienced among them, the remembrance of which is still precious." Apart or hidden from whites, African Americans enjoyed spiritual communion with less fear of white violence and oppression. They could also proclaim openly their faith in a God who would liberate them. "We wish you to consider, that God himself was the first pleader of the cause of slaves," Richard Allen preached. "God, who knows the hearts of all men, and the propensity of a slave to hate his oppressor, hath strictly forbidden it to his chosen people."[23]

With the end of slavery in the United States following the Civil War, roughly four million Southern blacks celebrated their newfound freedom. For many of them, freedom from their masters also meant freedom from worshiping with whites. Given the context of inequality, the vast majority of former slaves were not interested in integrated congregations, and more than one-half of blacks who had worshipped with white Southerners had left mixed churches by the end of 1866. This great "exodus" and the establishment of African American congregations throughout the South provided freed men and women much-needed social and religious autonomy from southern whites. These congregations served as locations for unified social and political activities where African Americans debated public issues, formed

[21] Frederick Douglass, *My Bondage and My Freedom* (1868 [1855]), 353–54.
[22] Curtiss DeYoung et al., *United by Faith: The Multiracial Congregation as a Response to the Problem of Race* (2003), chapter 3.
[23] Douglass 1968 [1855], 353–54; Allen 1983, p. 70.

consensus, and elected representatives. As historian Evelyn Brooks Higginbotham maintains, "the church itself became the domain for the expression, celebration, and pursuit of a black collective will and identity." Black ministers focused on political issues of particular relevance to African Americans, while church magazines devoted themselves to "the interests of the Negro Race in general."[24]

Although separating themselves from white congregations, most blacks did not seek to bar whites from joining the newly formed African American churches. The black church was a segrega*ted* institution, but not a segrega*ting* one.[25] Following the Civil War, some whites participated in predominately African American congregations. When over 3,000 white men and women from the Northern states traveled to the war-ravaged lands of Dixie as missionaries to the freedpeople, they worked alongside African Americans in a variety of venues: they established schools together, they labored on farms together, and they attended worship services together. For a number of white missionaries, moments of interracial religious community moved them emotionally and spiritually. One New England white woman wrote that she was struck when a freed person "prayed for black and white, for rich and poor, for bond and free." Another female missionary was equally touched when a local elder "prayed that 'the little white sisters who came to give learning to the children might be blessed.'" A missionary in Mississippi probably summed up the impact of interracial worship most poignantly when she recalled, "As I walked home in the beautiful moonlight, I could but think that perhaps God was as well pleased with that lowly group in the humble cabin, as with many a gilded throng in splendid cathedrals."[26]

During the decades following the Civil War, racial segregation became entrenched in state and local laws throughout the South. Jim Crow statutes dictated that whites and blacks should be separated in almost every public arena. Most African Americans lost their voting privileges; they were forced to attend poorly funded schools; and they were barred from restrooms, restaurants, libraries, hospitals, and railroad cars that were reserved for whites. The late nineteenth century also witnessed increasing segregation in congregations. The evange-

[24] Katherine L. Dvorak, *An African-American Exodus: The Segregation of the Southern Churches* (1991); Evelyn Brooks Higginbotham, *Righteous Discontent: The Women's Movement in the Black Baptist Church, 1880–1920* (1993); J. R. Oldfield, ed., *Civilization and Black Progress: Selected Writings of Alexander Crummell on the South* (1995), p. 37.

[25] Liston Pope, "Caste in the Church: I. The Protestant Experience" (1947a), p. 60.

[26] Edward J. Blum, *Reforging the White Republic: Race, Religion, and American Nationalism, 1865–1898* (2005), chapter 2.

list Dwight Moody, founder of the Moody Bible Institute, did not seg-regate his revivals in northern cities, but in the 1880s and 1890s he accepted racial separation in the South. In response, African American ministers roundly criticized him for religiously energizing Jim Crow. As one African Methodist Episcopal Church leader put it, "His conduct toward the Negroes during his Southern tour has been shameless, and I would not have him preach in a barroom, let alone a church. In Charleston he refused to give the Negro churches rep-resentation at his evangelical meetings." Moody, this minister fumed, had "placed caste above Christianity." At the same time, southern white evangelicals such as Methodist preacher Sam Jones openly bragged about bullying African American voters and endorsed the Ku Klux Klan.[27]

The loss of political rights led many African Americans to prize their own religious congregations even more dearly. Black churches be-came "havens in a heartless world" where African American culture was celebrated, not castigated. They were places where men and women of color celebrated themselves as children of God in defiance of an American society that treated them as pariahs. For these rea-sons — and because they were one of the few organizations that Afri-can Americans could control for themselves — black churches became central locations of political and social activity. In his pioneering work of urban sociology, *The Philadelphia Negro*, W.E.B. Du Bois described the black church as "a centre of social life and intercourse." It "acts as newspaper and intelligence bureau, is the centre of amusements — indeed, is the world in which the Negro moves and acts. So far-reaching are these functions of the church that its organization is al-most political." Along with Du Bois, two other African American lead-ers, Mary Church Terrell and Kelly Miller, further honored the black church as "the most powerful agency in the moral development and social reform of 9,000,000 Americans of Negro Blood."[28]

In addition to supporting their own congregations, many African Americans questioned the depth of religious belief and community among whites. Ida B. Wells, who vocally opposed racial violence in the late nineteenth century to the extent that she could not return to her home in Memphis, clearly believed that African Americans were true Christians and that whites were not. As she told one reporter,

---

[27] See Blum 2005, chapters 4 and 6.

[28] W.E.B. Du Bois, *The Philadelphia Negro: A Social Study* (1996 [1899]), p. 201; W.E.B. Du Bois, ed., *The Negro Church: Report of a Social Study Made under the Di-rection of Atlanta University; Together with the Proceedings of the Eighth Conference for the Study of the Negro Problems, Held at Atlanta University, May 26th, 1903* (2003 [1903]), p. 208.

she was "prouder to belong to the dark race that is the most practically Christian known to history, than to the white race that in its dealings with us has for centuries shown every quality that is savage, treacherous, and unchristian." Other African Americans also responded to white supremacy by challenging the genuineness of whites' Christianity. After the lynching of one black man in 1906, an African Methodist Episcopal Church minister denounced whites in the United States as "the demon of the world's races, a monster incarnate. . . . The white is a heathen, a fiend, a monstrosity before God." [29]

Still, the deterioration in race relations during the late nineteenth and early twentieth centuries did not lead to a complete congregational separation of blacks and whites. In the early twentieth century, the Pentecostal movement and its focus on a life-changing baptism of the Holy Spirit brought more whites and blacks together in integrated revival meetings and church services. As historian Grant Wacker has observed of the early Pentecostals, "Whites and blacks routinely came together for worship and fellowship, and often seemed genuinely fond of one another." [30] Some other churches, moreover, appeared to treat their African American members with a great deal of respect. Du Bois, who in 1895 would become the first African American to receive a Ph.D. from Harvard University and who led one of the most outstanding academic careers in twentieth-century America, attended a primarily white Congregational church with his family in North Barrington, Massachusetts. Later in life, Du Bois recalled that this church and especially his Sunday school classes were places untainted by racism. "[T]here were celebrations in Sunday School, and I was always there," he reminisced. "I felt absolutely no discrimination, and I do not think there was any, or any thought of it." Despite his appreciation for the black church, and even after Du Bois had spent more than fifty years battling racial and economic discrimination to the point that he embraced Communism and rejected the United States, he attended an interracial church in Brooklyn. Du Bois felt so close to his pastor, the white Episcopal priest William Howard Melish, that when nearing his death Du Bois arranged for Melish to obtain a special passport to conduct the funeral service in Ghana.[31]

[29] Edward J. Blum, "'O God of a Godless Land': Northern African American Challenges to White Christian Nationhood, 1865–1906," in Edward J. Blum and W. Scott Poole, eds., *Vale of Tears: New Essays on Religion and Reconstruction* (forthcoming).

[30] Grant Wacker, *Heaven Below: Early Pentecostals and American Culture* (2001), p. 227.

[31] W.E.B. Du Bois, *The Autobiography of W.E.B. Du Bois: A Soliloquy on Viewing My*

Throughout the early twentieth century, the vast majority of white
and black Catholics and Protestants attended racially separated
churches, further proving to African Americans that white Christians were not their brothers and sisters in the faith. Most white
Christian leaders remained silent on issues of racial discrimination,
prejudice, and violence. One study of race relations in the church
found that white Protestant denominational leaders made only six
pronouncements against segregation between 1908 and 1929.[32] During this same time period, more than 1,000 African Americans were
lynched.[33] American Indians, Mexicans, Chinese, and others likewise experienced extreme individual and institutional discrimination, limiting their life chances.

Even yet, religious voices of opposition to racism and church separation were never completely silenced. In the late 1930s, members
of the Fellowship of Southern Churchmen denounced segregation as
anti-Christian and supported federal legislation against lynching.[34]
Black leaders, including Du Bois, also continued to attack church segregation. "I can conceive of no more pitiable paradox than that of a
young white Christian in the South to-day who really believes in the
ethics of Jesus Christ," Du Bois lamented in 1907. "What can he
think when he hangs upon his church doors that sign that I have often
seen, 'All are welcome.' He knows that half the population of his city
would not dare to go inside that church. Or if there was any fellowship between Christians, white and black, it would be after the manner explained by a white Mississippi clergyman in all seriousness:
'The whites and Negroes understand each other here perfectly, sir,
perfectly; if they come to my church they may take a seat in the
gallery. If I go to theirs, they invite me to the front pew or the platform."[35]

During the 1940s, a host of voices arose from the Christian communities assailing racial discrimination in society and in the
churches. The horrors of World War II — particularly the Holocaust —

Life from the Last Decade of Its First Century (1968), p. 89; Edward J. Blum, "The Soul
of W.E.B. Du Bois," *Philosophia Africana* (August 2004).

[32] Frank S. Loescher, *The Protestant Church and the Negro: A Pattern of Segregation* (1948), p. 28.

[33] On lynching, see Edward L. Ayers, *Promise of the New South: Life after Reconstruction* (1992), pp. 156–59 and 495–97, nn. 69, 70; Philip Dray, *At the Hands of Persons Unknown: The Lynching of Black America* (2003); W. Fitzhugh Brundage, *Lynching in the New South: Georgia and Virginia, 1880–1930* (1993).

[34] Tracy Elaine K'Meyer, *Interracialism and Christian Community in the Postwar
South: The Story of Koinonia Farm* (1997), p. 19.

[35] Booker T. Washington and W.E.B. Du Bois, *The Negro in the South: His Economic
Progress in Relation to His Moral and Religious Development* (1907), pp. 176–77.

spurred greater religious interest in racial violence and discrimination within the United States. The number of public religious pronouncements increased dramatically. For example, from 1940 to 1944 the leadership of white Protestant denominations made more than seventy pronouncements condemning Jim Crow. In 1946, the Federal Council of Churches renounced the "pattern of segregation in race relations as unnecessary and undesirable, and a violation of the gospel of love and human brotherhood." It went even further, calling for both "a non-segregated Church and a non-segregated society."[36] In a powerful appeal to white Christians to oppose segregation in their churches, the director of the United Church Press Fred D. Wentzel wrote in 1948, "*Segregation in the church makes difficult, if not impossible, the practice of Christian fellowship.* Good will on the part of the white Christian, and an honest desire for friendship and cooperation, are not enough." Wentzel contended that white Christians must divest their interest in white supremacy and join hands with African American Christians in the struggle for racial equality.[37] Catholic bishops also began responding to segregation with public pronouncements. For instance, Joseph Rummel, archbishop of New Orleans, declared that segregation was "sinful and wrong," and backed up his statement by sending black priests to say Mass in his white Louisiana parishes.[38] Sociologist Frank S. Loescher echoed Wentzel's call in his own study of race in Protestant churches. American Christians, he wrote, "need to have the goals of brotherhood and justice proclaimed by their churches. But they also need to be shown how to achieve the goal of integration. When the church states certain ends to be good, it has a moral obligation to try to find the means. Social research is one method of finding the means of building 'a non-segregated Church and non-segregated society.'"[39]

Along with these pronouncements came several movements among Christians for interracial fellowship. A handful of churches were formed throughout the nation in the 1930s and 1940s with the specific intention of uniting whites and blacks. These included the Detroit Church of All Peoples, the San Francisco Fellowship Church of All Peoples, and the South Berkeley Congregational Church.[40] In 1942, Baptists Clarence Jordan and Martin England established an agrarian community in southwestern Georgia named "Koinonia Farm." There, Jordan, England, and other white Christians endeavored to

---

[36] Loescher 1948, pp. 34, 42.
[37] Fred D. Wentzel, *Epistle to White Christians* (1948), p. 53.
[38] See chapter 4 of DeYoung et al., *United by Faith* (2003) for exact reference.
[39] Loescher 1948, pp. 116–17.
[40] Homer A. Jack, "The Emergence of the Interracial Church" (1947), pp. 31–37.

forge ties with local African Americans. They held summer camps where black and white children participated in activities together. A number of local blacks applauded the efforts. As one put it, "I wanted to be there. I liked it there. It was a nice place to live—the right way of living." In the 1960s, Koinonia became a popular meeting ground for civil rights organizations such as the Student Non-Violent Coordinating Committee. Local African Americans, however, refused to become full members of the Koinonia community. They cheered the efforts of these white Christians, but looked to their own church fellowships for social and political empowerment.[41]

Public pronouncements against segregation and interracial religious meetings ultimately did little to unify larger numbers of Christians of different racial backgrounds. For example, in 1948 sociologist Frank S. Loescher estimated that of the 14,000,000 African Americans in the United States at the time, 8,000,000 belonged to some type of Protestant Christian church, but of these, fewer than 500,000 (about 6 percent) were part of churches with whites in the congregation. The general pattern seemed clear: "If there are Negroes in the local churches at all, they are in very small and inconspicuous numbers."[42] A survey of Congregational ministers conducted in 1945 supported Loescher's findings. Of 3,800 canvased Congregational ministers, only 388 (10 percent) indicated that their churches had any non-white members. Follow-up research on 189 of these 388 churches found that only 14 had non-white memberships of more than ten individuals.[43] Baptist preacher and civil rights leader Martin Luther King, Jr., described the typical lifestyle of African American Christians in 1963 this way: "If your family attended church, you would go to a Negro church. If you wanted to visit a church attended by white people, you would not be welcome. For although your white fellow citizens would insist that they were Christians, they practiced segregation as rigidly in the house of God as they did in the theatre."[44]

The level of general interracial interaction rose enormously during the late 1950s and 1960s as civil rights organizations stormed the citadels of white power and privilege. African American churches provided the primary organizational locations for the movement and spirit for the crusade. They became hot spots of interracial activity, opening their doors to whites who sought to enlist in the struggle for

[41] K'Meyer 1997, p. 97.

[42] Loescher 1948, pp. 51, 68.

[43] Liston Pope, "A Check List of Procedures for Racial Integration" (1947b), pp. 38–43.

[44] Martin Luther King, Jr., *Why We Can't Wait* (1964), p. 48; Richard Lischer, *The Preacher King: Martin Luther King, Jr., and the Word That Moved America* (1995).

social justice. Throughout the South, white and black civil rights workers and leaders convened in predominately African American churches to sing, to pray, and to organize. Blacks and whites marched together on picket lines and sang in unison, "We shall overcome, Black and white together, we shall overcome someday." At the March on Washington in August 1963, church groups including more than 40,000 white people swelled the masses that heard King's now-famous "I Have a Dream" speech. As we noted earlier, the dream for many of these civil rights workers was, in the words of King, to create a "beloved community" where "the dark clouds of racial prejudice will soon pass away and the deep fog of misunderstanding will be lifted from our fear-drenched communities."[45]

During the Montgomery Bus Boycott of 1956, which began when Rosa Parks refused to give up her seat to a white man on a segregated bus, a white Lutheran pastor of an African American church, Robert S. Graetz, supported the boycott by using his station wagon to carpool blacks to work or home. In return, Graetz and his family were viciously attacked by white supremacists in Montgomery. Their house was bombed repeatedly, and their children threatened. But the animosity of the local whites was matched by the support of local blacks who went to great lengths to defend the Graetz's. Amid the struggle, he and his wife felt as if they were full-fledged members of the African American community. As Graetz recalled of his church services with local blacks, "Here was a white man, standing in front of an almost totally Negro gathering, saying, '*We* are going to have to find a way to make it *ourselves*. *We* are going to have to reach down into *our* own pockets and pay *our* own money if *we* want *our* freedom movement to succeed.' Jeannie and I felt totally part of the Negro community. It had never occurred to me that there was anything unusual about the pronouns I was using. Apparently other people almost viewed me as a Negro, as well."[46] Others were influenced by the movement to the point of working to integrate their congregations, such as Father Nick Perusina and the congregation of St. Pius X Catholic Church in east Texas. This congregation, like some others, began racial integration during the early 1960s, when segregation was still maintained by law.[47]

Although thousands of white church people joined the struggle,

[45] Aldon D. Morris, *The Origins of the Civil Rights Movement: Black Communities Organizing for Change* (1984); James F. Findlay, Jr., *Church People in the Struggle: The National Council of Churches and the Black Freedom Movement, 1950–1970* (1993); King 1964, p. 61.

[46] Robert S. Graetz, *A White Preacher's Memoir: The Montgomery Bus Boycott* (1998), p. 86.

[47] DeYoung et al. 2003, chapter 5.

other white religious leaders equivocated in response to the civil rights movement, while some African American ministers opposed church integration. Along with a number of white Christians, the popular evangelist Billy Graham did support the Supreme Court's landmark decision in *Brown v. Board of Education, Topeka, Kansas* (1954), in which the Court declared segregation in primary and secondary education unconstitutional. Graham even referred to Dr. King and the black participants in the Montgomery Bus Boycott as "setting an example of Christian love." But Graham also urged moderation and slow change. In response to King's dream that his four children "one day will live in a nation where they will not be judged by the color of their skin, but the content of their character," Graham commented, "Only when Christ comes again will the little children of Alabama walk hand in hand with little black children." At the same time, a young Baptist and soon-to-be powerful minister Jerry Falwell used his pulpit in Lynchburg, Virginia, to denounce integration as the beginning of the end for the white race.[48]

Some African American leaders also expressed reluctance to accept church integration, especially the kind that would merely fold black Christians into predominately white churches. Drawing upon the teachings of African American religious leaders such as Richard Allen and Frederick Douglass, a number of black intellectuals, including James Cone and Albert B. Cleage, Jr., created a "black liberation theology" that stressed God's connection with oppressed peoples. To them, the African American church and even a "black Christian nationalism" held the keys to a true understanding of Christianity. As Willie White, an African American pastor in North Carolina, wrote, "White men must be made to realize that the black church is the instrument of God in this world, not just a group of nigger churchgoers who are separated unto themselves until the good graces of white men call them back into fellowship with white congregations." White further contended that it was vital for African Americans to remain in their own congregations, because God still had much to teach the world through them. "God's revelation in the black experience calls for continued development of, and continued commitment to, a theology that will counter oppression and uphold justice the world over." The black church, he concluded, was necessary for such a theology.[49]

---

[48] William Martin, *With God on Our Side: The Rise of the Religious Right in America* (1996), pp. 42–45, 57–58, 80; William Martin, *A Prophet with Honor: The Billy Graham Story* (1991), pp. 167–71.

[49] James H. Cone, *Liberation: A Black Theology of Liberation* (1970); Albert B.

By the late 1960s, American congregations were far from overcoming racial segregation in their congregations, perhaps farther than they had been in the 1860s. American society, through the civil rights movement and changes in laws, had made progress reducing segregation in public arenas. Yet, in 1968, the nation was rife with racial tension. King was assassinated in Memphis. Race riots bloodied the streets of northern cities. A group of leaders at the National Black Economic Development Conference cried out against "the racist white Christian church with its hypocritical declarations" and called for white churches to pay $500 million to African Americans in "reparations."[50] In response many white Protestants retreated from the support they had once given the civil rights movement. As one white Protestant put it, African Americans "should be treated fairly at all times but WE DON'T OWE THEM ANYTHING."[51]

Even this statement of defiance, however, demonstrated some change, because it acknowledged that African Americans should receive equal treatment. Because of the courage of black and white civil rights workers and the pronouncements from major religious leaders, worship-attending whites could no longer be unaware that their congregations were deeply divided by race. At the same time, many African Americans recognized that although they lived in a racialized society that privileged individuals deemed white, there were whites who would join them in their struggle against Jim Crow. The nation was also diversifying racially. Changes in the immigration laws led to the increase in immigrants from Latin America and Asia, especially since 1970. The resurgence of American Indians in local and national politics brought Native American issues to the forefront. The United States was no longer mainly black and white.

But when the racial composition of congregations is surveyed today, little seems to have changed since the civil rights movement. As we will see in detail in the next chapter, most congregations remain racially segregated. Since the 1960s, a proportionately small number of congregations have struggled to be multiracial, and a few seem to have succeeded, but they are the exceptions to be sure (as detailed in chapter 2). No research has yet systematically studied these multiracial congregations, to understand why they exist, how they work, and what they mean.

Cleage, Jr., *Black Christian Nationalism: New Directions for the Black Church* (1972); Willie White, "Separate unto God" (1974), pp. 179–81.

[50] R. S. Lecky and H. E. Wright, eds., *Black Manifesto: Religion, Racism, and Reparations* (1969), pp. 125–26.

[51] Findlay 1993, p. 206. The emphasis was added in the original text.

TRAVELING

This book reports on the first systematic study of multiracial congregations. Given the importance of religion and religious congregations in American life and armed with a historical understanding, my purpose was clear. I needed to go to the organizations labeled as the most racially segregated of all—religious congregations—and study specific cases where they were not segregated.

My colleagues and I spent six years studying multiracial congregations.[52] We began by conducting more than 2,500 telephone interviews with Americans. We talked to a random sample of adult Americans who speak English or Spanish (most everyone in the United States), whether they were religious or not. This gave us excellent information about who is in multiracial congregations and who is not, and how such people differ. Also as part of our surveys, we asked people who attended a religious congregation for the name and address of their congregation. We then sent surveys to these congregations, in order to study the congregations themselves. The survey responses provided broad information of a good cross-section of U.S. congregations, helping us to understand the differences between multiracial and other congregations. It also helped us identify a sizable pool of interracial congregations from which to select thirty to study in-depth.

For this in-depth next portion of the research, we traveled to a variety of congregations, spending at least two weeks in each location, and often having the opportunity to return at a later time. We attended worship services and meetings, interviewed parishioners and the clergy, read historical documents about the congregations, studied the neighborhoods of the congregations, and gathered other information shedding light on the experiences of the congregations. Finally, to gain a richer understanding of change over time, I spent five years in a congregation that was in the process of transforming from a uniracial to a multiracial membership.[53]

[52] On the Lilly-funded project, these colleagues included George Yancey and Karen Chai Kim, as well as a number of graduate and undergraduate assistants mentioned in the preface. Other important colleagues that I worked with included Korie Edwards and Brad Christerson.

[53] For the details of the research design, see appendix C. As noted in appendix C, after our national survey of all Americans, we limited our collection of congregational data and interviews to those from Christian traditions. We initially intended to include all faith traditions, but the number of non-Christians was far too small to make generalizations from our data (I do use the National Congregations Survey to look at other faith traditions). Although the United States is religiously diverse in terms of the num-

My desire to communicate my quest to understand multiracial congregations led me to structure this book somewhat unconventionally. To provide a foundation from which to understand the national findings, we will enter into the life of one congregation as it transforms from a uniracial to multiracial membership. Although I spent five years in this congregation, I rely heavily on the perceptions and words of the senior congregation clergy person, the Reverend Dr. Rodney Woo.[54] Beginning in chapter Two, we follow Rodney Woo through the transformation, complete with his congregation's and his own struggles, victories, doubts, and joys. From this narrative, I examine the larger issues, comparing and contrasting the experiences of this one congregation with others around the country. This congregation, then, is the thread used to weave together the findings of this book, and to make the findings more understandable.

The turbulent 1960s ushered in a new United States, a post-civil rights nation. Not only was this decade the beginning of the dramatic increase of non-European immigration, which continues to change the face of racial and ethnic categories, but it also saw the growth feminism, assassinations, riots, youth counterculture, the realization of suburbs as the primary place where Americans live, and the emergence of a new alignment in U.S. religion, including the decline of denominational loyalty.[55]

The 1960s encapsulated decades and even centuries of questioning about what the United States was and hoped to be, who belonged, and how Americans should relate to each other. The questions were not answered during that decade and they remain unanswered, but especially in the 1960s the questions exposed the tensions that the United States has always had to negotiate. The nation's motto, *e pluribus unum* — out of many, one — reveals both an early recognition of diversity and the value of unity arising from this diversity. But the motto also is sufficiently vague to leave much room for debate and change

---

ber of traditions and groups (Eck 2001), most of the diversity is found in different forms of the same tradition — Christianity (Beaman 2003). About 90 percent of religious people in the United States claim a Christian affiliation, with no other religion having more than a 3 percent share (Emerson and Kim 2003). As R. Stephen Warner (2004, p. 20) has argued, at least to date, "the new immigrants represent not the de-Christianization of American society but the de-Europeanization of American Christianity."

[54] Dr. Woo granted me multiple interviews. I also gave Dr. Woo several topics and questions to address in writing. He wrote nearly two hundred typed pages in response to my inquiries. Because of his central contribution to gaining an inside look at a congregation transforming, he serves as a "with" author. Except when Dr. Woo's voice is directly quoted, all interpretations and analyses in the book are mine, and do not necessarily reflect Dr. Woo's perspective. For a more detailed discussion, see appendix C.

[55] Wuthnow, 1988.

over time. What does it mean to say from many, one? There have been many different answers over the nation's history (see appendix A for a much fuller discussion); we continue today asking and trying to answer that question. It is within this churning context that the multiracial congregations my colleagues and I studied are attempting to make a way.

Why "People of the Dream"?

This attempt to make a way in shifting, uncertain times led to the book title, *People of the Dream*. The word "dream" is used in many ways, with multiple meanings. In the United States, the "American dream" is one of the nation's most central metaphors. "The American dream that we were all raised on is a simple but powerful one — if you work hard and play by the rules you should be given a chance to go as far as your God-given ability will take you," said former President Bill Clinton.[56] Most U.S. presidents, in fact, refer to the American dream as the great promise of the country. People growing up in the United States spend much of their time pursing this dream, and people from around the world migrate to the United States for the chance to do the same.

Dreams are also often thought of as visions or hoped-for directions that guide people from a problematic place to a better one. At a very individual level, this partly captures the meaning of the American dream. King also used the word "dream" in this way, saying his dream was deeply rooted in the American dream. But his dream was much larger than the American dream. His dream was the creation of what he called the Beloved Community, "where brotherhood is a reality" and there is "genuine intergroup and interpersonal living — *integration*."[57] By an integrated society, he meant one in which people "relate to each other across those nonrational, psychological barriers which have traditionally separated them in our society," and there is a complete sense of the interrelatedness of humanity.[58] In an integrated society — the Beloved Community — not only will *all* people be free to pursue the American dream, but they will care for one another, work for justice, and come to talk and walk as if "[w]e are tied to-

[56] Bill Clinton as quoted in Jennifer L. Hochschild, *Facing Up to the American Dream: Race, Class, and the Soul of the Nation* (1995), p. 18.

[57] Kenneth Smith (one of King's professors in seminary) and Religious Studies professor Ira Zepp, Jr. explore this question in detail in their book, *Search for the Beloved Community* (1998), p. 130.

[58] Ibid., 131.

gether in the single garment of destiny, caught in an inescapable net-work of mutuality."[59] They will truly believe and live as if "injustice anywhere is a threat to justice everywhere."

There are still other meanings of the word "dream." Some dreams are scary. To be a dreamer can also mean to be someone who never comes "down from the clouds" to get things done or who lives in a make-believe, fantasy world. In such cases, dreams are not good. Malcolm X strongly communicated the negative side of dreams: "What is looked at as an American dream for white people has long been an American nightmare for black people."[60] "No, I am not an American. I am one of 22 million black people who are the victims of Americanism."[61] "We didn't land on Plymouth Rock — that rock landed on us."[62] "I am not interested in being American, because America has never been interested in me."[63] When it came to religion, Malcolm X said:

> Brothers and sisters, the white man has brainwashed us black people to fasten our gaze upon a blondhaired, blue-eyed Jesus! . . . The white man has taught us to shout and sing and pray until we die, to wait until death, for some dreamy heaven-in-the-hereafter, when we're dead, while this white man has his milk and honey in the streets paved with golden dollars here on this earth![64]

This book is called *People of the Dream*. But an important question eventually to answer is, "Which dream?" Are the people of multiracial congregations people of Bill Clinton's American dream, Dr. Martin Luther King, Jr.'s Beloved Community dream, or Malcolm X's nightmare? And what difference does that make for American religion and race relations? To answer that question, the pages that follow have us travel to a variety of places, learn from multiple methods, and explore many levels of life.

[59] Ibid., 131.
[60] Quoted in Cone, *Martin and Malcolm and America* (1991), p. 89.
[61] Quoted in Cone 1991, p. 1.
[62] Taken from Cone 1991, p. 197, and see p. 339.
[63] Quoted in Cone 1991, p. 38.
[64] Speech in Harlem, 1954, quoted in Cone 1991, p. 151.

MULTIRACIAL congregations in the United States are highly unusual. In this chapter, I consider how common such congregations are, which faith traditions are more likely to include multiracial congregations, and reasons for why some congregations are multiracial.

In the congregations my colleagues and I studied, effective, committed leadership was essential for thriving as a multiracial congregation. Often this leadership started with the senior clergy members of the congregations, typically individuals with the background and experiences that make them desire a multiracial congregation and provided them with the necessary tools to lead. But it also takes a willing congregation. The story of Wilcrest, the congregation introduced in the Prelude, is representative.

RODNEY WOO AND WILCREST BAPTIST

Trying to survive as a congregation amid the drastic changing racial context of their neighborhood, the leaders of Wilcrest Baptist in 1991 had a major decision to make. Should they move to a whiter neighborhood or stay in their racially diversifying neighborhood? Most every economic and social indicator told them they should leave. Their pastor told them the same. They took a vote. After the tally, one of the leaders stood up to announce the results. "Allow me to have your attention please. The votes have been cast; we have made a decision. We're stayin', ya'll."

Exactly why the leaders voted this way is not clear. One leader I interviewed simply told me that he felt the congregation should stay in the community, even though he did not specifically know why or even what staying would entail. Another told me he felt "God had called" them to be in that community, no matter who lived there.

The decision to stay was followed by a new discussion. The pastor clearly was not committed to the present neighborhood, but the congregation had just decided it was. After serious discussion, the church leaders voted to ask Pastor Windom to resign. They went to Pastor Windom's home and informed him of their decision to keep the church in its present location. They suggested that perhaps it was time for him to resign from his position. According to the Wilcrest members I interviewed, Pastor Windom readily agreed. He felt ill prepared to go in the direction the congregation had elected to go. Shortly after that meeting, he announced his resignation to the congregation, and he left his Wilcrest pastorate in 1991.

The people of Wilcrest needed a new pastor. They formed a search committee to advertise the position, review applications, and decide whom to invite for interviews. The process took a year. The church was uncertain about what type of pastor could best lead the congregation. Committee members traveled around Texas to meet and hear candidates. Along the way, the committee thought they found the right candidate, but one committee member held out, insisting that it was not the right person. Because the committee had agreed their decision must be unanimous, they continued their search.

While they continued with the search process, a guest speaker, the Reverend Uvaldo Quintela, visited Wilcrest to tell about his work in one of Houston's barrios. He also told them about his young son-in-law, Rodney Woo, then a pastor in north Texas, but who, he said, might be someone Wilcrest would want to consider as a new pastor.

The search committee was intrigued, and asked Reverend Quintela to have his son-in-law send his résumé. After reviewing his résumé and talking to Dr. Woo by phone, the committee had two main thoughts: he seemed a good person to serve Wilcrest as their next pastor, and if he did, he would signal a major change for Wilcrest.

The Reverend Dr. Rodney Woo was well trained, the son of a missionary, and had eight years of pastoral experience. He spoke with boldness and confidence, and had a clear vision for the congregation's future. But he was merely twenty-nine years old, and had an unusual background and an even more unusual perspective. As the committee made the decision to invite him for an interview, they could not help but wonder: was this traditional Southern Baptist congregation ready for such changes?

The Shaping of Rodney Woo

It is unusual for someone only twenty-nine years of age to be considered for a senior pastor position, and even rarer that such a person would have already been a senior pastor for eight years. But unusual and rare accurately describe Rodney Woo, and his hope for Wilcrest. He grew up in Port Arthur, Texas, an area on the edge of multiple cultures — Texan culture, southern culture, the Cajun culture of southern Louisiana and spilling into the bordering region of Texas, white culture, black culture, and increasingly, Mexican American culture. Yet he did not particularly fit into any of these. During one of my first interviews with him, I asked him to describe his background:

My mother was white, from Virginia. My father was half-Chinese, who looked all Chinese. As an Asian in the South, my father understood what it meant to live as a minority. My parents, for example, could not legally get married in their home state of Virginia because of his Asian descent. They had to go to Maryland to get married.

My parents moved to Port Arthur where my father served as a missionary to impoverished Hispanics, African Americans, and after 1975, the Vietnamese. He had an inner city ministry, teaching English to immigrants, visiting jails, running after-school clubs for children, and going to the homes of people in need. So I grew up around lots of different cultures.

During elementary and middle school, I went to primarily African-American schools. Of the approximately 1500 students in my middle school, probably less than thirty were not African American.

Dr. Woo's experiences growing up taught him much about people, race relations, and racial divisions. For example, during a seventh-grade gym class, an incident taught him about racial ambiguity and the uncertain place of new immigrants in the black-white binary relations of the United States:

The coach had divided my class of 150 boys into groups of fifty and instructed the boys to choose teams of twenty-five. In my group of fifty, I was one of the two remaining boys yet to be selected. The captains who were selecting the teams were in an argument over who was going to be stuck with a white boy on the team. During their intense debate, I offered a critical bit of information that transformed their perspective of me. I told them that I was not white, but Chinese and my last name was "Woo." Both boys looked completely shocked. Finally one of them pointed at me and said, "I want him on my team." At that time, they knew they were to dislike whites, but did not know exactly what to do with a Chinese student.

Reverend Woo recalls feeling a sense of confusion about the role of race in the world around him. The church his family attended was nearly all white; his schools and the people his father worked with were nearly all non-white. "I often wondered why my church friends were a different color than my school friends and the people my father worked with. The racial distinctions seemed so sharp."

At the age of fifteen he felt compelled to follow in his father's footsteps as a missionary and perhaps a pastor. After he announced this, his father began involving him in his work. On weekends, they spent much time in the local city jail visiting inmates. At this still young age, what he saw in the jails, combined with what he experienced in his daily life, planted the seed of a desire to be part of a multiracial congregation:

At the city jail, I was befuddled by what I saw. In this era of the late 1970s, whites and blacks were segregated from one another in separate blocks of cells, so that they could neither see nor hear each other. I would talk to whole groups of prisoners, but would have to do so twice, once to the whites, once to the blacks. It was the same message, but given twice. I remember feeling a growing yearning to move beyond this division. Why, I thought, couldn't people worship together? Why couldn't they go to school together? Why did they have to be separated in jails?

Dr. Woo's desire and commitment to serve a multiracial congregation stems in part from the conditions that led to his interracial marriage. His wife, Sasha, is the daughter of Mexican immigrants. Their meeting and subsequent marriage were closely tied to his father's work in Port Arthur. Sasha's mother, a recent immigrant to the Port Arthur area, struggled with English. She ended up taking English classes at a local inner city ministry run by Rodney Woo's father. Shortly thereafter, she and her family began attending the same church as the Woos. A friendship between Rodney and Sasha began, and when they were in their teens, they began dating. Having grown up together, Rodney and Sasha had much in common. They married when he was twenty-one and she was nineteen.

When he left Port Arthur for college and seminary, his desire to pastor a multiracial congregation grew stronger. The more he learned in seminary, the more he dreamed of being a pastor of a multiracial congregation. While studying, he served as pastor of a tiny white church in a small town outside of Forth Worth, Texas. As the church grew, he attempted to bring in non-whites, but the congregation resisted. His experience in this small rural congregation only made him yearn more to lead a multiracial congregation and taught him valuable lessons about the difficulty in doing so.

Dr. Woo was thus unusual in his background, in his passionate desire to lead a multiracial congregation, and, as a result of his early experience as a pastor, in having some knowledge of what at least does not work in attempting to be multiracial.

Coming to Wilcrest

When they received a phone call from Wilcrest, Rodney and Sasha Woo were excited. Perhaps this was the opportunity they had been waiting for, they thought. They drove with much anticipation to Houston to interview. But they left dejected.

I'll never forget that first interview. As Sasha and I followed the committee through the church hallway, my heart almost exploded with excitement when I saw several Chinese people walking right by us. I finally found the multiracial church I have been looking for all these years! I did not care how small or how big this church was, this kind of church was for me. But my excitement quickly dissipated. I noticed a cold silence between the committee and the Chinese individuals walking by us. As soon as we sat down, I asked about the Chinese we had passed. They informed me that they were a separate congregation who used the Wilcrest building, and that only the former pastor had contact with them. The news got worse. In addition to the Chinese congregation, there was an African American congregation. Both were established by Wilcrest, and both had the effect of keeping these groups separate from the primary congregation. The ugly memories of my childhood flooded over me. Here we go again, I thought, the same old thing. It was a long trip home.

But for some reason, as much as he wanted to shut the door on the Wilcrest position, he could not stop thinking about it. Then he received a call from a member of the search committee, saying they wanted to recommend him for the position and to have him come back for the congregation-wide vote on their recommendation. Given what he had experienced during his interview at Wilcrest, he knew what he had to do:

I expressed my reservations, and then told the committee I would come, but only on a few conditions. I felt strongly that if Wilcrest was to move in an entirely new direction, I needed to share my vision with the entire congregation, not only with the eight members on the Pastor Search Committee. I needed to hear from the members before there was an official vote. I needed to see if they were willing to follow what God had placed in my heart to do. I needed to share my dream with the entire congregation.

The committee and the rest of the congregation agreed to this unusual alteration in procedure. On a Saturday in March of 1992 Rodney Woo met with the congregation and shared his vision of a church for all people:

I wanted to make it clear to the congregation that God wanted to lead them across racial lines and over cultural barriers. If the congregation as a whole did not want to pursue that direction, then I obviously was not the pastor for them. The church should not merely *reflect* the community surrounding the church, I told them, but it should *project* God into the community. Our love for each other across racial and cultural lines would announce to the world that God was present and working. To my surprise, they seemed to accept what I was saying. I will never forget the deep desire that I saw on their faces. In that moment, they radically transformed from hoping to survive "white flight" to grasping the God of the impossible.

After Rodney Woo had shared his vision, a vote was taken. Over 90 percent of the members voted to hire him. As he later told me, "whether they fully realized it or not, with that vote, they were not voting so much for me, but for the dream of a truly integrated church." In our interviews years later, members who had been at that meeting made it clear that they had *not* fully realized what they were voting for. One woman who was at the meeting in 1992 and later became a leading supporter of the vision put it clearly:

> We were excited about this vision, and having a man of God lead us, but we had no idea what it really meant to be a multiracial church. For some of us, the fact that Brother Rodney and Sasha were not white made us a multiracial church. I suppose most of us thought being an interracial church meant a few non-whites would come to worship with us, and be thankful that we let them. I am so embarrassed now to think we thought that way, but we did.

The whites of Wilcrest, like other whites, were firmly planted in a racialized world in which whites expected to be in control and saw themselves as the standard by which others must measure themselves.[1] As this woman indicated, the white members of Wilcrest expected that blacks, Hispanics, Asians, and others wanted to worship with them. If they "allowed" them to, non-whites would eagerly come to the congregation. Rodney Woo saw that much work was needed to overcome the dominate white perspective. Some members made comments to Rodney Woo after the vote that brought this point home to him. "After the vote, one woman came up to me and confessed, 'Pastor, I went ahead and voted for you, even though I am prejudiced.'" He also learned that one of the members had suggested to others that he add a "d" to the end of his last name. The name "Wood" would be much more palatable than the name "Woo." "Obviously," he said, "to realize our dream, miracles would have to happen!"

Where are They Now?

African Americans, Latinos, Asians, and others did not come to Wilcrest when they opened their doors. We will explore the processes that Wilcrest underwent for change to occur. But through much struggle and time, and despite many mistakes, a little more than a decade later, the Wilcrest congregation has fundamentally trans-

---

[1] An important literature establishes these claims. For example, see Bonilla-Silva 2001, 2003; Doane 1997; Duster 2001; Feagin 2000; Forman 2004; Gallagher 1997, 2003; Jackman 1994; Lewis 2004; Wellman 1993.

formed into a congregation of another kind. Demographically, the church is now about 20 percent black, 30 percent Hispanic, 42 percent white, 5 percent Asian, and 3 percent other race or ethnicity. And it has nearly tripled in size. Many in the congregation are immigrants to the United States, so Wilcrest has people from over forty different nations, including Argentina, the Bahamas, Belize, Brazil, Cameroon, Canada, Chile, China, Colombia, Cuba, the Dominican Republic, El Salvador, Ethiopia, Ghana, Guadeloupe, Guam, Guatemala, Guyana, Haiti, Holland, Honduras, India, Indonesia, Iran, Jamaica, Japan, Korea, Lebanon, Liberia, Mexico, Nigeria, Philippines, Puerto Rico, Sierra Leone, U.S. Virgin Islands, Taiwan, Trinidad, Venezuela, Vietnam, and the United States.

The story of Wilcrest and Rodney Woo helps us begin to understand why the Wilcrest congregation looks as it does today. But how does their story compare to the hundreds of thousands of other congregations in the United States? In later chapters we look at what is happening inside Wilcrest today. But first, we compare the demographics of Wilcrest to those of other congregations across the nation.

How Common Are Multiracial Congregations?

To answer the question, "How common are multiracial congregations?" I must define what I mean by multiracial congregation.[2] One

---

[2] When discussing congregations with multiple people groups, many terms have been used: multicultural, multiethnic, and multiracial, to name the most common terms. For my purposes, *multicultural* is an imprecise and misleading term. Though culture is often taken as synonymous with race or ethnicity, it clearly is not. I have two more reasons to avoid this term. By linking race and ethnicity with culture, the term assumes that any congregation with multiple ethnicities is also a congregation with people of multiple cultures. This is an empirical question. It is conceivable that such congregations have people who may have different ancestries but, through assimilation and amalgamation, have a common culture. The term *multicultural* also can imply that congregational life and structures are multicultural. As an example, a multicultural church may be one in which musical forms from two or more cultures are regularly drawn from during Mass or worship services. But this too is an empirical question. To define a congregation with a term subject to multiple untested assumptions, then, seems unsound.

Perhaps an even more common term is *multiethnic*. Because it is more specific, this term more accurately captures a congregation with parishioners from a variety of people groups. I do not use the term here because it is not the best term for what I wish to examine. I am not interested, for example, in including in my definition congregations that are made up partly of people of Swedish heritage and partly of people of Polish heritage, or those that are partly Honduran and partly Guatemalan.

The fundamental cleavage in the United States, in political, social, and religious can define congregations in binary terms—either they are or are not multiracial—or in continuous terms—they are more or less multiracial. I define and use both. The findings indicate that compared to other congregations, Wilcrest's multiracial congregation is highly unusual. The findings also suggest that Rodney Woo's dream, if not rare, is not often successfully realized.

My binary definition of a multiracial congregation is one in which *no one racial group comprises 80 percent or more of the people*. That is, to be classified as multiracial, more than 20 percent of the congregation must be racially different than the largest racial group. This is not an arbitrary figure. I use 20 percent as the cutoff because research in race and gender relations in multiple contexts suggests that 20 percent constitutes the point of critical mass. At this percentage, the proportion is high enough to have its presence felt and filtered throughout a system or organization.[3] In fact, at a 20 percent mix, assuming that each person in such an environment randomly comes in contact with twenty others, the probability of contact with someone of another race is .99.[4] My personal experience of studying these organizations concurs. More than 20 percent of the congregation must be of another racial or ethnic background for their presence to make noticeable differences.

My continuous definition of a multiracial congregation is based on a measure called the *general heterogeneity index*. It measures *the probability that two randomly selected people in a congregation will*

---

terms, is not ethnicity but race. The United States is the land of five melting pots (Hollinger 1995), and these pots are socially constructed racial categories. Different national groups, regardless of their ethnicities and their preferences, are expected to adopt a racial identity, to meld into one of the five main "racial" categories—white, black, Asian, Hispanic, and American Indian. Currently, the U.S. government classifies people of Hispanic descent as part of a trans-ethnic group who can be of any race. But once one looks beyond immigrants, in everyday life, in political organization, in social networks, in people's perceptions, and in religious life, the category "Hispanic" or "Latino" operates as a racial category, that is, a fundamental cleavage along common physical characteristics/ancestry lines. I do not deny the major and important differences between ethnic groups of Latin, Asian, African, or European descent. Puerto Ricans are different from Mexicans; Koreans are different from Filipinos. But these differences dissipate over the generations (partly by choice, partly by imposition), melding into socially constructed racial categories. For these reasons, I use the term *multiracial*.

[3] Kanter 1977; Pettigrew 1975; Pettigrew and Martin 1987. See also Gratton (1989), who found in his studies that when a congregation has more than 20 percent of its membership from a minority ethnic group, control and participation in the congregation begin to be shared among the different ethnic groups. More work needs to be done to know if the number of groups matters, as well as the percentage of non-majority groups.

[4] Sigelman et al., "Making Contact? Black-White Social Interaction in an Urban Setting" (1996).

Predominately
Single Race
93%

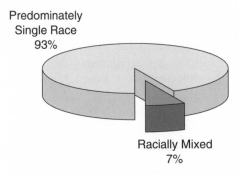

Racially Mixed
7%

FIGURE 2.1. Racial composition of U.S. congregations. *Source*: National
Congregations Study, 1998.

be of different racial groups. It ranges from zero—no probability that
two randomly selected people are of different racial groups—to one—
perfect probability that two randomly selected people are of different
racial groups. This measure gives weight not only to the relative mix
of racial groups, but to the number of groups.[5] Thus a congregation
that is 50 percent of one racial group and 50 percent of another would
receive a value of .5 (the probability that any two randomly selected
people are racially different). A congregation with four different
racial groups, each of which is one quarter of the total people, would
receive a value of .75. Realistically, then, we cannot expect congregations to be anywhere near 1. More realistically, any value approach-
ing .5 indicates a substantial racial mix.

Although the common assumption is that multiracial congregations are rare, and there have even been theories developed to explain why,[6] exactly how rare such congregations are has never been
established. Based on analysis of the National Congregations Survey,
and using the binary definition that no one racial group is 80 percent
or more of the people, I estimate that 7 *percent of American congregations are multiracial* (see figure 2.1). Thus, according to a binary
definition of multiracial, more than nine out of every ten congregations in the United States are racially homogenous.

Wilcrest, then, is unlike more than 90 percent of congregations in
the United States. Indeed, even this 7 percent of congregations estimated to be racially mixed is probably misleading. As I found in vis-

[5] It is calculated as 1 − sum of the squared group proportions.
[6] Emerson and Smith 2000, chapter 7.

iting congregations listed as multiracial, some simply were in the process of switching from one group to another. And others simply failed, not surviving as multiracial congregations. Although new ones may be started to take the failed ones' places, the number of stable racially mixed congregations is undoubtedly lower than the 7 percent estimated to be demographically diverse.[7]

When we turn to the continuous measure of multiracial congregations, we again see that Wilcrest is unusual. With .50 indicating substantial racial diversity, the average (mean) congregational diversity in the United States is merely .08. As a point of comparison, using the same measure, the mean racial diversity of public schools in the United States is .48 — suggesting that public schools, at the time of this writing, are six times more racially diverse than are religious congregations.[8] Wilcrest, with a general heterogeneity index score of .70, is impressively racially diverse and highly unusual among congregations.

This large value for Wilcrest points to a weakness of using the mean to summarize the average racial diversity in a congregation. Only a very few congregations are as racially mixed as Wilcrest—*less than one-half of one percent*. In fact, only 2.5 percent of congregations have general heterogeneity indexes above .5. Though only a few congregations are as racially mixed as Wilcrest, these "outlying" congregations drive up the mean congregational score. For example, if we had nine congregations, eight of which had zero racial mix and one of which had Wilcrest's score, the mean racial heterogeneity of these congregations would be .08, despite the fact that in our example only one congregation had any racial diversity at all.

A better measure of average diversity in such cases is not the mean but the *median*, which simply orders all congregations from the least racially diverse to the most racially diverse and then reports the score of the middle-ranked congregation. Calculated this way, the average racial heterogeneity of United States' congregations drops fourfold, from .08 (the mean) to merely .02 (the median). This demonstrates the unusualness of Wilcrest from a more revealing perspective — *Wilcrest is 35 times more racially diverse than the average congregation in the United States.*

---

[7] A similar conclusion was reached by Parker (2005) in his study of South African racially diverse congregations.

[8] See the work of James Moody (2001) for the analysis of school heterogeneity. Later in this chapter, I will compare the racial heterogeneity of congregations and the neighborhoods in which they reside.

WHY ARE MULTIRACIAL CONGREGATIONS SO RARE?

Why are so few congregations racially diverse? When I interviewed clergy and talked to people about this question, those not in multiracial congregations often said that they were in a denomination that had few people of diverse backgrounds—for example, Lutherans (a primarily white denomination) or National Baptists (a primarily black denomination). Others talked about the fact that people simply are more comfortable in racially homogenous congregations. And still others told me that they are not diverse because their neighborhoods are not diverse. This latter explanation was perhaps the most frequent response.

I explore these explanations and others here to see what influence such factors have on the likelihood of a congregation being racially diverse. Because people in the United States largely choose their congregations and tend to prefer to be with people like themselves,[9] the number of congregational options people have within given traditions likely shapes the degree of congregational diversity. The more choice of congregations, the more exact people can be in realizing their preferences.

According to the National Congregations Study, about 84 percent of congregations are Protestant, 7 percent are Catholic, and 9 percent represent a variety of other faith traditions, such as Islam, Judaism, Buddhism, and Hinduism.[10] Based on the number of choices available to people, and the tendency to choose to be with people like themselves, Protestantism should have the lowest percentage of racially mixed congregations. Given that the non-Christian category is composed of several different faiths between which people will rarely cross, these faiths generally offer the fewest congregations in a given area to choose from. This leads us to expect that those in such faiths will be more likely to be in mixed-race congregations.

Racial composition within broader traditions may also matter. The greater the racial diversity that exists within a tradition, the greater the opportunity there is for mixed-race congregations. According to my estimates from the Lilly Survey of Attitudes and Social Networks, Catholicism and non-Christian religions (a category again necessitated by small sample size) are both about two-thirds White; Protestantism is about 78 percent White.

[9] See chapter 7 of Emerson and Smith 2000.

[10] I use the unfortunate category "non-Christian" because the size of these individual traditions makes it inappropriate to estimate their proportion of congregations separately, given the sample size.

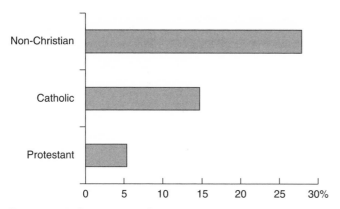

FIGURE 2.2. Percentage of congregations that are multiracial, by faith tradition. All percentages are significantly different from the others (chi-square tests of each comparison, p < .05).

Given these patterns, we should expect Protestantism to have the lowest frequency of multiracial congregations. The non-Christian category has a somewhat higher percentage of congregations than does the Catholic category, but only because it combines many faiths into one. Keeping in mind that people rarely change faith traditions, Catholics should have a higher percentage of multiracial congregations than Protestants, but not as high as the non-Christian traditions.

These predictions appear correct (see figure 2.2). I estimate that only 5 percent of Protestant congregations can be classified as multiracial. For Catholics, this figure triples, to 15 percent. And, combining all non-Christian congregations together, more than one-quarter (28 percent) are multiracial.

Based on these findings, I venture a further prediction: Other things being equal, the larger a faith tradition, the less racially diverse its congregations will be, both compared to other faith traditions, and compared to itself when it was smaller. This prediction leads to this conclusion: The more successful a faith tradition is in terms of relative size, the less successful it will be in having racially mixed congregations.

To further test this prediction, I divided Protestants into two groups — conservative and mainline — based on the theological orientation of the denomination of each congregation. Theologically conservative Protestants include those in the categories of evangelical, fundamentalist, Pentecostal, charismatic, all black denominations, and nondenominational congregations. Mainline Protestants include all others, such as congregations in denominations like Episcopalian and Presbyterian USA. Although there is some error in classification using denomination, this is an accepted and useful way to make our comparisons. As a percentage of Protestants, conservative Protestants constitute 62 percent and mainline Protestants 38 percent. According to the prediction offered above, conservative Protestants should have less racial mix in their congregations (because they have a larger share of people) than do mainline Protestants. But this is *not* the case. In this sample, 6 percent of conservative Protestant congregations are racially mixed, compared to 3 percent of mainline Protestant congregations.

This finding seems to contradict the hypothesis that other things being equal, the larger a faith tradition, the less racially diverse its congregations will be, compared to other faith traditions. But other things are not equal, and we must first equalize them before we can test the prediction.

The key factor that must be equalized, or accounted for, is *opportunity*: that is, the different levels of racial diversity within the faith traditions. To do this, researchers have developed measures of segregation. One such measure, the index of dissimilarity, is not influenced by the different levels of racial diversity within faith traditions. It simply asks how diverse the congregations within the faith tradition are compared to the racial diversity of the entire faith tradition. So if a faith tradition is 75 percent racial group A and 25 percent racial group B, zero congregational segregation would mean that every congregation had 75 percent racial group A and 25 percent racial group B. Perfect segregation would mean that no members of racial group A went to the same congregations as members of racial group B. Obviously, neither zero nor perfect segregation is likely to actually occur. So while the index of dissimilarity theoretically ranges from 0 (no segregation) to 1 (perfect segregation), actual values are almost always somewhere in between. In addition to adjusting for opportunity (the racial mix within the faith tradition), the index of dissimilarity also has the advantage of a clear interpretation. Its value is *the percentage of one racial group or the other that would have to switch congregations to end segregation*. Thus, if Hinduism had a dissimilarity score of .35, it would mean that 35 percent of racial group A (or 35 percent of racial group B) would have to strategically switch temples to end segregation.

When I calculated the index of dissimilarity for religious traditions within the United States, I found an extremely high level of segregation. As a basis for comparison, in research on neighborhood segregation, cities with indexes of dissimilarity greater than .60 are considered highly segregated. According to this definition, all religious traditions are highly segregated. Comparing the segregation of whites and non-whites, the non-Christian category has an index of dissimilarity of .75. The value for Catholicism is .81; for mainline Protestantism, .85; and for conservative Protestantism, .91. Especially for the Christian traditions, these values indicate more than high segregation; they indicate *hyper-segregation*. For all Christian groups, over 80 percent of whites (or non-whites) would have to strategically change congregations to end segregation. For conservative Protestants, over 90 percent of whites (or non-whites) would have to switch congregations. Given that there is always movement of people in and out of congregations, and that at any given time at least some congregations are in racial transition, these values push the theoretical limits possible. For example, the most extremely segregated cities in our nation's history approach the .90 value. Values this high could usually only be achieved through laws, discriminatory lending and real estate procedures, threats, and other racially unequal practices. According to the calculations, Catholicism and mainline Protestantism approach these extreme values, and conservative Protestantism actually exceeds these values. Even if someone were in control of all conservative Protestantism and had the power and will to consciously assign whites and non-whites to separate congregations across the nation, obtaining a value of over .90 would be a difficult feat. But in the context of millions of people making choices year after year about which congregations to attend, such segregation values are astonishing.

We can now return to the prediction that other things being equal, the larger a faith tradition, the less racially diverse its congregations will be, compared to other faith traditions. Continuing to use the four faith traditions I have been discussing, I calculated the share of all religiously involved people that each tradition has, what we can call the *religious market share*.[11] I then plotted the relationship between

[11] I adjusted the adherent market share by each tradition's congregational share. Because of the way in which Roman Catholicism is organized—to have larger and fewer congregations than congregations in other traditions—its adherents have less congregational choice relative to its adherent size. Conversely, with its many small and storefront congregations, adherents of conservative Protestant have somewhat more choice relative to its adherent size. To account for this, I performed what I call a "gentle adjustment." That is, I first calculated an *adherent-to-congregation share* ratio for each tradition (adherent share/congregation share). If the ratio was greater than 1, I subtracted the amount greater than 1 from the adherent share (so for Catholicism, with a ratio of 3.69, I subtracted 2.69 from its adherent share of 25.1). For ratios less than 1, I added the difference between the ratio and 1 to the traditions' adherent share (so for mainline Protestantism, with a ratio of .99, I added .1 to its adherent share of 25.8).

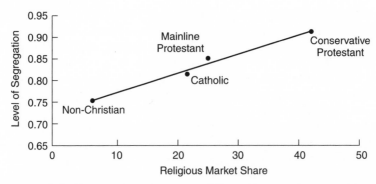

FIGURE 2.3. Relationships between religious share and index of dissimilarity, adjusted for congressional share

religious market share and the level of segregation (the index of dissimilarity). As figure 2.3 shows, the relationship between relative size and level of segregation is nearly perfect, and gives strong support to the prediction.[12] The non-Christian category has both the smallest number of adherents and the least amount of segregation, followed by Catholics, then mainline Protestants. Conservative Protestantism, the largest tradition of the four, also is the most segregated of the four.

DOES NEIGHBORHOOD RACIAL DIVERSITY MATTER?

When my colleagues and I talked with clergy and other congregants about the question of racial diversity in congregations, they rarely argued that they wanted to be uniracial. Most lay people gave the topic little thought, so for them it was not really an issue either way. Most clergy, especially if they were not in immigrant congregations, seemed to take the position that having at least some racial mix would be positive, even if they were committed to being a black church or a Chinese church.

Yet we have just learned how few congregations are racially mixed. For clergy in uniracial congregations who thought racial diversity in their congregation would be a positive step, we asked them why they thought their congregations were not racially mixed. A common response (often given in conjunction with other responses) was that

[12] For the statistically minded, the R^2 when regressing level of segregation on the religious market share is .98.

their neighborhoods were not racially diverse. This lack of neighborhood diversity, they told us, meant their congregation was limited severely in its ability to attract people outside their current dominant racial group.

By linking census data with the congregational data, we can examine the racial diversity of the neighborhoods in which the congregations reside. First, though, implicit in citing the lack of racial diversity in the neighborhood as a key limiter of racial diversity in the congregation is the assumption that people primarily attend congregations close to where they live. The National Congregations Study asked key informants in each sampled congregation to estimate the percentage of people they thought lived within a ten-minute walk, a ten-minute drive, and a more than thirty-minute drive from the congregation's worship site. According to these key informants, about three-quarters of their congregants live within a ten-minute drive from the congregation's worship site. Though a ten-minute drive from the worship site is larger than what most people would consider a neighborhood, it is not so much larger as to challenge the assumption by the clergy that the racial diversity of their surrounding area matters.

Given the ten-minute-drive finding, instead of using the immediate neighborhood (the immediate few blocks) surrounding the worship center, I will use what the U.S. Census Bureau calls a census tract. Census tracts are larger than an immediate neighborhood; they roughly approximate the size of an area that would take ten minutes or less to drive. Census tracts usually contain between two and eight thousand people. For the rest of the chapter when I use the word "neighborhood," I am measuring it as a census tract.

Using the general heterogeneity index—the probability that any two randomly selected people will be from different racial groups—I examined the racial diversity of the neighborhoods. Also, for comparative purposes, I compared the level of racial diversity of neighborhoods and congregations to public schools. I found that the neighborhoods in which the congregations reside are only about half as diverse as the nation's public schools. However, these neighborhoods are substantially more diverse than the congregations.[13] If I measure the average as the mean, the congregation's neighborhoods are three times more diverse than the congregations (.25 compared to .08); if I measure the average as the median, the congregation's neighborhoods are *ten* times more diverse than the congregations (.20 com-

---

[13] The congregational data was gathered in 1998. Because organizations take a period of years to adjust to their environment, I use census data from 1990.

pared to .02). Recall the simple interpretation of these numbers: the probability that any two people randomly selected from the neighborhoods of these congregations will be of different racial groups is 20 percent, but for any two people randomly selected from the congregations themselves is only 2 percent. Obviously, *the vast majority of congregations are substantially less racially diverse then the neighborhoods in which they reside*.

That the neighborhoods of religious congregations are, on average, substantially more diverse than the congregations may mask a more important pattern. Perhaps the higher average racial diversity of the neighborhoods is primarily the result of the neighborhoods of racially mixed congregations. In such a case, congregations without significant racial diversity would be in racially homogenous neighborhoods. When I examined this possibility, I found some interesting patterns.

The neighborhoods of white congregations indeed are less diverse than the neighborhoods of multiracial congregations (about one-half to one-third as racially diverse, depending on whether I use the mean or median). But this is not the case for black and other non-white congregations. The neighborhoods of black congregations have the same average level of racial diversity as do the neighborhoods of multiracial congregations. The neighborhoods of other uniracial congregations (primarily Asian and Latino) are actually more diverse than the neighborhoods of multiracial congregations. This likely reflects two realities. First, Asian and Latino Americans are less residentially segregated than white and black Americans, so the neighborhoods in which they live are more racially diverse. Second, because such high percentages of Asians and Hispanics—compared to whites, blacks, and American Indians—are first generation, they may seek out immigrant (and thus racially homogenous) congregations, regardless of the racial diversity of their neighborhood.

But knowing the diversity of the neighborhoods in which the congregations reside is only one way to examine whether a lack of neighborhood racial diversity is associated with a lack of congregational diversity. Perhaps just as interesting is the ratio of how racially diverse the congregation is to how racially diverse its neighborhood is, that is, the heterogeneity of the congregation divided by the heterogeneity of its neighborhood.

This approach gives a different picture. Primarily white congregations, though they reside in the least racially diverse neighborhoods among the four categories of congregations, are only about one-fourth as diverse as their neighborhoods. Black and other congregations are even less diverse compared to their neighborhoods. In strong contrast, multiracial congregations are actually 40 percent *more diverse* than their neighborhoods. Multiracial congregations are unique then not only because they are racially diverse, but because they *tend to be more diverse than the neighborhoods in which they reside*. One key will be to understand how it is possible to achieve this. We will explore that question in the next chapter.

Neighborhood diversity, then, seems an important factor in developing multiracial congregations, but it is neither a necessary nor a sufficient factor. Most congregations in racially diverse neighborhoods are not themselves racially diverse. Not all multiracial congregations are in highly diverse neighborhoods. About 13 percent of multiracial congregations are in neighborhoods that are 95 percent or more white; about one-quarter are in neighborhoods that are 85 percent or more white; 5 percent are in majority black neighborhoods; and an additional 15 percent are in majority Latino neighborhoods. Using the general heterogeneity index of the neighborhoods in which multiracial congregations are located, 15 percent of these congregations are located in neighborhoods with racial diversity as limited as those found in the average neighborhood of white congregations.[14]

Wilcrest is a multiracial congregation that is located in a multiracial neighborhood. In 1990, its neighborhood was 36 percent black, 28 percent Latino, 24 white, 14 percent Asian, and 2 percent other. Recall that in 1990 Wilcrest had not responded in its membership to the changes in its neighborhood; it was an all-white church. Through many factors explored in subsequent chapters, Wilcrest in 2000 was well on its way to responding to its neighborhood, but the neighborhood continued changing. According to 2000 census data, the neighborhood diversity score had actually declined. The percentage Latino and Asian had grown, and the percentage black stayed the same. But as is common in neighborhood transition, the neighborhood became less white: less than 10 percent of the neighborhood was white in 2000 (24 percent was white in 1990), and many of these whites were older residents who had moved to the neighborhood in the 1960s and 1970s. Few white families currently are moving to the neighborhood.[15] This means that most of the whites at Wilcrest, if they are under sixty, now come from somewhere outside the neighborhood.

[14] The zero-order correlation between tract racial heterogeneity and congregational racial heterogeneity is .26, a statistically significant but moderate association. The zero-order correlation (non-canonical) between tract heterogeneity and being a multiracial congregation or not (using the definition that no one racial group is 80 percent of the congregation) is .19.

[15] These figures were calculated from the www.census.gov website, accessed April 9, 2003. I attempted to keep the tract sizes constant over the ten-year period, but due to changes in the Census Bureau classifications, the 1990 Wilcrest neighborhood (calculated by combining two block groups) is slightly larger than in the 2000 tract, extending about 2 blocks further west, but identical in all other directions.

Though many non-whites now do so as well, the neighborhood people in this congregation are almost solely non-white.

CONCLUSION

In this chapter, words such as "unusual," "rare," "unique," and "different" have appeared frequently. That the people of Wilcrest decided to stay in their racially changing community—despite the congregation's declining size—and survived as a congregation is rare. That they hired a mixed-race, interracially married pastor with a unique background and vision is rarer still. And that Wilcrest is now more racially diverse than 99.5 percent of all U.S. congregations obviously makes Wilcrest highly unusual.

Congregations in the United States are hyper-segregated. The average level of racial diversity in congregations is near zero, and the average level of segregation between congregations is nearly perfect. Only 7 percent of all congregations in the United States can be classified using a binary measure as demographically multiracial. Within Christianity, the percentage is smaller still. For Protestantism, the percentage is even smaller. In an attempt to make sense of these segregations levels, I found an ironic twist. *The more successful a faith tradition is in terms of its overall number of adherents, the more segregated are its local assemblies. Moreover, nearly all congregations are substantially more segregated than the neighborhoods in which they reside. The exceptions to this rule are multiracial congregations, which are internally more diverse than the neighborhoods in which they reside.*

And so we can summarize this chapter's theme: Multiracial congregations, on multiple levels, appear to be distinctive. They are unique, different from most of the hundreds of thousands of congregations in the United States. But we still have more to explore. Importantly, *how* do congregations like Wilcrest become multiracial? What factors seem to matter? We will explore these questions and others in the next chapter, drawing on in-depth study of multiracial congregations around the country.

CHAPTER 3 • Paths

GIVEN THEIR RARITY, how do multiracial congregations come to be? In this chapter I explore what key factors are associated with racial diversity in congregations. I begin by examining traits of more than 1,200 randomly selected U.S. congregations. This provides us a good overview but does not tell us much about the process of becoming a multiracial congregation. For a better understanding of that process, we turn to the thirty congregations that my colleagues and I studied in depth and explore the paths these congregations took to becoming what they are. And then, to give a more detailed, inside view of the transformation process, we return to and follow Wilcrest and Rodney Woo as they start down their path to becoming a multiracial congregation.

THINKING BIG

Organizations are not self-sufficient. They depend on their environments to survive. Environments, constantly changing, can serve to shape the goals and boundaries of organizations. The last chapter explored two environmental factors that seemed important in understanding the level of racial diversity in congregations. One was the faith tradition of the congregation. The larger the numbers of people in a tradition, the less diverse, on average, are congregations in that tradition. We also found that the racial diversity of congregations' neighborhoods seems to matter, at least to some degree.

Other factors are often thought to explain racial diversity in congregations. When I began this research, I heard repeatedly that I should find out why "the Charismatics and Pentecostals are so likely to be racially mixed." I found this request odd, given that we had no data to support this claim. It made more sense first to find out if indeed such groups were more likely to be racially mixed. When we measure this as the likelihood that a racially mixed congregation belongs to a Charismatic or Pentecostal denomination, contrary to popular belief, congregations are in fact no more likely to be racially mixed than other faith traditions. However, if we consider worship style, we find a different story. I measured charismatic worship style by combining four indicators—during worship in the past week, saying "amen"; raising hands; jumping, shouting, or dancing spontaneously; and, anytime in the last twelve months, "speaking in tongues" (that is, speaking in languages unknown to the speaker). Using this measure, those congregations with more upbeat, charismatic-like services are indeed more likely to be racially mixed. This holds true no matter what the tradition of the congregation. For example, mainline congregations with a charismatic style are as likely to be racially mixed, using the binary measure discussed in the last chapter, as are congregations in Pentecostal denominations with a charismatic style. Charismatic worship style seems to matter. But multiracial congregations also tend to be younger, on average, than other congregations. Perhaps it is the younger membership that leads to both a more charismatic worship style and a greater likelihood of being racially diverse. The problem with comparing one variable at a time to see if it is associated with congregational diversity is that we do not know which factors really matter.

To avoid this problem, I used *multivariate analysis*, a set of statistical techniques that allow us to consider all potentially pertinent factors simultaneously, to see which factors among them really matter and which do not. Attempting to explain the racial diversity of congregations—using the general heterogeneity index—I included factors thought to matter by social scientists or by the people I talked to in the congregations. These factors include the religious tradition of the congregation; congregational characteristics, such as number of attendees, age of its worshipers, theology, and worship style; neighborhood characteristics, such as racial composition, percentage of immigrants, percentage urban, percentage single parents, median household income, and average age; and the region of the nation in which the congregation was located. (Many people have asked whether congregations in the South are less likely to be racially diverse.)

The results—summarized in Table 3.1—are illuminating.[1] Compared to mainline Protestants congregations (Episcopalians, Presbyterian USA, United Methodists, and related denominations), the non-Christian traditions (again put into just one category because of sample size) and Catholic congregations are more likely to be racially diverse, even after accounting for all the other factors mentioned above. These findings follow from what we explored in the last chapter. Interestingly, once we account for other differences, namely worship style, congregations in Pentecostal/Charismatic denominations are less likely to be racially diverse than are mainline Protestant congregations. This is perhaps due to the fact that the two largest Pen-

---

[1] The full statistical results are reported in table B3.1 in appendix B.

TABLE 3.1
Factors Associated with Racial Diversity in U.S. Congregations

Variable	Variables association with racial diversity of congregation, when effects of other variables have been removed
Religious Tradition[a]	
Non-Christian	Increased Diversity
Catholic	Increased Diversity
Penecostal/Charismatic	Decreased Diversity
Black Denomination	Decreased Diversity
Evangelical/Conservative Protestant	No Effect
Congregational Characteristics	
Attendance	No Effect
% of congregation over 60	Decreased Diversity
Theology	No Effect
Worship style	Increased Diversity
Small group[b]	Increased Diversity
Year congregation was founded[c]	No Effect
Neighborhood characteristics	
Racial diversity of neighborhood	Increased Diversity
% White	Decreased Diversity
% Black	Decreased Diversity
% Urban	Increased Diversity
% Renters	No Effect
Median HH income	Increased Diversity
% employed in managerial or professional	Increased Diversity
% Aged 18 or under	No Effect
Region of Country[d]	
Northeast	No Effect
Midwest	No Effect
South	No Effect

[a]All variables in this category are compared to Mainline Protestant.

[b]Within the past 12 months, any groups of people from the congregation meeting *once a month or more* for religious, social, recreational, or other purposes, not including governing or administrative committees.

[c]Several methods of entering founding date were tried, none had a significant effect.

[d]All variables in this category are compared to the West region.

tecostal/Charismatic denominations are racially based. The Church of God in Christ denomination is overwhelmingly black, the Assemblies of God denomination is largely white. Not surprisingly, congregations in the black Protestant denominations are less likely to be diverse than our comparison group, mainline Protestants.

As we found earlier, the more charismatic the worship style, the more racially diverse, on average, is the congregation. Even controlling for worship style and the other factors, higher percentages of people over sixty in the congregation are associated with less racial diversity. Once accounting for other factors, the theology of a congregation—be it conservative, liberal, or somewhere in between—does not predict a congregation's diversity. Congregations that meet in small groups are more likely to be racially diverse. Sociologist Kevin Dougherty, who also found this small-group effect, argues that the potential for multiracial congregations to survive long term is enhanced to the degree that their members develop interracial ties. The opportunity for such ties is enhanced through the social arrangement of small groups, which stress close relationships among participants.[2]

Six neighborhood factors help explain the level of racial diversity in a congregation. Three measure racial diversity. The more racially heterogeneous the neighborhood, the more racially diverse the congregation. However, this is not a one-to-one relationship. Specifically, according to the estimates, each 10 percent increase in neighborhood racial diversity leads to, on average, about a 1 percent increase in racial diversity.[3] So, though there is an association between these factors, congregational diversity does not keep pace with neighborhood diversity.

The overall level of racial diversity is not all that matters. Because the most segregated groups in the United States are whites and blacks, and because they have the strongest traditions of separate congregations and denominations, I suspected that the percentage white and black in the neighborhood would also shape the level of congregational diversity. The results support this idea. Both greater percentages of whites and greater percentages of blacks in the neighborhood are associated with less racial diversity in the congregation.

---

[2] See Kevin Dougherty's 2003 and Dougherty and Huyser's forthcoming articles on racially diverse congregations. See especially the latter article for a fine review of the literature on the topic of factors associated with racial diversity in congregations.

[3] This estimate comes from OLS regression equation estimates (not shown). This estimation technique allows the sort of interpretation given here. However, because OLS is not the best estimation method given the distribution of the dependent variable (though in actuality the OLS and Tobit methods gave the same substantive results), this ten-to-one relationship must be viewed as an approximation.

This finding foreshadows an important finding for our study of multiracial congregations, one I will discuss in chapter 6. The percentage of recent immigrants in the neighborhood, once we account for the other factors, does not shape the level of diversity in the congregation.

The results of the multivariate model also suggest that the more urban an area, the more racially diverse a congregation will be, on average. Importantly, the higher the average household income and the higher the percentage of people in managerial and professional occupations in the neighborhood, the more racially diverse the congregation tends to be. This may mean a wider variety of people are more willing to attend congregations in neighborhoods with higher average socioeconomic status, or it could be an indicator that racially diverse congregations are less likely to be poor. Some have argued that if congregations are to be racially diverse, they will have to hold other factors in common, such as class.[4]

In the data set my colleagues and I constructed of 490 congregations, including more multiracial congregations than we would get in a simple random sample (to allow for adequate numbers for analysis), we asked the key informant — usually the senior clergy person — to rate on a scale from 1 to 7 how economically similar or diverse their members were. Although the key informants certainly do not know the incomes of every person in their congregation, they do have a general sense of whether their congregation is economically diverse. They use markers such as the occupations of their parishioners, where they live, and the car(s) they drive or do not drive. Using this question, informants (regardless of the dominant racial group of their congregation) said that although their congregations had some class diversity, their parishioners were more economically similar than different. The lone exception to this pattern was multiracial congregations. Here, informants reported that their congregations were *more economically diverse than economically similar*.[5] Unless we think that racially mixed congregations report more economic diversity than other congregations for reasons other than actually being more economically diverse, the belief that racially mixed congregations will only form if they are homogenous on class measures is not supported by these data. The in-depth study of congregations by my colleagues and I also confirms this conclusion. The racially homogenous con-

---

[4] C. Peter Wagner, *Our Kind of People* (1979).

[5] With 1 meaning no economic diversity and 7 meaning maximum economic diversity, the mean score for homogenous congregations was 3.47, and the mean score for multiracial congregations was 4.68, a statistically significant difference (t = 6.36, p < .001).

gregations we studied appeared to have more uniformity in the class of their members. And while we certainly found exceptions to the rule, most of the multiracial congregations we studied were economically mixed, certainly more so than the racially homogenous congregations we studied. Wilcrest is a good example of why this may be. As Dr. Woo discusses later in the chapter, when he arrived Wilcrest was both racially and economically homogenous. When new groups began attending, the racial changes also introduced class differences into the congregation.[6] And as discussed in chapter 5, as the congregation became more racially diverse, a wide variety of people were attracted to the congregation because they felt accepted there.

Finally, when I account for the other variables in the model, region of the country does not predict the level of racial diversity in congregations. Some people believe congregational diversity might be lower in the South, given its racialized history. Congregations in the South are highly segregated, but so too are congregations in every other region of the country, such that they are statistically equally segregated.

Taken together, religious tradition, congregational characteristics, and neighborhood characteristics can explain nearly one-half of the variation in the level of racial diversity in congregations (see table B3.1 in appendix B for the full statistical results). These factors, then, are useful in helping us understand racial diversity in congregations. But what explains the other one-half of the variation? Clearly, something more matters that these factors are not capturing. To understand what else is important, and to begin looking at the actual process of transformation, I turn to a systematic analysis of the congregations that my colleagues and I visited.

Congregations Transforming: A Qualitative View

For a more complete understanding of how congregations are transformed, we must understand that, most generally, religious congregations are *organizations*, like businesses, schools, or local YMCAs. Organizations are characterized and defined by three unique features.[7] First, they are *goal directed*. When they are functioning well,

---

[6] This of course can cause additional problems. For example, one white professional man at Wilcrest, who came after Wilcrest was diverse, abruptly left the church when his children reached youth group age. He told Pastor Woo he left because the types of people in the youth group were not the best people for his children to associate with. I will discuss such problems in chapter 6. See also Christerson, Edwards, and Emerson (2005) for a fuller analysis of the role youth have on adult decisions to attend, stay, or leave multiracial congregations.

[7] Howard Aldrich, *Organizations Evolving* (1999), pp. 2–5.

they have a focused agenda around which members organize their activities. One way to accomplish this is for organizations to formally state their goals in mission statements. Next, they are *boundary maintaining*. Organizations must have boundaries to define who and what is part of the organization and who and what is not. All sorts of factors can push organizations to blur these boundaries, but organizations must have them to survive, so they must engage in boundary maintenance. Congregations may do this through formal membership classes that teach what is unique about being part of their congregation, and discussion in worship services and other meeting times. Finally, organizations have *activity systems* to accomplish their goals and maintain their boundaries. In religious congregations, such activities often include a regular time for worship or study, youth events, and annual celebrations. For many congregations, paid staff, a board of volunteer leaders, a committee structure assigned specific tasks, and many more volunteers carry out the work of implementing the goals and maintaining uniqueness.

In our in-depth study of over thirty congregations — twenty-two of which were multiracial — I found that, at least on the surface, every congregation appeared unique, and began in its own way. However, looking at congregations as organizations with the three unique dimensions noted above, and as organizations influenced by their environments, two main factors appear to underlie the manner in which multiracial congregations develop: (1) the primary impetus for becoming a multiracial congregation (this combined the goal direction and boundary maintenance dimensions); and (2) the source of the minority population (environment). By minority population I mean any groups which are not the majority group in the congregation. For an Asian congregation, all non-Asians are part of the minority population. The particular combinations of these variables result in not one but seven multiracial founding types, and also shape the chances for their long-term survivability as multiracial congregations. Importantly, all of these congregations had to have effective activity systems to carry out the tasks necessary.[8]

The Primary Impetus for Change

Often, the primary impetus for a congregation becoming multiracial comes from its *mission* — its theological, cultural, and/or symbolic orientation. In short, its goals are the impetus. In this case, a con-

---

[8] For comparison, we studied eight racially homogenous congregations as well. For simplicity, they are not discussed here, but they were used to compare congregations that became multiracial and those that did not.

gregation's becoming multiracial is consistent with the very purpose for its existence, either directly—"we desire to be multiracial"—or indirectly—"we wish to serve all people." Another possible impetus stems from the process of *resource calculation*. Changes in the congregation's resource levels—whether a decline in membership (sometimes driven by neighborhood population changes), budget constraints, or perceived opportunity due to an abundance of a new resource—can spur congregational adaptations that lead to a multiracial membership.[9] A third possible impetus for a congregation becoming multiracial originates in the *external authority structure* in which the congregation exists. In this case, denominational leaders can tell a church to become multiracial in order to meet a goal at the denominational level. The primary impetus for change comes from outside the congregation but may still be consistent with its mission. In organizations, there may be a variety of impetuses for change. Therefore, it is important to note that I am discussing the *primary* impetus for change. (See figure 3.1 for a summary.)

In order for the efforts toward a multiracial membership to *succeed*, there must be an available population of racially different persons from which to draw new members—that is, there must be population opportunity. These new members, who are of a different race from the majority of members of the congregations in question, may be drawn to the church for a variety of reasons. First, the population may be drawn by *proximity*, if in this new situation, members are drawn from the same neighborhood as the congregation, but the neighborhood itself undergoes changes in racial composition. There may be evangelization of or social programs developed for neighbors, but the primary draw is the proximity of the congregation, as in the case of a geographically based Catholic parish. Proximity is never enough, in and of itself, for congregations to racially diversify, but in combination with an impetus for change, such as the congregation's mission, it can lead to change.

[9] The term *resource calculation* best captures Penny Edgell Becker's (1998) work. In her case studies of the congregations in Oak Park, IL, an inner ring suburb of Chicago, she argues that congregations respond to environmental change (in this case, their neighborhoods becoming more racially diverse) either by (a) ignoring it, and ultimately declining, (b) moving away, (c) adopting a regional strategy for survival and growth (with these congregations remaining racially homogenous), or (d) adopting a *local growth strategy*, then drawing on their tradition to set the stage for being more broadly inclusive communities. Her research is helpful for understanding the options available to congregations in racially changing communities. In our study of congregations from a variety of places around the nation, my colleagues and I found the local growth strategy to be part of a wider array of strategies by which some congregations became multiracial.

Second, the minority population may be drawn by the appeal of the *culture and purpose* of the congregation. This can involve outreach or evangelization on the part of congregation targeting a particular niche and attracting a diverse membership across racial lines. Congregations that draw racially diverse people because of their culture and purpose typically draw from the region rather than simply locally. In this sense, such congregations create population opportunity, even if their immediate neighborhood is not diverse. This begins to help us understand the earlier finding that multiracial congregations, on average, are more diverse than their immediate neighborhoods.

Third, diverse membership can be the result of *preexisting organizational packages*. This is the case when two or more congregations merge. The membership diversity comes from the joining together of preexisting congregations, not by an increase in new membership. In fact, mergers are often accompanied by membership declines, as some members reject the merger.

Figure 3.1 presents a typology of different types of multiracial congregations that my colleagues and I have identified through our study, and the paths of the underlying variables that lead to each congregational type.[10] The table shows the relationships between the primary impetus for change (mission, resource calculation, or external authority structure) and the source of diversification (proximity, culture and purpose, or preexisting organizational package). Unique combinations of these two variables lead to seven main multiracial congregational types. Although many multiracial congregations exhibit characteristics consistent with more than one type, there is usually one primary category that describes the mechanisms through which a congregation became multiracial.

Not all combinations between the two variables are possible. When the primary impetus for change is the congregation's mission, the source of diversification does not come from preexisting organizational packages.[11] Likewise, when the primary impetus for change is an external authority structure, the source of diversification does not appear to come from culture and purpose.

Slightly more than one-half of our twenty-two multiracial congregations became or began multiracial because of their sense of mission. But from this dominant underlying variable, we found four distinct types of multiracial congregations, each with a different route to diversification. As the figure shows, five of our sample congrega-

[10] These types were first proposed and discussed with my colleague, Karen Chai Kim. See Emerson and Kim 2003.

[11] See Finke and Stark 1992, chapter 6 for why this is so.

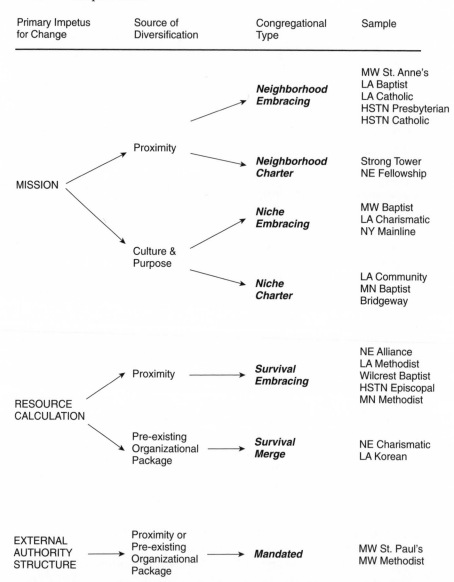

FIGURE 3.1. Impetus for change, diversification source, and multiracial congregational types

tions transformed from uniracial to multiracial due to the implications of their mission as their local neighborhood's population changed. I call this a *Neighborhood Embracing* multiracial congregation. For some congregations it is their mission to actively reach out to anyone in the neighborhood through programs or evangelism. For others, it is a reinterpretation of the mission of their church in light of the changing neighborhood.[12] And, for some, this mission is to accept and serve any who come.

Houston Catholic is one of these congregations. Today about 50 percent African American, 45 percent white, and 5 percent Latino and Filipino, the church began in the mid-1950s as a largely Italian congregation. Over time, Catholic African Americans who were moving from Louisiana increasingly populated parts of the parish. The dioceses established a separate church for them, but with fewer resources than Houston Catholic. During one especially long hot summer in the early 1960s, some African Americans, attracted by the air conditioning at Houston Catholic, came to visit. Although this was the era of segregation by law, in the black parishioners' own words the parish priest, Father Nick Perusina, met them welcomingly. Known as someone with an extraordinary love for people, Father Perusina's goal for the church had always been to embrace any who lived in the parish, and he had been preparing his white parishioners for this day. So, despite the times, the original black parishioners that we interviewed said the congregation as a whole accepted them. Because of the welcome (and the air conditioning) they came back, bringing other family members. Within just a year of their arrival, Father Perusina began asking African Americans to be involved in leadership. One such person was Delilah, one of the very first African Americans to come to Houston Catholic. Raised in the strict racially segregated environment of the South, when she was asked to teach a religious education class, she was shocked:

> I was skeptical because of the fact that (in the outside world) we were called Negroes, and considered low class. And I was uncomfortable because I didn't have a very good competence level. I had very low self-esteem because of what it [the racial system] had done. But with Father Perusina and some of the ladies here, I worked through it. I then realized—I can do this! And over the years my husband and I have continued to be involved. And I sit back now on Sundays and realize . . . it's beautiful, all the groups we have here, and I also realize, this parish is a part of me. I have given myself here and this is my parish and these are my friends.

[12] Becker 1998.

A *Neighborhood Charter* multiracial congregation differs from a Neighborhood Embracing congregation in that it *began* as a multiracial congregation, rather than being remade into one. Northeast Fellowship began as a mission to convert and rehabilitate homeless men. A white pastor lived among homeless men in the city, mostly African Americans and whites, requiring them to follow a strict program and teaching them about Christianity. His ministry then evolved into a congregation of homeless men, often with criminal records and histories of drug abuse, and others from this multiracial neighborhood. The multiracial nature of this congregation points to an important fact: congregations can be multiracial because the issue of racial inclusiveness is a central aspect of their mission, or they can be multiracial as a result of a more central aspect of their mission, such as reaching the homeless, providing services, or evangelizing.

Strong Tower Church is an interesting example of this point. The Reverend Chris Williamson, an African American, was on staff at a white Presbyterian church. Seeing the needs in the black community, he set out to start a black church. But something unexpected happened.

> We started a black church and the Lord from the onset said it's going to be integrated. When I would have prayer meetings about starting the church, whites would show up, saying "Let's pray" and "We want to be part your church if you start one." This kept happening. So my plan to reach the black community by starting a black church drew many white folk in support of our mission. I thought, "Loooord, you're telling me something here. I don't want to be in your way, so let me change my thinking. Strong Tower will be multidimensional, our term for multiracial, multieconomic, multicultural, multiministry."

Despite Pastor Chris Williamson's original mission to reach African Americans, his former involvement in a white church led to many whites joining him. This ultimately led to changing the mission to be more directly focused on reaching all people of the local area.

Midwest Baptist is an extreme example of becoming multiracial as an outgrowth of a different mission. A fundamentalist church with strict dress and grooming codes, this congregation's driving mission is to "save every soul" in their small metropolitan area. A white congregation with a white staff located in a primarily white neighborhood in a rural-looking area outside the city limits, but driven by its mission, Midwest Baptist began a bussing ministry in the mid-1970s. Going door to door in every neighborhood of the city, members of Midwest Baptist talked with parents and invited their children to get on the Midwest Baptist bus that would come through Sunday morning to bring their children to Sunday school. What began with one bus and a few children has now, over 25 years later, evolved into 28 buses each sent out twice on Sunday mornings, involving the efforts of 200 members each Sunday to bring over 1500 children for four separate hours of Sunday school and worship services. Most of the children are black and Hispanic, and it has been that way, the pastor told us, since the start. Over time, parents started attending the church, and some of the original children, now adults, stayed, transforming the congregation into a multiracial one.

Midwest Baptist is a clear example of a *Niche Embracing* multiracial congregation. Its mission led it to programming and outreach efforts that draw diverse people from the entire region. Its niche is its bussing ministry and now well-known children's Sunday school.

Minnesota Baptist is a niche church as well, but because it began as a multiracial church, it is a *Niche Charter*. Its African American pastor began with the goal of establishing a multiracial church that would reconcile people of different racial groups. Driven by this mission, the pastor spoke to any existing congregations that would let him — Latino churches, black churches, white churches, Chinese churches, and so on. He told these congregations about his goal to start a multiracial congregation and invited people to join him. When the church opened its doors for its first service, the congregation was multiracial, which it has remained.

For about one-third of the congregations in our study, the primary impetus for change was not their mission, but resource calculation, typically due to declining membership as the neighborhood racial composition changed. Oftentimes, when neighborhoods change, congregations sell their church building and move, or they stay and close their doors when members no longer remain. But a few take a different strategy.

Houston Episcopal is an example of a congregation that took a different strategy. This *Survival Embracing* multiracial congregation, originally a well-to-do congregation of professional whites with young families, saw its neighborhood racial composition turn from white to black almost overnight. Fearful of the reaction of white neighbors, the first black family to buy a house in the neighborhood, upon the recommendation of the realtor who sold them the house, moved into their house under the cover of darkness, at three in the morning. When the neighbors discovered what had happened, "For Sale" signs went up en masse, and in a relatively short time, the neighborhood was 98 percent African American.

The effects of this dramatic neighborhood shift on Houston Episcopal were profound. This growing congregation full of young families and children dwindled to only a few families, with almost no money to pay the staff. Rather than close the doors or move, the congregation decided to open its doors to black parishioners. The primary impetus for this decision was its resource calculation — they had to do something new to survive. Because of this calculation, they then altered their understanding of their mission, and began programming (such as changes in worship) to attract black parishioners. They have been successful. The church is now about 70 percent African American and Caribbean black, and 30 percent white.

Resource calculations can lead some congregations, faced with the desire to survive, to combine with another congregation. If the congregations are predominately of different racial groups, the result is a *Survival Merge* multiracial congregation. A Los Angeles Korean ethnic church merged with a multiracial church several years ago. The merger was precipitated by the lack of an English-speaking pastor for the Korean church's English ministry. At the same time, a nearby multiracial church of the same denomination was in need of a church building. Because the multiracial church's pastor was Korean American, he was a suitable candidate to lead the new merged congregation. In this case, both congregations were able to survive from the merge, but in different ways — one gained an English-speaking pastor, the other a building.[13]

The final type of multiracial congregation — the *Mandated* congregation — originates not from internal decisions, but from decisions made by an authority structure outside the congregation. The source of racial diversification can be either the immediate neighborhood or a preexisting organizational package. The latter was the case for Midwest St. Paul's Catholic church. The bishop of the diocese, in consultation with others, made the decision to close five churches, creating one new parish with a new building and bringing together the five congregations — one African American, two German white, one Latino, and one Polish white. The result was a mandated multiracial congregation that currently has (unofficially) co-pastors — one black

[13] Although this Survival Merge congregation began as a multiracial one, it did not stay that way as the result of two factors. First, the new congregation shared facilities with and maintained close ties to a Korean-speaking immigrant congregation. Second, the large number of Korean American members in the merged congregation and the close link between the church and Korean ethnic identity (including a Korean American senior pastor) eventually caused non-Korean members to leave the congregation and form their own congregation — still in the same building — with an African American pastor. A uniracial congregation and a multiracial congregation merged to share resources, but the end result was a uniracial congregation, Los Angeles Korean American Church, and a new multiracial congregation.

and one white, eclectic music, and a mass conducted partly in Spanish. This particular church appears, on the surface, to be healthy and operating smoothly. However, in interviews with the pastors and the parishioners, there are questions as to whether the congregation will remain multiracial. In particular, the African American population is aging, as the congregation is not successfully drawing new African American members.

Though all multiracial churches face forces that make them at risk of instability, *Mandated* multiracial congregations seem to face even more initial risk. This is due to the source of the change, from outside the congregation, sometimes producing resistance within the congregation. For example, Midwest Methodist, a congregation of older whites now in a Latino and African American neighborhood, has twice bristled at the mandate that they become multiracial. As African American and Latino staff were successively appointed, African American and then Latino locals began attending. However, the elderly white members refused to make any adjustments to their worship service or to their church operations to accommodate the new attendees. Feeling unwelcome and alienated by the longtime members, the African Americans and Hispanics left to join their respective uniracial congregations. Denominational leaders have since resigned themselves to the fact that this church will die when the current members do.

IMPLICATIONS OF THE MODELS FOR SURVIVABILITY

The equilibrium point — the natural place of social stability — for most congregations is a uniracial condition. Given that so many factors predispose congregations to be uniracial, what gives rise to multiracial congregations? I identified seven models that describe the origination of multiracial congregations. Key to understanding these models are the two main variables that underlie their creation — the primary impetus for change (mission, resource calculation, and external authority structure) and source of diversification (proximity, culture and purpose, and preexisting organizational package). The particular combinations of these variables lead to different models.

Attempting to generalize, it seems that the model which led to the creation of the multiracial congregation impacts its survivability as a multiracial congregation. When the change originates outside the congregation (external authority structure-driven Mandated churches), these churches appear less likely to remain multiracial. Conversely, congregations that become multiracial out of their sense of mission (internal locus) will, on average, be more likely to sustain their multira-cial composition than those that become so out of resource calculation (a mix of external and internal locus), which in turn will be more likely to sustain their multiracial composition than those that become so from an outside authority structure (external locus).

Given that neighborhood populations are often dynamic, it also seems that, apart from the influence of other factors, the broader the area from which a congregation draws its racial diversification, the greater the likelihood that it will sustain its multiracial composition. If a congregation relies on the immediate neighborhood for racial di-versity, its multiracial composition can only last as long as the neigh-borhood remains racially diverse. I did find evidence, though, that some congregations that initially drew their diversity from the im-mediate neighborhood gained a reputation over time as racially di-verse, which then led to people coming from a broader area.

Congregations that derive their racial diversity from preexisting or-ganizational packages tend to form at least in part from an external locus. Also, they draw their diversification not from a neighborhood or region per se, but from what used to be independent congrega-tions, meaning the source of continued diversity is uncertain. What is more, bringing together two or more congregations each with their own unique cultures, social networks, and internal authority struc-tures is fraught with potential difficulties. Hence, apart from the in-fluence of other factors, I hypothesize that *Survival Merge* and *Man-dated* multiracial congregations are the least likely of the multiracial congregational types to survive as multiracial congregations.

I found evidence for this hypothesis in this research. Of the two multiracial congregations that reverted to uniracial status during the time of our study, both had become multiracial through preexisting organizational packages. One was a *Survival Merge*, the other a *Man-dated* congregation. And the long-term sustainability of our other two study congregations that became multiracial from preexisting orga-nizational packages seemed tenuous.

My colleague George Yancey used our survey of congregations to produce a somewhat different typology of multiracial congregations. Our survey asked key informants of congregations what they thought were the main factors in their becoming multiracial. Analyzing their responses through a statistical method called factor analysis, George Yancey identified four main types: Leadership multiracial congrega-tions, which are based around a leader or leaders who attract a di-versity of people, Evangelism multiracial congregations, which use proselytizing strategies to reach a diversity of people, Demographic multiracial congregations, which become multiracial largely through a changing neighborhood that provides the diversification source, and Network multiracial congregations, which grow racially diverse through an expansion of social ties. Of these four types, he finds that Network multiracial congregations are the most likely to grow. This appears to be the case because people come with social ties already in place and have greater confidence in joining.[14]

INSIDE CHANGE

Discussing the main origination types of multiracial congregations is helpful, but we are still left without a full sense of the processes involved. What are the actual on-the-ground steps taken in transforming into or beginning as a multiracial congregation? Let us turn to an in-depth look at Wilcrest, the congregation we have been following in this book. Wilcrest is a congregation that has used and relied on aspects from all four types of multiracial congregations George Yancey discusses, so exploring its development not only allows us to see its impetus for change and its racial diversification source, but also gives us a glimpse into how leadership, proselytizing, demographics, and networks matter for diversifying.[15]

In the Beginning

How did Wilcrest move from being a uniracial church to today being more racially diverse than more than 99 percent of all congregations? Given what we discussed earlier in the chapter, Wilcrest faced some key challenges. Their impetus for change was resource calculation: they needed to survive and were willing to hire a pastor with a different kind of vision in an attempt to do so. As time moved on, we see this original impetus translate into the core mission of Wilcrest. The source of diversification was also a question. To learn about the beginning of this process, I talked with Rodney Woo. Yes, he had a dream to transform from a uniracial to a multiracial congregation. But how was this dream realized, at least demographically? I asked him to describe what happened, beginning with his very first day at Wilcrest.

[14] See chapter 4 of George Yancey's book, *One Body, One Spirit* (2003a).

[15] For a more in-depth discussion and model of the actual stages congregations go through in racially diversifying, see the work of Parker (2005), who closely studied the transformation processes of three South African congregations. In addition, see the work of his mentor, H. J. Hendriks (1995). See also my discussion of these stages in the final chapter of this book.

I walked into my office the first day bent on acclimating myself to the place and the culture. One of the first things I did was visit the people who were part of the congregation, to get to know them, and for them to get to know me. I soon learned that the members that remained were almost without exception in their later forties and fifties. As so many white congregations of this age are, it was also a middle class group of people. I spent a lot of time with the youth (at age 29 I was closer in age to many of them than to most of the adult members), talking with them, playing basketball with them. Strategically, I thought if change were going to come, it would be easiest if it began through the youth. They were the ones with friends in the local schools, which were now so very racially mixed. They had more connections to people they could invite to our congregation, or whom I could meet.

I also encouraged the members of our congregation to join me in praying for change, and to invite people of different backgrounds to the church. If they knew people through work, through their involvement in the local school, or in their racially changing neighborhood, I asked them to consider inviting them to Wilcrest. A few did. And we benefited from our location. Near the intersection of two main streets, I found that we would get a few non-white visitors on Sunday mornings. In the past such visitors had been told they would be more comfortable elsewhere, or they were not welcomed, and so they did not return. Those practices had to change.

With enthusiasm I committed to this: I visited anyone who came to visit our church. Especially if they were not white, I went the extra mile to visit them soon after they visited us, sharing our faith and dream with them, and encouraging them to become part of Wilcrest. Racial change was slow going these first years, for I was asking people to be pioneers.

Rodney Woo had a goal—to become multiracial—but he needed the means. The means were twofold: changes within the congregation and efforts to reach outside the congregation. These means are not always mutually exclusive. What they had in common was heightening the impetus for change and reaching sources of racial diversification. Congregations that transform from uniracial to multiracial, as opposed to beginning multiracial, must make *several* changes. Simply changing one aspect or another is never enough to overcome organizational inertia. Multiple changes are required. These changes can neither come too slowly nor too fast.

Successful transition to diversity is exponential. Demographic and other change starts slowly with little overall change, typically high turnover, and low retention rates of the congregation's non-majority members and majority members who do not want such change. Through this period, if more changes are made, the attraction for non-majority members increases, and the growth rate of such people increases, as does the retention rate. The growing presence of non-majority members further enhances the transformation potential as they encourage other internal changes that attract people and invite people in their networks to attend. Certainly this has been the case for Wilcrest.

Although Wilcrest does not keep records of people migrating out of its congregation, they do keep careful records of people entering. Baptists classify new congregants in two ways—those who join by transferring from another congregation, and those who newly join by baptism. Joining by baptism means the person was not previously a baptized member in another evangelical Christian congregation. In the first year and a half that Dr. Woo came to Wilcrest, given the size of the congregation—slightly fewer than 200—Wilcrest had a large number of new members join. A total of 242 people joined through transfer or baptism during this period (mid-1992 through the end of 1993). Of these 242 people, 78, or approximately one-third of the new members, were non-white. Of the 78 non-Anglos, only 10 were Asian (some in the congregation feared that in hiring Rodney Woo, the church would become all Asian), while 31 were black and 37 were Latino. Some of the non-Anglos who joined were middle class, but many were not. So the growth meant increasing class differences as well. In some congregations that we studied which attempted to become multiracial, many people in the congregation resisted. In more than one case, their resistance was enough to keep others away. For example, recall Midwest Methodist discussed a few pages earlier. The resistance of the whites in that congregation was so strong that non-whites rarely visited any more. I asked Dr. Woo about his experience with the Wilcrest members as the initial changes happened:

> Yes, there was some resistance, but I experienced more support for these changes than I did opposition. Several factors contributed to the dominant theme of support. The church was under new leadership and prior to that had been in decline for several years, so people were willing to support, at least initially, new ideas and practices. Perhaps in part because I had been upfront about the direction that Wilcrest must go, most of the people who would strongly resist a move toward becoming a multiracial congregation had already left before I arrived. The infusion of growth, even if it involved non-white people, created much excitement among the longer-time members. And even though one-third of the growth was non-white, two-thirds of it was white, so we were living up to our call to be a church for all people. I also taught about the rightness of becoming multiracial, providing the beginning of a theological understanding for the changes. Finally,

while one third of new people joining our congregation in that first year and half were non-Anglos, the church remained overwhelmingly Anglo. Anglos were still 95 percent or more of the congregation, minimizing long-time parishioners' feelings of being threatened by the changes.

Despite this early support by Wilcrest members, not all went well. They made mistakes and had much to learn. Moreover, just because people came did not mean they stayed. During the beginning stages of a transformation, not all key changes are in place. For example, Wilcrest's worship during this time remained exactly as it had been in the past. So non-whites came, but not many stayed. According to Woo, "of the original 78 that came in the first year and a half, probably less than 20 stayed more than a year or two. Obviously, we had problems, and to address them, more fundamental changes had to be made."

Formalizing the Dream

With Rodney Woo leading, the members of Wilcrest took a number of important steps that aided their racial diversification. These steps had the function of institutionalizing racial diversification. That is, they built racial diversity into the very character of their organization.

The church formed a task force to communicate and institutionalize their goal into a vision statement. In preparation of writing their vision statement, much background work was done. One of the members involved in this process, a white woman then in her fifties, recalls:

> We created a task force. Our eventual goal was to produce a vision statement. We first had Sunday night meetings for several months when Brother Rodney first came. We focused on understanding how God works. As part of this discovery process, we talked with some families living in the neighborhood around the church. The most striking result to me was that many did not know that Wilcrest existed.
>
> After some months of studying and talking to people in the neighborhood, we went on a retreat, to write a vision statement. It was a big deal. Over fifty of us set aside whatever other responsibilities we had for the weekend, and we went on the retreat to come up with a vision statement. By the time of the retreat, we were fairly settled on the components we wanted the vision statement to have. Over wording and order, though, we had a good deal of debate, but we came up with one that we could all agree to. It has been important for our congregation, and I am so thrilled to have been apart of writing it.

Rodney Woo reflects on the vision statement writing process:

We all agreed that we saw three core components to our faith, one of which was that we must be intentionally multiethnic.[16] This was essential to living out our faith to reach and minister to all people, and to overcome the sinister barrier of race. After much discussion, work, and revision, we arrived at our final vision statement, which has come to be so important to our congregation: "Wilcrest Baptist church is God's multiethnic bridge that draws all people to Jesus Christ, who transforms them from unbelievers to missionaries."

Though certainly there are elements in our vision statement that would not appear in other faith traditions, this vision statement perfectly captured our hope and our dream. Our congregation would be a bridge to the central figure of our faith, the one who provides our basis for unity despite our many differences. But this bridge must draw all people, regardless of ethnicity or race. This was not an option; it was a requirement. We did not want to become a multiracial congregation by taking people from other congregations. Rather, we wanted to be transformed by reaching out to the many people in our surrounding neighborhoods not currently involved in a congregation. Finally, by the term missionaries we had a twofold meaning. The first is the traditional sense of going to foreign lands, but the second is that everyone in our congregation must be able and willing to cross cultures in our own city and in our own congregation.

Implementing the Vision Statement

Armed with their concise vision statement, the vision statement development task force returned to Houston, excited to present it to the rest of the congregation and begin implementing it. The congregation voted unanimously in support of the new vision statement. Rodney Woo described what happened next:

> Several things then fell into place, or as I would look at it, God worked in directed ways. The son of one of our elders had a Korean friend who was an artist. He heard about the vision statement, and to our joy, designed a logo for us. This logo—with its embedded phrase "Love in any language"—wonderfully captured our vision. One of our leaders took it upon him to have a large placard made that displayed our logo and vision statement. We placed the placard on the wall in the lobby where people enter the worship hall building. We were announcing to all who entered our doors who we hoped to be. This was an important step in saying, "You are welcome!"

[16] The other two were a central focus on Jesus Christ, and growing in faith maturity.

FIGURE 3.2. Cross logo

We went a step further and had the logo and vision statement serve as the cover of our worship bulletins. I began asking the congregation to memorize the vision statement. We repeated it in our services, over and over. I am sure at least some in the congregation thought we said it too much, but I wanted it to burn in their hearts. I began teaching a new members class, where we would go over the principles of the faith and the meaning of the vision statement in great detail. Every new member had to memorize and be able to recite the mission statement (good thing it is relatively short!). Every few weeks, I found a way to have the congregation say the mission statement together during a worship service.

The constant question now asked was: What should they do to be true to their vision statement? Two key aspects to change were identified: music and the leadership. The Wilcrest leaders reasoned that the music could not remain as it had been if all were to be welcomed. Not changing the music would be asking for people to assimilate to a single style. Second was the need to diversify the leadership. Initially Dr. Woo thought making these changes would lead to racial diversity in the congregations, but later he learned it had a different impact:

> Oh my, I knew these changes would take time. You see, when I came the music was, to say the least, staid. Some people think of Baptists as if they are Pentecostal. This was certainly not true of Wilcrest. The interim music director when I arrived never led the congregation in hymns or songs written after 1955. He told me so.
>
> A year after my arrival, we hired a full-time associate pastor of worship, Monty Jones, an Anglo from Louisiana. I had worked with Monty at the

previous congregation I had served, and knew he possessed a deep passion for a great diversity of musical styles. In Monty's first month at Wilcrest, we called a group of church leaders together to gather feedback on the potential changes in the music and worship. I asked the group of leaders to be open and patient as we attempted to make some innovative adjustments.

Change in this area did come, but slowly. The first thing Monty did, which took a period of a couple of years, was to introduce a more contemporary style of worship. Being innovative in this early context meant a variety of styles, but still primarily white music. The big issue was to introduce variety. But looking back, we didn't address it thoroughly enough, didn't think it through intentionally enough.

Over time, we tried new forms of music. It took us nearly ten years to move out of simply doing various forms of white music. The help of new members especially aided us with different types of music. We began singing some songs in Spanish, we sang some black gospel songs, we did Caribbean music. Adding a drummer, a bass guitar player, and a conga player from Cameroon helped us do a wider variety of music. Our choir became more and more racially diverse, allowing us to continue trying new forms of music.

Not everyone was pleased with these changes. For some they came too fast. For others, they simply were viewed as wrong. According to a white man I interviewed one year before he left Wilcrest:

> If our worship changes much more, I will be embarrassed to invite others to come. The pace of some of the music, the loudness, it is just not right. I alternate between being sad and mad. Anyone is welcome at our church, but when they start changing the worship, that is when it has gone too far. Honestly, I don't know how many more changes my wife and I can handle.

While the congregation lost some people because of the changes, most people I interviewed said that they had come to appreciate the different types of music, or that they were glad that others now got to worship with the types of music most meaningful to them.

Music was one important component in implementing the vision. The other was racially diversifying leadership. Dr. Woo recounts one early leadership change.

> At about the same time that Monty Jones became our associate pastor of worship, I asked Wilcrest to consider taking a decisive step toward our multiracial vision by considering the hiring of an African American youth minister, James Darby. During the course of the church-wide interview, the members expressed fear that James would take the youth group to an all-black church, thus possibly exposing them to a style or form worship that they felt was not appropriate for their children (remember, this in-

terview was early in our transformation). There was nervousness about having a black man in charge of the member's teenagers. Witnessing this, I saw again how very far we would have to travel to becoming authentically multiracial, embracing all people.

James patiently responded to the questions. When the day of the vote came, I distinctively remember sitting in the front row of the auditorium, alone, wondering what would happen if the majority of the congregation did not vote in favor of James coming to Wilcrest. The final vote was seventy-five percent in favor of calling James to Wilcrest. I knew it was going to be a long road, but on that eventful day the congregation took one decisive step toward the goal that God had set before us. This step not only affirmed our vision statement but it was further evidence that we were moving in that direction.

From my perspective, I thought this change in leadership would immediately help us make new inroads to our local community. It did not. However, a transformation did occur within our congregation. James told the congregation that African Americans would not come to the church based on the hiring of an African American youth minister. I did not want to admit this assessment, but he was right. I realize now that in order to be a multiracial congregation, the process does not come from an "Affirmative Action" type of maneuver, but must emerge from more fundamental transformations in the church—both the people and its structure.

James contributed to Wilcrest in powerful ways. He was not timid, and for that I am thankful. He was a strong presence in our congregation. Throughout the time that James was with us, there would be members who would intermittently confess to him how prejudiced they were and asked him for his forgiveness. This happened so often that both James and I wondered how it was that seventy-five percent of the congregation had voted to hire him.

Each confession of prejudice represented a small victory in the deep and slow transformation of the congregation. Before God could lead us in our multiracial vision, we had to remove our blinders of prejudice and racism. The arrival of James as our youth minister challenged this exclusive mindset each and every day.

An Important Event: The 20:20 March

Not long into the tenure of Pastors Woo, Jones, and Darby, a drive-by shooting that resulted in the death of a black teenager occurred in the Wilcrest neighborhood. This murder was connected with gang activity in the area. James Darby was moved to lead the entire congregation on a march, beginning at the church and concluding at the very spot where the young man was shot. The march was called the

20:20 March because, as Rodney Woo told me, "it was based on a Bible verse (Acts 20:20) encouraging us to preach publicly, from house to house." The 20:20 March took place at night with approximately 125 Wilcrest members ready but not exactly sure what was going to occur. Dr. Woo picks up the story:

> As we began our march, two patrol cars from the Houston Police Department unexpectedly converged on our group and then escorted us through the entire neighborhood. When we arrived at the intersection in which the young man was shot, with his bloodstains still visible on the street, we knelt down and prayed and wept for our entire area. This was the most visible our church body had been in the community since I had arrived. People peered out of their windows to observe us. Eventually some came out of their houses and apartments. A few even joined us.
>
> The 20:20 March served as one of the most powerful markers in the history of Wilcrest as we entered the surrounding community at a critical time, representing our faith and presence to a neighborhood full of fear. It also allowed our congregation and our neighbors to see something important. Here was an African American youth minister leading an almost-all-white group of believers through a racially diverse area to pray over a neighborhood that had just lost an African American young man to a gang shooting. There are images in that march that will be etched in my mind forever. For a few moments, we all saw the power of transcending the limitations of racial division and inequity. The very lines used for demarcation, God used as a rallying point to get people on their knees over the bloodstains of a slain young man. This was our community. As Dr. Martin Luther King, Jr. might say, an attack on any one of us was an attack on every one of us. We took with us a powerful image that we were called to walk by faith across racial and cultural lines, to live a common humanity.
>
> The 20:20 March was just the start. Subsequent walks through our immediate neighborhood became a consistent practice as we passed out fliers concerning upcoming events, asked people if we could pray for them, and let them know we were there if they needed support. Racially diverse people from the neighborhood began coming to our church—sometimes just to drop off their children at one of our events or for Sunday school, sometimes to attend an event themselves. But over time, more and more people came and joined us, and this time, more stayed. Our congregation had begun to change.

As we know in hindsight, change they did. A full 70 percent of Wilcrest's members since Dr. Woo's arrival have been "switchers," people not previously involved in the same faith tradition as Wilcrest. Quite often these were people who may have attended some religious services as a child but had not as an adult. Still another 10 percent of the growth at Wilcrest has come from people not before involved in any religious tradition. These sources of growth make Wilcrest unusual. Nationally, the majority of growth experienced by congregations occurs through transfers, that is, people moving from one congregation to another within the same faith tradition.[17]

I obtained data on the racial background of all persons baptized at Wilcrest since 1992, the year Rodney Woo arrived. For Wilcrest, baptisms are a good measure of those joining the congregation either as switchers or as persons new to the faith tradition. In 1992, Rodney Woo's first year, two-thirds of those baptized were white. In 1993, the year that saw the arrival of Monty Jones and James Darby, 55 percent of those baptized were white. Except for one atypical year, 1993 was the last year whites were the majority of those baptized. Since 2000, less than 30 percent of those baptized have been white. Latinos and African Americans each represent about one-third of those baptized, and Asians nearly 10 percent.

This demographic diversification of Wilcrest did not occur without bumps and wrong turns. But looking backward, the congregation became multiracial by making changes internal to the congregation and reaching outside the congregation. These changes involved meeting with congregational members individually and corporately to encourage their support of the changes to come, preparing congregational members for the changes through times of teaching, encouraging congregational members' involvement by asking them to invite racially diverse others, and participating in the creation of the orienting document of the congregation, the vision statement.

With the creation of the vision statement came strategic changes in an effort to conform to its meaning. These changes included over a decade of changing the music (the changes continue) and diversifying the leadership (this, too, continually evolves). Many efforts were made to connect to the surrounding community, including marches, visits to homes, hosting festivals, movie nights, and creating programs for parents of young children, for teens, and for non-native English speakers, to name a few. These efforts did not go unnoticed by people in the area, and increasingly, by people well outside the local neighborhood. I talked with more than one new member of Wilcrest who said they first came to Wilcrest because of a program they had attended at the church, or because their children had attended an event with friends and wanted to go back, or because they had heard

---

[17] The figures in this paragraph come from the U.S. Congregational Life Survey (2000). This national survey of people in congregations included Wilcrest. As part of the benefit for participating, each congregation was sent a summary report about their congregation specifically, with comparisons to the national findings.

that Wilcrest was racially diverse. As the congregation grew more diverse, it became easier for others to come. The comments of one woman, an immigrant from the Caribbean, are particularly telling because she had visited both before and after the changes at Wilcrest:

> When I first came in 1988, it was not diverse, and I did not feel welcomed. So I did not stay. I came back ten years later to visit, and so much had changed. I felt welcomed. There were people from around the world. And I was hungry to learn the Word in this diverse place. These are the things that kept me here.

Conclusion

This chapter began by asking what key factors are associated with racial diversity in congregations. It examined religious tradition, congregational characteristics, and neighborhood characteristics. Religious traditions matter, especially being a factor in non-Christian and Catholic traditions. Worship style matters as well. The more upbeat the worship style, the greater the average level of racial diversity. Theology, measured on a conservative-to-liberal continuum, does not matter. The racial diversity of the neighborhood matters, but most certainly does not determine the level of racial diversity in congregations. Region of the country that the congregation is located in does not predict congregational diversity.

For a better understanding of the paths congregations take to become multiracial, we turned to the thirty congregations that my colleagues and I studied in depth, especially the twenty-two multiracial congregations. Seven models were identified. These models are differentiated based on two main factors — the impetus for change and the source of racial diversification. The path taken by a congregation in becoming multiracial appears to influence its chances for long-term survivability.

Finally, to get a detailed inside view of the transformation process in one case, we examined the steps taken by Rodney Woo, his staff, and the Wilcrest congregation. Among the seven models, Wilcrest is classified as a Survival Embracing congregation. But it has been so successful in diversifying that it appears to have actually transformed itself into a Niche Embracing congregation, the model type predicted to have the greatest likelihood of long-term survival.

We have examined congregations in this and the prior chapter. The next chapter introduces some of the individual people in Wilcrest and other multiracial congregations to see how they compare to Americans overall.

Chapter 4 · Folk

WHO ARE the people in multiracial congregations? How did they get there? Are they different from those attending uniracial congregations and from other Americans? As suggested in the last chapter, it takes more than paid staff to transform a congregation. It takes people identifying with, supporting, and making the vision their own. It takes people to give life to the vision. This chapter begins by examining the experiences of three members of Wilcrest, three men whose life stories are quite divergent.[1] For different reasons, all three ended up in Houston, at Wilcrest, and through their membership, became close friends. The second half of the chapter analyzes their stories in light of broader trends in multiracial congregations, and we meet people from these other congregations. The findings of this chapter suggest a different kind of American may be on the horizon.

MEET THE PEOPLE: THREE MEN'S STORIES

Glynn Hogan was born in a small town in Texas, about halfway between Fort Worth and Waco. This typical Texas small town of 1,500 people was about half white, a quarter black, and a quarter Hispanic. The darkness of Glynn and his family's skin suggests very few non-blacks have been part of his family's past. He grew up poor, in the 1960s and early 1970s, and he grew up racially segregated. As he put it, "everybody had their side of town." He and his brother were raised by his grandmother from age three to eleven, and his grandmother would take them to a small black church that Glynn remembers as being "real upbeat" with lots of singing and swaying. When he began the first grade in 1967, the town dealt with the school integration law

[1] In this section, I trace the life stories of three men who end up at Wilcrest. Later in the chapter I focus on two women who are part of a different congregation. For my analysis of Wilcrest, I describe the life stories of men rather than women for two main reasons. First, being male, I had much more access to men—their prayer and Bible study groups, their social gatherings, the sharing of their inner thoughts and feelings, and the like—than I did women. Second, religion is often seen as predominately a women's sphere, where women are the main attendees, invest the most in their faith and congregation, and are more likely to develop deep relationships within congregations (e.g., see Gilkes 2001). To show that patterns of deep friendship formation and spiritual bonding across race are not limited to women, I explore the lives of these men.

by closing down the black school. Thus Glynn was part of the first group of African Americans to attend the white school. Although he and his black classmates were separated somewhat from the other students, he recalls otherwise being treated fairly.

At age eleven, Glynn's mother remarried, to an army man. This led to significant changes in Glynn's life. He and his brother went to live with their mother and her new husband. Because his stepfather was in the military, they had to move, often—first to Kansas for junior high school, then to Bamberg, Germany for high school, except for his senior year, which was completed in Kentucky. Germany, of course, was culture shock for Glynn. Germany looked and felt vastly different than central Texas and the plains of Kansas. The people looked, talked, and acted differently. He and his "new" family lived on the army base. In terms of people, the army base in Germany was larger than his hometown. It also was middle class, and racially integrated. He attended high school on a military base, and the school too was highly racially diverse. But that fact did not mean peace, love, and harmony:

> My friends in high school were mostly of my own race. I think back on that and I don't know if I was racist or discriminatory, but I had issues. I had race issues, especially going from a small country town to a situation where everybody was mixed together. I didn't get along with some whites. I don't think we were called gangs then. But we were groups, and we had jackets. I never got expelled in high school for fighting or anything but I was involved in some fights and they were usually black against white.

Another change from his life in Texas was that he and his family no longer attended church services, and when Glynn enlisted in the Air Force after high school, he drifted into drinking alcohol heavily and eventually other forms of substance abuse. He recalls that that such a lifestyle was common in the military in the years he was enlisted. He also remembers that "the blacks pretty much hung out with the blacks, the whites with the whites. I still had issues."

After leaving the Air Force, Glynn went back to his original hometown in Texas, where he got a job and spent spare time carousing with friends and acquaintances. A few years of this convinced Glynn that he needed a change in his life, as he felt like he was in a rut and going nowhere. He had a few relatives in Houston, so he made the decision to move there.

Two weeks after moving to Houston, he met MaryAnn, a woman of Italian descent who had just moved a week earlier from the Boston area. They hit if off immediately. Glynn said it was love at first sight, and he credits his relationship with her as helping to begin changing his outlook on white people. Despite initial opposition from family members, they married four years after they first met. Glynn also attended and finished tech school, and began a job that he stayed at for fourteen years, until he was laid off.

In 1990, Glynn and MaryAnn had their first child, a son. But the elation of having their first child soon gave way to intense grief when their two-month-old son died of SIDS. Glynn recalls that while many coworkers and other acquaintances offered their condolences, one coworker seemed especially supportive. It was the overtly Christian white man Ted, whom Glynn and his other coworkers would "persecute mercilessly" for his Christian beliefs: "We passed up no opportunity to ridicule that brother." Glynn, still going through bouts of drinking and depression, was struck that this man would help him in his time of need, despite the mistreatment Glynn had doled out to him.

Two and half years later, while going to visit the grave of their son, Glynn and MaryAnn took a different route. They drove by a church named Wilcrest. Though they had occasionally attended a Catholic church since their marriage, Glynn had not given religious faith much thought since he was a child. While at work the next day, Glynn told Ted he had driven by this church called Wilcrest. Ted said he had heard of that church, that his wife worked in an IRS office with Wilcrest's recently appointed new part-time youth minister, James Darby, an African American. Ted told him that he had heard good things about the church.

Hearing that there was at least one other African American there, Glynn and MaryAnn decided to give the church a try. "They just showered us with love," Glynn says of their first visit, and MaryAnn adds, "Being mixed-race, my husband and I, it has always been an issue when we go to group functions. . . . When we came here, we were greeted so warmly and so lovingly." Two days later Pastor Woo came over to visit them. The visit was memorable, and Glynn prayed with Pastor Woo to convert to Christianity. The next Sunday, they were back at Wilcrest, where MaryAnn converted as well. At the end of the service, to announce their decisions, MaryAnn said, "they had us stand at the front of the sanctuary. The people came up to greet us, and I can't tell you all the kind, loving words people said. My husband and I were in awe."

Glynn and MaryAnn became faithful attendees, and more involved in the church. They began attending adult Sunday school and teaching children's Sunday school, and were involved in other children's programs at Wilcrest. Their involvement with children afforded them many opportunities to meet the parents, and to make new friends.

Glynn's fun-loving personality and true care for children, no matter their background — and in turn, the kids' unanimous love of Glynn — became a symbol for the new and changing Wilcrest.

David Adcock came to Wilcrest about five years after Glynn. An ordained pastor, he left the pastorate in the mid-1990s to earn a Ph.D. in religious studies, and is currently teaching philosophy and religious studies at Houston Baptist University. Exactly the same age as Glynn, David was born and raised in southern Louisiana, in Cajun country. Although he is white and grew up on a sugar plantation, his family was working class at best.

The second youngest of seven children, David's father was the plantation overseer, in charge of running the plantation for the owner. In exchange for this work, David's father was given a home on the plantation, a truck, some basic food items, and a small monthly check. David's father managed the workers of the plantation, most of whom were black, though the workers also included a few whites, such as David's uncle. David's mother was a devout Christian, and in an oddity for the region, was Protestant. As David recalls, "there was a Baptist mission for the four white Baptist families in the area and a black Baptist church, but otherwise everyone was Catholic." Then, as now, congregational segregation by race was the norm.

The time and region meant that most people, including most in David's family, assumed a world of white superiority and black inferiority. But David's mother was, for her time, different. Her faith had eventually led her to view all people as equal, and she continually stressed this to her younger children (the older ones were already grown at this point). David says that if he used any language that divided people or made them unequal, his mother would always correct him. "Everyone must be treated with dignity," she said, and, like the golden rule, "treat others as you want them to treat you." David remembers his mother listening to an album of sermons by black preachers. He said he learned much from these preachers, including a young one by the name of Dr. Martin Luther King, Jr.

His interracial contact was high during his formative years. He worked on the plantation from a young age, and so spent much time with black men. Despite the stratification inherent to the plantation system, one man in particular took him under his wing and taught him many things, from farming to math. In the third grade, David's school was required to racially integrate. This led to some interesting experiences for David. Already exhibiting his traits of deep thought and taking ideas seriously, he was nicknamed "professor" by classmates. But in grammar school, such a nickname was not positive and was often used as a reason to pick on him. During recess time, the boys would play baseball. As captains picked teams, they usually ended up with one white team and one black team. However, white kids did not pick David. But the black kids would, and they befriended him, giving him a chance to participate. The experiences of his mother's teaching, his time with the black men on the sugar plantation, and his experiences at school all provided atypical racial training for David.

In his senior year, David was selected to take part in a statewide pilot program for advanced students, allowing the participants to attend college early. The participants of this program became close knit. It is here that David met and married Lisa, a white woman who was raised about one hundred miles from David's home.

After graduation from college, newly married David and Lisa moved to New Orleans, where Lisa began medical school and David began attending seminary. It also is here that David says he learned some valuable lessons about race. One evening after returning from the grocery store, Lisa told David about a woman she met while waiting in the checkout line. This woman and Lisa had a fine time chatting, as they found they had much in common. Some weeks later, Lisa and David were shopping at the same grocery store. Walking down the baking goods aisle, Lisa gasped in delight when she saw her newfound friend coming from the other direction down the same aisle. David was taken aback. The woman was black.

Because Lisa had never mentioned that the woman was black, David assumed she was white. Although this likely would not be that significant an event to most people, shockwaves went through deep-thinking David. If race was not mentioned in describing a person, he realized, he assumed the person to be white, as if to be white was to be without race, the norm, the standard. David was troubled. "If I unconsciously assumed the standard to be white, I was separating people, likely putting differential value on their worth. If I was making such value assumptions, and was not aware of them, what other unchristian assumptions and beliefs might I be holding?"

This episode led David to a period of deep reflection, a time to question what he truly thought and believed, and a time in which he came to see how deeply affected he was by the racial system in the United States. "I asked God to reveal to me these false assumptions, and to eliminate them," David told me. "From that grocery store experience, I became much more cognizant of how race worked, and I found myself seeing racial inequality and how deep it ran." He relayed an experience he had while in New Orleans to illustrate what he meant.

I was working at a hospital, and was in charge of hiring for some positions. The personnel office was to forward me the applications received for these positions. After the positions had been open and advertised for a while, I grew more and more puzzled. I was hardly receiving any applications at all. I waited some more time but nothing was changing. I went down to the personnel office to see why we were receiving so few applications. I found out. They were not forwarding to me any black applicants, of which we had many! I was angry. Even though I was not a high-ranking person at that hospital, I demanded to see *all* the applications. I found three wonderfully qualified candidates, all black, and hired them. They were three of the best staff at the hospital. This sad beast called racism was institutionalized, to the point of providing inferior personal to take care of sick and hurting people.

After Lisa finished medical school, her residency brought them to Houston. David took a position as a pastor in a small town west of Houston while finishing his seminary degree. Four years later, he became the pastor of a struggling Baptist church in a racially diverse suburb southwest of Houston. The church grew a good deal during his time there, but was not very racially diverse. David was in the same Baptist district as Rodney Woo, and the two had met and David knew some about Wilcrest. When David left the pastorate to work on his Ph.D., he and Lisa looked for a church to attend. Because of his prior contact with Rodney Woo, David suggested to Lisa that they give Wilcrest a try. They were not necessarily intending to stay, but "we fell in love with the vision and the people. That is what kept us there." Although heavily involved at Wilcrest, David stays in the background, quietly living out the vision through his encouragement of staff to be true to the mission, counseling people one-on-one in his spare time, and many other activities. Perhaps his most public participation is his involvement in Wilcrest's choir, where he can be seen singing the loudest and with the most enthusiasm during songs with a gospel, African, Caribbean, or Latin feel, and during songs of any culture that have deep theological meaning. Many people I have interviewed at Wilcrest commented that they much appreciate the passion with which he sings.

Fernando Medina was born and raised in the Dominican Republic. Five years younger than Glynn and David, he was the second youngest of ten children born to Pastora and Domingo. His youngest brother, Juan Manuel, died when Fernando was nine years old, making Fernando the youngest living child. When I asked him if he was raised poor, he said, "if you wish to understate it, yes. My grandparents lived with us, my oldest sister had a child, and they lived with us, plus my siblings. We had four people per room, which we shared with cockroaches and mosquitoes." His father, despite having only a fifth-grade education, was something like an accountant at the local sugar refinery. His mother stayed home raising the children and doing the many chores necessary to keep the household functioning.

When his father, Domingo, was laid off from the sugar refinery a few years after Fernando was born, complete poverty was the result. Because Domingo's father was born in Puerto Rico, and Puerto Ricans are American citizens, a relative suggested to Domingo that he use his status as the son of a Puerto Rican to move to the United States for work. After doing the necessary paperwork, Domingo was allowed to migrate to the United States on a work visa, but his family was not allowed to accompany him. The United States was looking for workers, he was told. Only when his children were of working age and would not be a burden to U.S. taxpayers would he be allowed to bring them.

Needing to provide for his family, Domingo spent most of Fernando's childhood in the United States, with his family in the Dominican Republic. Fernando says his father would come back as often as possible, impressing his children by saying the three or four words in English that he knew. Spanish speakers in a Spanish-speaking country living in a poor town, the fact that their father knew a few words in another language seemed exotic. Over the years, as Fernando's siblings reached working age, they migrated to New Jersey, to join Domingo where he lived and worked. Eventually Pastora joined her husband in New Jersey. Fernando and the younger children stayed behind with grandparents and one older brother.

When Fernando was fourteen, his parents succeeded in getting him the proper papers to join them in New Jersey. Although they continued to be poor—he remembers his family getting welfare checks for a short time—the Medinas found that life in the United States afforded much more opportunity for their children. They stressed to their children—all struggling to learn English in the American schools—that education in the United States would open more doors. Domingo also became a Protestant while in the United States, and many in his family followed, including Pastora and Fernando.

With respect to school, fourteen-year-old Fernando was in a difficult position, however. His peers in the United States were entering the ninth grade. But Fernando had only completed the fifth grade, and had not attended formal schooling since he was eleven. So when he came to the United States, and was reentering school, he faced a dilemma: "I could go into sixth grade, and look like Yao Ming [a seven-foot-six-inch basketball player], or try to go to school with kids my own age and size, but with much more education." His parents decided to have him take a test to see if he could be placed in a higher grade. Despite his lack of formal schooling and despite knowing almost no English, Fernando was placed in the ninth grade, and through classes taught in Spanish and ESL (English as a Second Language) courses, he did well enough to pass and move on. This odd set of events may make Fernando one of the few high school graduates never to attend junior high.

Fernando recalls being thrilled to have a chance to be educated, and he longed to go to college. When he graduated from high school, he went to the New Jersey Institute of Technology, and earned a B.S. in civil engineering. He also met Lorraine, a student at a nearby nursing school. Half Puerto Rican, half second-generation Polish, she was raised in the same area of New Jersey where Fernando's family lived. They were married in 1989. Their first child was born with spina bifida, and this immediately changed Fernando and Lorraine's lives. Close calls on their child's life were frequent, and they relied heavily on their faith and church friends to help them through the difficult times and the many operations.

When their daughter was about five years old, Fernando was attempting to push her in her wheelchair across an ice- and snow-covered parking lot. He kept slipping and sliding, and at that point thought, "this is not the right kind of climate for my daughter. She will eventually have to move around on her own, and if I cannot even move on this ice, what will she do?" After talking it over with Lorraine, they made the decision to leave New Jersey for a southern climate. Fernando had a brother in the Houston area, and after finding out that it does not snow in Houston, the family packed up their belongings and moved there. Fernando found work with the city of Houston, Lorraine found work in her profession of nursing, and together they began looking for a church home and for friends.

They were living in an apartment near Wilcrest, so, after visiting a few other churches, they gave Wilcrest a try. The music reminded them of the church they had attended in New Jersey, and by this time there was a bit more racial mix than at the church back home (which was 90 percent white and about 10 percent Hispanic and Portuguese). Their daughter took a strong liking to her Sunday school teacher, Glynn Hogan. Through his daughter, Fernando met Glynn, and a friendship developed.

Despite the relationship with Glynn, the Medinas were struggling to feel included at Wilcrest. Fernando, very much a doing kind of person, was eager to get involved in the church. But all did not go well.

As I wrote elsewhere,[2] one particular experience crystallized how Fernando and Lorraine were feeling about Wilcrest:

> Wilcrest had a mission trip planned to Canada and they asked for volunteers to drive the people to the airport. So I volunteer my van, I cleaned it up, I vacuumed it. I was like the kid looking forward to a trip to the beach; I was getting to serve. I volunteered because it used to be that if you wanted to be included, you had to try to include yourself, you had to be a servant and that was my attitude. So I get my van, I line it up in the row outside of the church, I even put the AC running so that when they get in it will be nice and cool. I'm looking forward to it. I even had loaded some of their baggage in my van.
>
> We all get in a circle, hold hands, and pray. Then it is time to get in the vans. I am excited to serve. Everybody is laughing with friends and family. They all get in vans, but nobody is getting in mine. I'm like "Hey, how about here?" But everyone got in different vans and left.
>
> There I was, left alone in the parking lot. I felt low. I felt like a nothing. It was like a kid who had candy taken away from him by a bully. I said to myself in Spanish, "You know, this is a good example of why my family shouldn't be here. We've got to move on. We're not really welcome here. Hey, they have a clique, and we're not part of it." I went home and told my wife, who was already feeling like an outsider at the church, what happened. She said, "What?! They did that? We're not going there anymore." So we left.

And indeed they did leave Wilcrest, feeling like they were not part of the core group, the Anglos of the church. They most probably would never have returned to Wilcrest, except for a series of events involving Glynn and Pastor Woo.

> Someone from Wilcrest called me to tell me that I had some things in the van that the Canada team needed. So I took the stuff to Glynn, who was my friend. When I brought the stuff to him, I broke down and I cried. And Glynn, being my friend, felt so bad. He talked to me for a long time, telling me how sorry he was. I told him we had decided to leave, and couldn't come back. He said, "I am not giving up that easily."
>
> He called Pastor Rodney and told him what had happened. Pastor Rodney called me right away. I told him I couldn't talk to him now. I told him my family was going to try other churches, and after we did we could talk.
>
> So we go to another church, and I couldn't believe what the sermon was about. The preacher said, "Some of you are being sensitive, some of you are hurt by things and want to run away, because you are looking sideways.

---

[2] Christerson, Edwards, and Emerson 2005, pp. 43–44.

You have to look up. Persevere. Ask God for strength to change things for the better." I mean, it was a message that God spoke to me. And Lorraine and I said, let's let Pastor Rodney come talk to us.

Pastor Rodney came right away, we met, and he apologized for what happened. I told him, I said, "Pastor Rodney, what I think is, I think we're going back." But I also said, "We need to analyze the situation. There are too many cliques here. The goldfish are going with the goldfish and the tropical fish are with the tropical fish. We gotta be inclusive."

Through Glynn's friendship, the persistence of Rodney Woo, and a timely sermon, the Medinas returned to Wilcrest. Fernando and Lorraine have played vital roles ever since in helping Wilcrest move toward its vision. Fernando volunteered as a children's Sunday school teacher, and then taught the Spanish Sunday school class. He has taught ESL courses at the church and SSL (Spanish as a second language) courses for native English speakers. He started the Translation of the Service Ministry, so that Spanish-speakers could listen in their native language via a portable receiver and headphone. He and a few others do the actual translation. Lorraine sings in the choir and Fernando is now a deacon, one of the leaders of the congregation. What is more, he and Lorraine are on several committees at the church.

Fernando credits Glynn with playing an important part in the Medinas decision to return to Wilcrest. Not only did he help them when they had left, but Fernando says an important event happened when Glynn and MaryAnn invited the Medinas over for a church get-together.

> I was struck at how friendly he was to everyone, regardless of the person's color. And here was this dark-skinned man, even darker than me, and I watched how well the others in the church treated him. Here were people of all colors and backgrounds in the home of a black man and a white woman, and they all seemed to care about each other. We wanted to be a part of that.

Fernando and Glynn became close friends, meeting for Bible study, attending ball games together, and talking on the phone nearly every day. Shortly after their friendship developed, David, the white man we met earlier in this chapter, began attending Wilcrest. Fernando went up to David after worship service one morning to introduce himself. As David remembers, "Fernando is such an outgoing friendly person, he really helped pull us into the church. He is such an organizer, so good at getting things done and getting people involved. He invited me to a number of events, had us to their home, and soon we reveled in deep theological discussions." They became good friends, and that friendship played a part in the deep friendship between Glynn and David.

When Glynn had a recurrence of substance abuse, it was a trying and difficult time, both for Glynn and for the church. Given David's gifts for listening and counseling, Fernando and Pastor Woo asked David if he would meet with Glynn. That began what both Glynn and David describe as one of their closest friendships ever. "I love that brother," they each told me in separate interviews. Glynn credits David for helping him get back on track, and when David's wife Lisa was diagnosed with cancer, David credits Glynn for "giving me more support than I ever gave him."

To a Broader View

These three men are a small slice of the people of one multiracial congregation located in one corner of one community. Together with the other people at Wilcrest, they shape the meaning of Wilcrest's vision, and live its reality. None of these three men is originally from Houston, and they all came to the city for different reasons. But they did have a few things in common. In Houston, they did not have a home church in which they grew up, and they had varied backgrounds that made being in a mixed congregation at least conceivable. Undoubtedly, they only would have met and become friends through their involvement in Wilcrest. Each had unique experiences that brought him to Wilcrest and kept him there. And while they certainly knew people of other racial groups before attending Wilcrest, their membership in this racially diverse church led to a greater racial diversity in their friendships and social networks. Some of their views—religiously and socially—seemed to have changed as well. Are the patterns of these three men an anomaly, or do they represent common patterns found among people participating in multiracial congregations? These are the broader questions addressed in the following pages.

I first ask how common the experience of Glynn, David, and Fernando is. What percentage of those who attend church are in racially mixed congregations? We learned in an earlier chapter that only about 7 percent of the nation's religious congregations are demographically interracial, defined as no one group being 80 percent or more of the congregation. Do we get a different answer if we focus on the individual? In other words, how many people attend congregations in which their own racial group is not 80 percent or more?

I would expect the figure for people to be higher than the 7 percent for congregations for this reason: A person can be in a congregation that is defined as racially homogenous from the organizational viewpoint, but not from the individual viewpoint. For example, a Latino can be in an otherwise homogenous Asian congregation, but the Latino member will be classified as being in an interracial congregation — according to the definition that the congregation is not 80 percent or more Latino. Because of this difference between the organizational and individual viewpoints, when I talk about racially mixed congregations — no one racial group 80 percent of more — I use the term *multiracial* congregation. But when I talk about individuals being in congregations where their own racial group is not 80 percent or more, I use the term *interracial* congregation. To repeat, the term interracial congregation means that from *the viewpoint of the individual, the congregation is not 80 percent or more of their race*. It can be 21 percent of another race or it can be 99 percent of another race or any other combination in between.

My colleagues and I conducted a nationally representative, random-sample telephone survey. We asked all Americans who regularly attended religious services the following question: "Though hard to know for sure, would you say that [respondent's race] make up more than 80 percent of the worship service that you normally attend at your place of worship?"[3] We then asked a follow-up question of those who said "no" to the first question: "About what percent of the people at the worship service that you normally attend would you say are [respondent's race]?" Respondents that reported a figure less than 80 percent were classified as attending a mixed-race congregation (again, even if the congregation itself was not mixed-race).[4]

Overall, 15.5 percent of Americans who regularly attend worship services said they attend a congregation where their racial group is

[3] We defined regularly attending as attending religious services twice a month or more (46% of the total sample). We only asked the racial-makeup-of-the-congregation question of regularly attending respondents who had been attending their congregation at least three months (98% of the regular attenders). We did this to reduce measurement error, as those not regularly attending or new to a congregation would be less likely to know the racial makeup of their congregations.

[4] Based on background work I have done, people tend to overestimate the diversity in their congregation, usually by rounding to the next highest 5 percent. For example, two or three families of a different race than the majority in a congregation of 300 often is reported at 5 percent of a different race. For this reason — the propensity to round up the degree of diversity — I classified anyone who said they were in a congregation that was 75 percent or more their race as being in a racially homogeneous congregation. Using the 75 percent figure as the cutoff meant reclassifying ten people.

not 80 percent or more of the congregation.[5] So the racial composition of Wilcrest puts Glynn, David, and Fernando in the definite minority. But for each of these men, their religious tradition and race impact how deeply they are the minority. Figure 4.1 shows the variation in being part of mixed-race congregation by the religious tradition and race.

For the most common category—white Protestants—only 5 percent say they are in racially mixed congregations. Whites are more likely to be in mixed congregations if they are Catholic or in another religion. Blacks and Asians are also most likely to attend a mixed congregation if they are Catholic. The reverse is true for Hispanics. They are the least likely to be in a mixed-race congregation if they are Catholic.

What accounts for these differences? As we saw in our exploration of racial diversity in congregations by religious tradition, the more choice people have, the more they end up in homogenous congregations. There are many more white Protestants than white Catholics and Others, so it is not surprising that white Protestants are the least likely to be in racially mixed congregations. There are many more Hispanic Catholics than Hispanic Protestants and Others, so it is not surprising that Hispanic Catholics are the least likely to be in racially mixed congregations. Conversely, there are far fewer black and Asian Catholics than black and Asian Protestants and Others, so it is not surprising that it is in Catholic congregations that they are the most likely to be in mixed congregations.[6]

For Glynn, David, and Fernando, the fact that they are Protestant means their being in a multiracial congregation makes them a rare breed indeed. Because he is a white Protestant, David's participation in a multiracial congregation is the most unusual. Because Fernando is a Hispanic Protestant, his participation in a multiracial congregation is less unusual than for Glynn or David. Latino Protestants are two-and-a-half times more likely to be in multiracial congregations than are African American Protestants, and seven times more likely than white Protestants. Because Fernando is Protestant, as a Hispanic he is 50 percent more likely to be in a multiracial congregation than are Catholic Hispanics. Thus, while these men have their individual life stories, the socially defined categories of religious tradition

[5] The 95% confidence interval is +/− 2.2%.

[6] The Catholic parish model, which focuses on geography, likely shapes outcomes as well. The influence of the parish model in the United States, however, is declining as more and more Catholics seek out a church that matches their preferences, even if it means crossing parish boundaries.

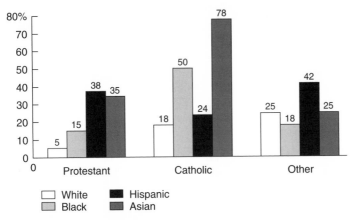

FIGURE 4.1. The percentage of people in interracial congregations varies by religious tradition and race

and race shape the likelihood that their individual life histories will lead them to an interracial congregation.

Fernando is part of another significant category. He is an immigrant to the United States. Does being an immigrant matter for ending up in interracial congregations? As figure 4.2 shows, immigration status makes a large difference. Too few white and black Americans are immigrants to make meaningful comparisons, but large percentages of Hispanics and Asians are immigrants, so figure 4.2 uses these groups to compare the percentage in interracial congregations by immigration status. Within each religious tradition, U.S.-born Hispanics and Asians are much more likely to be in interracial congregations than are their foreign-born counterparts. For Protestants, the difference is most stunning. The percentage of Latino and Asian immigrants in interracial congregations is as low as the percentage of African Americans in such congregations. So the fact that Fernando is in such a congregation makes his experience quite unusual compared to other immigrants. For U.S.-born Latinos and Asians, such as Fernando and Lorraine's children when they become adults, about two-thirds are in interracial congregations. This dramatic change suggests rapid assimilation, acculturation, or a strong desire to avoid ethnic congregations for the second and further generations of Hispanics and Asians. Should the pattern continue, it also suggests that multiracial congregations will become more common, their growth driven by immigrants, and especially by their children and future generations.

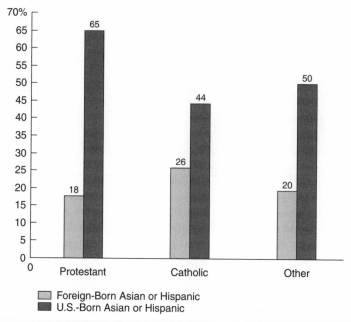

Foreign-Born Asian or Hispanic
U.S.-Born Asian or Hispanic

FIGURE 4.2. The percentage of Asians and Hispanics in interracial congregations varies by immigrant status
Note: All differences, using chi-square tests, significant at .05 level or less.
Source: Lilly Survey of Attitudes and Social Networks, 1999–2000.

What is the racial background of the senior clergy person of mixed congregations? If we look at congregations themselves, and compare them to non–racially mixed congregations, there are only two differences. Multiracial congregations are less likely to be headed by an African American — about 4 percent of multiracial congregations compared to 20 percent of uniracial congregations — and more likely to be headed by a senior clergy person of mixed racial background — 12 percent of multiracial congregations compared to 1 percent of uniracial congregations. My colleagues and I witnessed these differences when we visiting multiracial congregations around the country. As noted in chapter 2, the head clergy persons of these congregations were often of mixed racial background, interracially married, grew up in a mixed-race environment, or had other cross-race experiences that made them particularly adept at leading such congregations. This was the case with at least sixteen of the twenty-two senior pastors of our multiracial study congregations. By comparison, in our eight uniracial study congregations, these categories seem to fit only one of the senior pastors. Also in multiracial study congregations, we originally only had two black senior pastors (to increase this number, we specifically sought three more). From each of these African American clergy persons we heard about the difficulties of leading a diverse congregation—especially, challenges to their leadership. I explore this in more detail in chapter 6.

For the *people* in the congregations, the race of the senior clergy person varies by the person's racial backgrounds. Only African Americans in interracial congregations are at all likely to have an African American as their senior pastor. For African Americans in interracial congregations, nearly half have an African American senior clergy person; for all other groups, the percentage having an African American senior clergy person is 5 percent or less. Except for African Americans, who are equally likely to have a black or white senior clergy person, all groups are most likely to have a white senior clergy person (85 percent for whites, 75 percent for Latinos, and 65 percent for Asians).

I have only nonrandom data on the racial backgrounds of other clergy and staff of these congregations, but it is often the case that they do not match the race of senior clergy person. For example, at Wilcrest at the time of this writing, in addition to the racially mixed heritage of Rodney Woo, the staff consists of an African American associate pastor, a Korean American children's director, and a white youth pastor and white worship leader. I found this pattern to be common among the multiracial congregations with multiple staff members, especially if they were intentionally multiracial rather than merely transitioning from one group to another. Of the nineteen multiracial study congregations with multiple staff members, seventeen of them had racially diverse staffs. This high figure may be due to survival and attrition of congregations. As I have witnessed, any congregation claiming that being multiracial is important to them, but with a staff from only one racial group, finds it difficult to maintain its multiracial character.

Does the likelihood of having others of the same race in interracial congregations differ by a person's race? It does. In interracial congregations, for whites the average (median) percentage of members who are white is 50 percent; for blacks the average percentage of members who are black is 30 percent; for Latinos the average percentage of members who are Latino is 25 percent; and for Asians, the average percentage of members who are Asian is 10 percent. All groups, then, are in quite racially mixed environments, but especially for Asians, the percentage of their own group tends to be small, though double the size of the national percentage Asian.

As I did for congregations in chapter 3, I wanted to see for individuals what factors predict whether they are in interracial congregations. Again using a multivariate statistical method, I can find what
factors still matter after removing the influence of other factors. For
example, if both education and income seem to matter, by placing
them in a multivariate model, I can find out if each matters independent of the other, or if it is really only education or only income
that predicts involvement in interracial congregations, net of the
other.[7]

As summarized in table 4.1, I found that that factors predicting attendance at an interracial congregation differ for whites and non-
whites, so I looked at these groupings separately.[8] For whites, factors
associated with attending interracial congregations, as opposed to
uniracial congregations, include having lived in an interracial neighborhood or attending an interracial school when they were younger,
being interracially married, having attended an interracial congregation in the past,[9] being part of a faith tradition other than Protestant
Christianity, and currently living in an interracial neighborhood.[10]
Just as instructive are factors that do *not* predict attendance at an interracial congregation: sociodemographics and region of residence
variables.

In contrast, for non-whites socioeconomic status does matter. Higher
socioeconomic status for non-whites is associated with a greater like-

[7] I used logistic regression, because the dependent variable was binary: attending
an interracial congregation or not. The data source is the *Lilly Survey of and Attitudes
and Social Networks*, 1999–2000. The full results can be found in appendix B. For a
discussion of the data source and the interview protocol, see appendix C.

[8] The estimated percentage of variation explained with the equations differed for
whites and non-whites as well. About one-third of the variation is explained using the
equation for whites. For non-whites, about 45 percent of the variation is explained.

[9] It makes intuitive sense that prior interracial experience may be associated with
contemporary interracial involvement, and I find that relationship with these data.
Perpetuation theory formalizes the connection between past and current interracial
contact, specifying the causal mechanisms. This micro-macro theory of racial segregation originally developed by Jomills Braddock (1980) says that segregation tends to
repeat itself "across the stages of the life cycle and across institutions when individuals have not had sustained experiences in desegregated settings earlier in life" (McPartland and Braddock 1981:149). This theory acknowledges the real structural constraints
to interracial interaction, but focuses on how individual agents adjust their behavior
to accommodate and thus perpetuate these constraints. Exposure to integrated settings can change this behavior and start a process by which people seek such environments and relationships across succeeding stages of the life course. As knowledge,
experiences, and connections across race are developed, they heighten the likelihood
of future involvement with racially diverse persons and organizations.

[10] At least for some of these variables, causality is not clear. I explore this further
later in the chapter.

TABLE 4.1

Factors Associated with Attending an Interracial as Opposed to a Uniracial Congregation, When Effects of Other Variables Have Been Removed, for Whites and Non-Whites

Variable	Whites	Non-Whites
Other Interractial Involvement		
In the past, lived in a racially mixed neighborhood or attended a racially mixed school	+++	
In the past, attended a racially mixed congregation	+++	+++
Married to someone of a different racial background	+++	+++
Racial diversity of current neighborhood	+++	+++
Religious Tradition[a]		
Protestant	− − −	
Catholic		
SocioDemographics		
Live in a central city		
Live in a suburb		
Immigrant		− − −
Black		− − −
Have children under 19 at home		
Male		
Age		
SES (income and education)		+++
Region of Residence		
South		+++
Midwest		

Note: A +++ sign indicate statistically significant positive association (p < .05) with attendance at an interracial congregation as opposed to a uniracial congregation, after removing the effect of the other variables. A − − − sign indicates a statistically significant negative association (p < .05) with participation in an interracial as opposed to a uniracial congregation, after removing the effect of the other variables.

[a]Comparison category is all non-Christian traditions.

[b]Comparison category is the Northeast and West, which do not differ from each other.

Source: Lilly Survey of Attitudes and Social Networks, 1999–2000.

lihood of attending an interracial as opposed to a uniracial congregation. Later in this chapter and in chapter 5 I explore why this association exists and look at issues of causality. At least part of this association seems to be due to rising socioeconomic status after coming to the congregation, partly because of a widened social network. Also unlike for whites, non-whites living in the South are less likely to attend interracial congregations. The odds of non-whites in the South attending interracial congregations are only 36 percent that of non-whites living in the Northeast and the West. For non-whites, being an immigrant decreases the likelihood of attending an interracial congregation. In comparison to Latinos and Asians, blacks have a smaller likelihood of attending an interracial congregation. Whereas for whites prior living in an interracial neighborhood or attendance at interracial schools was associated with a greater likelihood of attending an interracial congregation, no such association exists for non-whites. Like whites, however, the other interracial involvement measures are associated with a greater likelihood of being in an interracial as opposed to uniracial congregation.

SOCIAL TIES AND BRIDGE ORGANIZATIONS

What implications might multiracial congregations have for the individuals and groups involved in them and for communities and societies? To begin exploring this question, I must first step back to consider a few key concepts.

Social ties, an academic term for webs of interpersonal relationships, are a driving concept in understanding groups, organizations, and society. As social creatures, our relationships are central for nearly all of us. We sing about them, think about them, work to develop them, lament when they fail, use them to find work or lift our spirits, create and pass on our culture through them, and live in them most of our waking hours.

Social ties are central to producing what researchers call *social capital*, a key good that comes from successful relationships.[11] A concept first popularized by the French sociologist Pierre Bourdieu and American sociologist James Coleman, social capital can be thought of as resources that accrue from social networks.[12] Sociologist Pamela Paxton argues that social capital has two main components: (1) objective associations between individuals that are (2) reciprocal, trusting, and display positive emotions.[13] When these are both present, Paxton and others argue, the capacity for action—such as getting a job or having

---

[11] Robert Putnam, *Bowling Alone* (2000).

[12] For Pierre Bourdieu, see for example his article in the German journal, *Soziale Welt* (1983), and his article "Forms of Social Capital" (1985); for James Coleman, see for example his article, "Social Capital in the Creation of Human Capital" (1988).

[13] Pamela Paxton, "Is Social Capital Declining in the United States?" (1999).

a neighborhood garage sale — is enhanced and the production of some good is facilitated. Social capital can be something held by an individual, a small group, an organization, a community, or an entire society.[14] No matter the level, social capital derives from social networks, the web of interpersonal relationships.

Political scientist Robert Putnam identifies two types of social capital. *Bonding social capital* comes from the micro-bonds between individuals within already well-established groups. Such capital is "inward-looking" and is "good for undergirding specific reciprocity and mobilizing solidarity."[15] Given the homogenous nature of volunteer organizations, such bonding typically takes place among homogenous people. *Bridging social capital* comes from the bonds that form between people across groups. Such capital is externally focused, crosscutting, and bridges gaps between disparate individuals and groups, or more specifically, individuals and groups that do not share common histories or identities.

We have an inherent dilemma in attempting to foster these two types of social capital — developing one often curtails developing the other. For example, as theorists Peter Blau and Joseph Schwartz write, "What benefits ingroup bonds [and bonding capital] may have for individuals, from a macrosociological perspective they are a disintegrative force because, far from integrating the diverse segments of a society or community [and bridging capital], they fragment it into exclusive groupings."[16] Further, as the work of cognitive and social psychologists show, the development of bonding social capital is associated with the rise of prejudice and discrimination in favor of one's own group over other groups,[17] and the creation of out-group antagonisms.[18] And strong bonding capital has been connected with maintaining segmented social networks and generating and reproducing inequality between groups.[19]

Conversely, if volunteer organizations attempt to overcome the bonding social capital bias by emphasizing bridging social capital, and therefore looking outside the organization, the very survivability of the organization is threatened. The less attention given to the development, identity, and maintenance of an organization in terms of

[14] See Portes 1998, 2000.

[15] Putnam 2000, p. 22.

[16] Peter Blau and Joseph Schwartz, *Crosscutting Social Circles* (1984), p. 12.

[17] Billig and Tajfel 1973; Hamilton and Trolier 1986; Hewstone, Jaspers, and Lalljee 1982; Hogg 1992; Hogg and Abrams 1988; Sagar and Schofield 1980; Tajfel 1978, chapter 3; Taylor and Jaggi 1974; Turner and Turner 1978; Wilder 1981.

[18] Putnam 2000, pp. 21–24, 350–63.

[19] Emerson and Smith 2000.

bonding social capital, the greater the risk that the organization will die.[20]

Hence, we have a bridge-bond dilemma. Both types of social capital are presumed beneficial to individuals, groups, and whole communities. As Putnam states it: "Bonding social capital constitutes a kind of sociological superglue, whereas bridging capital provides a sociological WD-40."[21] But developing one seems to work against the other.

One clear means around this bridge-bond dilemma is to have *bridge organizations*. By bridge organizations I mean those organizations with diverse members, such as a racially and economically integrated school, or in our case, a racially diverse religious congregation. Such organizations, to the degree that they succeed in building bonding social capital, provide the context within which that bonding social capital can be at the same time bridging social capital. In short, if social relations develop within the organization, where most all social relations occur, they have a good chance of simultaneously generating both bonding and bridging capital.[22] These organizations, then, provide the opportunities for the development of bridging social capital, getting around many obstacles that limit the simultaneously generation of bonding and bridging social capital. Such congregations are neither one culture nor many separate cultures, but exhibit *mestizaje* culture and identity—that is, the cultural complexity of a community in which the mixtures of people and cultures become part of the congregation's identity.[23] What is more, because congregations are "connected communities," the members of these organizations are typically linked to other voluntary associations and organizations.[24] For instance, the congregant may also be a city hall employee, local softball coach, neighbor, and parent-teacher association member. Insofar as congregants develop relationships across race in their own congregations, it may enable them to diversify their relationships outside the congregation as well, and build bridging capital outside of the congregation.

But in making these claims about the benefits of multiracial congregations, I am also making a substantial assumption—that people

[20] Michael Hechter, *Principles of Social Solidarity* (1987).

[21] Putnam 2000, p. 23.

[22] Feld, "The Focused Organizations of Social Ties" (1981) and "Social Structural Determinants of Similarity among Associates" 1982.

[23] See R. Stephen Warner's 1996 essay, "Religion, Boundaries, and Bridges." Warner argues for the importance of "embodied ritual" as a key means by which connections and collective identity—cognitive and emotive—are created.

[24] Ammerman and Farnsley 1997, pp. 360–62.

actually develop networks across race within these congregations. Certainly this is true for Glynn, David, and Fernando at Wilcrest. These men get together at one another's homes, go to movies together, pray together, support each other during times of stress, eat out together, and babysit each other's children. But the assumption that people develop social ties across race must be formally tested at the national level.

Are Social Ties More Racially Diverse for Those in Interracial Congregations?

We can measure social ties at a variety of levels, from close friends to entire webs of relations. My colleagues and I designed our survey to examine expanding rings of social life, as illustrated in figure 4.3. Beginning at the most intimate level—in the case for married people, their spouse—to people's two closest friends, to their friends in their congregation, to their circle of good friends no matter where they are located, to their overall social network (all the people they have contact with and enjoy being around, including people in their neighborhood, place of worship, workplace, school, and any associations or clubs). Let us compare those who attend uniracial congregations to those who attend interracial congregations on each of these measures.

For each ring of social ties in figure 4.3, figure 4.4 compares people in racially homogenous congregations (uniracial) and those not regularly attending congregations (no congregation) to people in racially mixed congregations (interracial).[25] The figure shows that dramatic differences exist between those in interracial congregations and the other two categories. Nearly everyone who is married and in a homogenous congregation or not in a congregation is married to someone of the same race (98 percent and 92 percent respectively). For married people in interracial congregations, that figure drops to 73 percent, a substantial difference from those in homogenous congregations or not regularly attending a congregation.

The next ring of social ties is a person's two closest friends. Nearly nine out of ten people (88 percent) in homogenous congregations and

[25] The sample size for the Spouse variable is 1513, for Circle of Friends and Social Network variables, 2550. The sample size for the 2 Closest Friends variable is 2518, and for Friends in Congregation, 1139. For all variables the percentage for the interracial congregation category significantly differs from the percentage for no congregation (do not regularly attend a congregation) and from the uniracial congregation category (ANOVA, using post-hoc tests, $p < .01$).

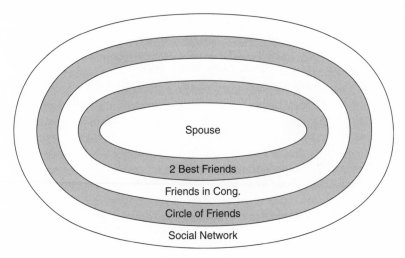

FIGURE 4.3. The rings of social ties

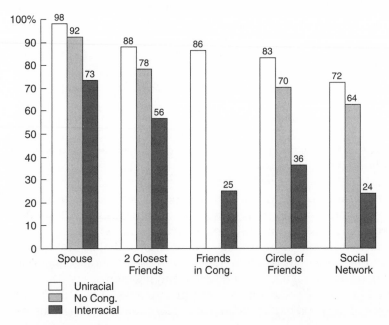

FIGURE 4.4. People in interracial congregations have more racially diverse ties that other Americans: Percentages saying most or all are of the same race

Note: The 2 closest friends variable reports the percentage of people who said both of their closest friends are of the same race.

Source: Lilly Survey of Attitudes and Social Networks, 1999–2000.

nearly eight out of ten (78 percent) of those not regularly attending a congregation say that their two closest friends are the same race as are they. However, for those in interracial congregations, just over half (56 percent) say that their two closest friends are of the same race.

Moving to the ring of friends in the congregation, we again find a stark contrast. Although 86 percent of people in homogenous congregations say that all or most of their friends in their congregation are of their race, this figure plummets to 25 percent for those in interracial congregations. The lack of racial diversity in congregational friends for those in homogenous congregations of course follows from the racial composition of the congregation. But the substantial racial diversity in congregational friends for those in interracial congregations need not follow. As often happens in desegregated schools, friendships in racially mixed organizations can remain largely homogenous.[26] But this clearly is not the case for those in racially mixed congregations. Racially mixed congregations, then, either are bridge-building institutions, attract bridge-building people, or both. I explore these possibilities in the next section.

When we expand outward in the ring of social ties, to people's circle of friends — defined for our respondents as persons they like to do things with and have conversations with, whether they do this in person, by calling, writing, or other means — we find the same dramatic pattern of difference. People in homogenous congregations have little racial diversity in their circle of friends. Those not regularly attending a congregation report a somewhat more diverse circle of friends than those in homogenous congregations, but neither category of people comes close to the level of diversity reported by those in interracial congregations. And the same is true when we look at the last ring, social networks. Importantly, even when I account for other differences, such as prior interracial contact, education, age, socioeconomic status, and other variables, attendance at an interracial congregation is a powerful predictor of the racial diversity of people's social relations (See table B4.1 in appendix B).

In short, on any ring of social ties, *people in mixed-race congregations are, on average, considerably different from other Americans*. In fact, this pattern of difference goes beyond measures I have presented here. First, the differences found in figure 4.4 hold for every major racial group, from whites, to blacks, to Latinos, to Asians (there are too few American Indians in the sample to analyze here). What is more, people who are in mixed-race congregations now *and* in their

---

[26] For example, see Hallinan and Williams 1989.

previous congregations have more racial diversity in their social relations than people who are in their first mixed-race congregation. Those in their first mixed-race congregation have more racial diversity in their social relations than those who used to attend a mixed-race congregation but no longer do. And those who used to be in a mixed-race congregation but no longer are have more racial diversity in their social relations than those who do not now and have not ever attended a mixed-race congregation.[27]

Determining respondents' zip codes from phone numbers and then looking up census information for the zip codes, I found that respondents who attend mixed-race congregations also currently live in more racially diverse zip codes than do respondents who attend racially homogenous congregations. Here, then, is yet another area of life to experience racial diversity. Moreover, those in interracial congregations were more likely to have lived in a racially mixed neighborhood in the past and to have attended a racially mixed school while growing up. Again, though, even when I remove the effect of prior interracial contact, people in interracial congregations have more racially diverse social relations than do other Americans (see table B4.1 in appendix B). Finally, there are solid correlations between these social tie variables, with those having more racial diversity on a social tie ring tending to have more diversity in the other social tie rings as well.[28]

As I analyzed the racial diversity of social relations, there appeared to be a group of Americans different from the others. On almost any and every measure of racial diversity in social relations, they are unique for their diversity. As historian and contemporary American analyst David Hollinger writes in his book *Postethnic America*, the United States is a melting pot to be sure, but it is a racial melting pot.[29] Immigrants come to the United States as ethnics, as people of

[27] For example, 84 percent of people who have never been in an interracial congregation say that all or most of their friends are the same race as them. For those who have been in an interracial congregation in the past but are not currently, this percentage drops from 84 to 64. For those currently in an interracial congregation, but had not been in one before, the percentage saying that all or most of their friends are the same race as them drops further to 44. And for those in an interracial congregation now and in the past, only 25 percent say that all or most of their friends are of the same race as them.

[28] Using the three continuous variables on the ring of social ties—racial diversity of one's congregational friends, one's circle of friends, and one's overall social network—the correlations range between .56 and .59, and the Cronbach's alpha standardized value of scale reliability is a quite high at .80. I found the same magnitude of relationship for both males and females.

[29] Hollinger's book *Postethnic America* was published in 1995.

a particular nationality or region. But they learn in the United States that for political, social, cultural, and even religious reasons, they are to meld into a racial group. They are expected to do so, and they garner advantages by doing so. For these reasons, Hollinger writes, there is not one, but five melting pots, corresponding to the major "racial" groups in the United States: Indian/Native American, African American/Black, European American/White, Hispanic/Latino, and Asian American/Asian. In this sense, Hollinger says, there are five types of Americans. Each type of American is defined using socially selected physical markers to imply a set of social, cultural, and psychological characteristics. People originating from the same general region of the world and having somewhat related physical characteristics come to be defined in the United States as a "racial group." Importantly, race is not the physical markers or region of origin, per se, but the *meanings* these markers have, including the rankings they imply. People are expected to conform to the culture of their socially defined racial category, and form social networks internally. Each racial group of Americans comes to have distinct ways of communicating and its own distinct subcultural traits. It often has its own neighborhoods and organizations. People marry others in their own racial group, make friends primarily with people in their own racial group, and prefer to socialize with people primarily in their racial group.

What we are uncovering in this chapter is another group, which I will call *Sixth Americans*. Although biologically they are part of one of the five melting pots Hollinger discusses, they seem to operate outside of their melting pot in most aspects of their social relations. Sixth Americans live in multiple melting pots simultaneously. Minorities among Americans to be sure, Sixth Americans live in a world of primary relationships and associations that are racially diverse. Like other Americans, the Sixth American may work in a racially diverse setting, see racially different others at the grocery store, and perhaps have a friend of a different race. But unlike other Americans, the Sixth American's "world of racial diversity" does not stop here. It is not a racially homogenous world with some diversity sprinkled in; the Six American's world is a racially diverse world with some homogeneity sprinkled in. It is a world, we can imagine, where one's friends, acquaintances, fellow parishioners, and perhaps even spouse, parent, or child are from multiple racial groups. It is a world where the lawyer, the bank manager, the clergy member, the construction worker, and the doctor can be of any race and often are of races different than one's own. It is a world where racially diverse others are present everyday, directly shaping the lives of Sixth Americans.

Sylvia, a member of NY Mainline, one of our multiracial study congregations, is an example of a Sixth American. She is classified as white, but lives in multiple melting pots. Her close friends are a mix of blacks, whites, Latinas, two Asians, and an American Indian. She lives near most of her friends, and spends a good deal of time at their homes, or they at hers. All of them send their children to the same school, a school designed to have racial and economic diversity. Sylvia spends much time at her church or volunteering with church members. Her senior pastor is an African American, as are many others on staff at her church. Her Latina friends are relatively recent immigrants to the United States, and through them she spends time learning about Hispanic culture and the difficulties of immigration. As Sylvia said in an interview:

> I had my stereotypes of Hispanics, stuff I had seen on TV or heard others say. But my friendships with Esmerelda and Juanita have shown me I really knew nothing. I have learned about true giving through them. They have very little materially, you know, but they have so much to give in every other way. From them I have learned about toughness, caring for family, and surviving.

Juanita too is a Sixth American. She has been attending NY Mainline for a little over two years, and through the church has met several non-Hispanics, including Sylvia. Of Sylvia, she says, "She is a dear friend. She has shown me how to talk to the government [deal with various offices of the government and the required paperwork], and I have learned very much about her culture here, how to live here. I have benefited from learning about Sylvia's culture. [How so?] Oh, the benefits of time management, the idea of freedom, of valuing myself as a woman, of new kinds of music and food and friends." Juanita, like Sylvia, lives in a racially diverse neighborhood. She has developed several non-Hispanic friendships through her congregation and in her neighborhood. Through her church, her residential location, and her racially diverse friends, her racially diverse social network continues to expand, and the organizations she is connected to are nearly all racially diverse.

Sylvia and Juanita are not merely Sixth Americans by choice, of course. It would be hard for them, even if they desired to have racially diverse social networks, to do so if they lived in a racially homogenous city or area of the country. Structural factors limit who can become a Sixth American, just as structural factors limit which congregations can be multiracial. Juanita ended up in New York because she had family there. Through her family connections, what she could afford, and what was available at the time, she ended up in her racially mixed neighborhood. She ended up at NY Mainline largely because it was close, and when she visited she felt welcomed. Through her congregation, she developed her friendships with Sylvia and several others. Sylvia chose to move to New York City from her racially homogenous upstate New York hometown mostly for work opportunities, but she also purposively sought out both a neighborhood and a church that were racially diverse, because she was "tired of only knowing one kind of person." Although she made a few friends through meeting people in her neighborhood, she said that she met most of her good friends at her church, and then was delighted to learn that many of them lived close to her.

There is much more to know about Sixth Americans like Sylvia, Juanita, Glynn, David, and Fernando. From the data analyzed earlier in this chapter, many people in multiracial congregations appear to be Sixth Americans. How did they end up in these congregations? Do they have different attitudes than others? But before we can turn to such questions, we must address the question of cause and effect.

CAUSE AND EFFECT

Although this work suggests a strong association between people being a part of a racially mixed congregation and the racial diversity of their social networks, we have a classic chicken and egg problem. We do not know which came first, or if each contributes to the other.

To address this dilemma, my colleagues and I conducted in-person interviews with approximately 160 respondents in congregations, asking them about the racial diversity of their circle of friends. If they had a diverse social network (less than 80 percent of the same race), we asked them whether the racial diversity of their friendships happened before or after coming to their present congregation.

First, consistent with our survey, those we interviewed in interracial congregations were substantially more likely to have a racially diverse circle of friends than those we interviewed in uniracial congregations. As to whether the friendships happened before or after coming to the congregation, the answer appears to be *both*. Many people had at least some racial diversity in their circle of friends before they came to their congregation. They then gained more racial diversity in their networks from participation in their congregation. As this immigrant woman from El Salvador told me when asked whether she had racial diversity in her friendships before she came to be part of her multiracial congregation in Los Angeles: "Yes, but not much. I would put it at about 10 percent before I came [to this church]. Since I have been at this church, the majority of my friends are of different races." And as this man from a multiracial congregation in the Northeast who said his friends were racially diverse put it, "With me, I didn't have a lot of close contact with anyone but white people until after I joined this church. That has changed since I have been here."

In analyzing the interviews, one conclusion is clear: the majority of people, regardless of their race, had greater diversity in their friendship circles *after* becoming part of their present congregation than before. That is, more than eight out of ten people we interviewed said at least some of their friendships with people of other racial groups were made after coming to their present congregation. I found the same pattern at Wilcrest. From a survey of the entire congregation of those 16 years or older, 82 percent said their social relations became more racially diverse after coming to Wilcrest. For most people we interviewed in interracial congregations, this racial diversification of their social relations was directly through friendships formed with others in their congregation. For some, their friendship networks diversified not only from friendships within their congregation, but outside of it as well. As one man from the South said, "Being in this church really opened me up to people of all different backgrounds. Now when I meet people of different races at work, I don't just say hello and move on. I am comfortable to get to know them. I've made new friends at work this way."

Although the racial diversity of nearly everyone we interviewed increased because of their participation in their racially diverse congregation, I did find racial differences in the percentage of those who said *most or all* of their friendships with people of other racial groups were formed *after* coming to their congregation. For 42 percent of white respondents, most or all of the racial diversity in their friendships came after coming to their congregation. In comparison, this was the case for 27 percent of African American and Latino respondents, and 14 percent of Asian respondents.

These percentages reflect in part the opportunity each racial group has to be in contact with racially different others. Because whites are the largest group in the United States at the time of this writing, they are the most segregated from other groups, and thus are more likely to experience changes in the racial composition of their friendships through their involvement in an interracial congregation. The opposite is true for Asians. As the smallest group, they are also the least segregated, and are more likely to have diverse networks before coming to an interracial congregation, even though nearly 80 percent say their networks became more diverse since coming to their present congregation.

Finally, are people who are part of multiracial congregations those who had more racially diverse social networks than other Americans, even before they came to be part of a multiracial congregation? My data are not perfectly suited to answer this question, but I do know that those currently in multiracial congregations are more likely to have attended at least one racially mixed school growing up. The majority of Americans attending multiracial congregations said they attended at least one racially mixed school, compared to the minority of Americans not in congregations or in uniracial congregations who did so. This difference remains even after accounting for regional, educational, sex, age, and racial differences between those in multiracial congregations and those not in such congregations. In our nonrandom in-depth interviews, we asked those in both multiracial and uniracial congregations about the racial diversity of their high school, the neighborhood they lived in the longest, their friends, and their church while growing up. After controlling for differences in sex, age, and race, those in mixed congregations were more likely to have lived in a mixed-race neighborhood growing up, but no other significant difference were found. Compared to those in uniracial congregations, those currently in mixed-race congregations were as unlikely to attend a mixed-race congregation growing up, have racially diverse friends, or attend significantly more racially diverse high schools.

As noted, the evidence is not as complete as we would like it to be, but what we do have suggests that people in multiracial congregations may have had greater exposure to racial diversity at some point in their growing up years. I do not find consistent differences across all measures, but find enough difference to suspect that although membership in a multiracial congregations leads to a substantial increase in the racial diversity of members' social ties, those members may have had more racially diverse social ties or experiences than other Americans before coming to a multiracial congregation.

CONCLUSION

This chapter followed the life paths of three Wilcrest members—Glynn, David, and Fernando—and more briefly, two members of New York Mainline—Juanita and Sylvia. We observed that their friendships with one another were formed because of their involvement in their multiracial congregation. These friendships were formed across racial lines. Are such patterns of friendships and other social relations common among those who attend interracial congregations?

The evidence points overwhelmingly to the answer, "Yes." So strong was the pattern of more racially diverse social networks for those in interracial congregations compared to those in uniracial congregations that I labeled them Sixth Americans. They constitute a category of people whose social ties are fundamentally more racially diverse than for other Americans, whether these other Americans are in congregations or not. For most people in interracial congregations, their social ties became more racially diverse after coming to such congregations.

But then we must ask: Why do people come to interracial congregations? What attracts them? And when they come, what happens? Do these people favor assimilation of races and cultures? And does their participation in interracial congregations affect not only the racial diversity of their social ties, but also their racial and religious attitudes and understandings? We turn to the next chapter in an attempt to find some answers.

CHAPTER 5 · Attractions

MOST AMERICANS, when they leave the public sphere of work and school, go home to neighborhoods that are filled mostly with people that are racially like themselves. They get together with their friends, who are almost always the same race as them. And for the many Americans who attend worship services, in houses of worship the people gathering with them are racially the same as them. It is in this sense that we have Five Americas, Five Melting Pots, and Five Americans.[1]

The Sixth Americans would seem to represent, at least in part, a realization of Dr. Martin Luther King, Jr.'s dream, that is, people whose lives are significantly intertwined with each other across racial lines and who serve as bridges between groups. But we must know more. With our focus on congregations, how did these people come to these congregations? Do they think differently than other Americans on some issues? Compared to their racial compatriots in uniracial congregations, do those in multiracial congregations have similar or different perspectives?

In this chapter, we first look at why people come to Wilcrest. This helps set the context for our national-level examination of why people attend mixed-race congregations, how they think of assimilation compared to people in uniracial congregations, how they differ demographically from people in uniracial congregations, and how, if at all, their attitudes differ from those in uniracial congregations.

WHY DO PEOPLE COME TO WILCREST, AND WHAT DIFFERENCE DOES IT MAKE?

The Wilcrest congregation had a committee design and conduct a survey of members and attendees. The survey was given to all those in attendance on a specific Sunday who were above the age of 15.[2] A total of 275 respondents completed the survey. One key question was, "What attracted you most to Wilcrest?" People wrote down what they felt was important, with 30 percent of the people writing down more than one response. As can be seen in figure 5.1, there were six pri-

---

[1] These ideas are discussed more fully in the previous chapter. See Hollinger 1995.
[2] The survey was conducted in May of 2002.

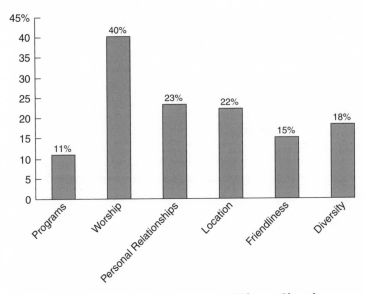

FIGURE 5.1. Reasons given for coming to Wilcrest Church

mary reasons given by the people for why they were initially drawn to Wilcrest: (1) worship; (2) personal relationships; (3) location; (4) vision of diversity; (5) friendliness; and (6) programs.

The least common reason given for coming to Wilcrest was programs. Wilcrest offers many programs that are used by congregants and non-congregants alike. Some learned about Wilcrest through their own or their children's involvement in one of these programs. But while such programs can draw people to Wilcrest, other factors were mentioned more often.

For all racial groups, the most common reason people gave for coming to Wilcrest was worship, including the music, the preaching, and the pastor. As Nancy Ammerman and Mark Chaves find in their exhaustive studies of congregations, while they perform many other functions, worship is the number one function of religious congregations.[3] It is what makes congregations unique and therefore draws people. Wilcrest appears to be no exception.

But worship can take on additional meanings in a multiracial congregation. Rodney Woo illustrates:

In a multiracial congregational setting, there are so many scriptural truths that may not have deep meaning in the American church context. For ex-

[3] Nancy Ammerman 2005; Mark Chaves 2004.

ample, the theology of persecution and suffering becomes flesh and blood when seen through the eyes of the believers who have come from third-world countries. One of our members from Liberia was in a refugee camp for ten years, sleeping in a tent so crowded that her legs could not be placed on the ground, but she had to prop up her legs on the pole in the center of the tent. Due to this woman's real life testimony and their connections to her, many of our members have begun developing a working theology of persecution and suffering, and it carries much deeper meaning to them. Now when we worship, we worship with more passion, as we have so much to celebrate, such as the woman being helped through her long trials.

There is also the variety in worship, to meet the needs of the diversity of people in the congregation. In addition to a variety of music styles, there are skits, testimonies, videos, baby dedications, and altered preaching styles. Pastor Woo says that he has "learned to preach dialogically, giving the congregation an opportunity to respond verbally to several questions and points throughout the sermon." Yet the preaching is not done in a true call-and-response pattern common in African American congregations, nor are the rhythms and songs those common to black gospel. According to Dr. Woo, African Americans have told him that not enough changes have been made to the worship—that it is too far from a black style. "Black Americans at Wilcrest often feel like they are giving up far more than other cultures when it comes to worship," he said. As one African American woman who grew up in a black church said about being at Wilcrest, "My family and I love the preaching and the vision, but we sure do miss our music." I explore this issue further in chapter 6.

After worship, the two most common reasons given for coming to Wilcrest are personal relationships and location. More than one in five people said they came because Wilcrest was close. This was especially true of the non-whites. Often the combination of being close and being invited to visit are what drew them to attend. As in most congregations, a significant number of people at Wilcrest said they first came because they were invited by a friend or family member. Personal relationships play an important role at Wilcrest. According to Dr. Woo,

> If a guest is connected with a member who invited them, then their willingness to engage in the multiracial experience dramatically increases. For the guests who have never been exposed to a multiracial congregation, it is vital that they are able to have an interpreter to help them process the experience.

He also finds, especially for the Latino members, that when one person joins Wilcrest, the whole family often becomes a part of the extended congregation:

Many of our Hispanic members have extended family members who eventually join. We have one Hispanic family that has approximately 20 to 25 members at Wilcrest. For them Wilcrest is a place where the family meets, ministers to each other, and to other members of the congregation.

Friendliness attracted some people to Wilcrest. A couple told me that because their marriage is interracial, they are always cautious in new social settings. "The first thing you look for is acceptance, how you are perceived. When we came here, we were greeted so warmly and so lovingly. . . . My husband and I were in awe." A man from the Caribbean islands said "[w]hat attracted us was the warmth of the people and the love that they showed. They greet you at the door, they try to find out things about you, be friendly with you, they even visit you." Friendliness was often mentioned in conjunction with the diversity in the congregation.

For people at Wilcrest, the vision of diversity was the fourth most frequently mentioned attraction. The frequency with which this reason was listed varies by length of time at Wilcrest. People who had been at Wilcrest for less than five years were nearly twice as likely to list diversity as a main reason they were attracted to Wilcrest than were those who had been at Wilcrest for five to nine years. (I did not look at those who had been at Wilcrest ten years or more at the time of survey, because they arrived before racial diversity became an emphasis).

Four main aspects seem to attract people to the diversity at Wilcrest: curiosity, consistency, acceptance, and rise of status. The many colors, outfits, accents, and languages at Wilcrest draw some people to want to learn more. One member told me that she was invited by friend, but came back because she was intrigued:

It just blew me away to see that worship service. There were Africans with their traditional clothing, youth with hip-hop clothing, Mexicans, whites, South Americans, Asians, American blacks, blacks from the Caribbean, and they were all speaking English with accents or in their native language. You know, what really caught my attention was seeing this mass of people talk to each other as if they had grown up together. I had to come back to see what was goin' on here. I had never seen anything like it before.

For those with prior interracial experience, Wilcrest was an important step in living consistent interracial lives. As a newer black member at Wilcrest said, "My wife and I work with different races, live in a diverse neighborhood, and my children are in diverse schools. I wanted the same in church. I believe my life would be much more consistent if all areas are multiracial." Such people already are Sixth Americans when they come to Wilcrest, and they come as a natural extension of how they live their lives.

According to Rodney Woo, many people are attracted to the racial diversity of Wilcrest because they are looking for acceptance.

> Especially for immigrants, they communicate to me that they feel accepted as they are. The congregation does not ask them to assimilate into a dominant culture, but rather wants to celebrate and learn from their cultural backgrounds. Worship is enriched in this acceptance. I have been told we communicate acceptance in many ways, from reading scriptures and praying in multiple languages, to having a diversity of music, translating our services into Spanish, and trips to their home countries in which we ask them to lead.

For whites and American-born blacks, Dr. Woo said they often are attracted to the diversity because they themselves feel ostracized. He noted that they are often divorced, single parents, alcoholics, and drug addicts, people who have come from broken homes, released inmates, and people whose lives have been scarred by neglect. As some members told me in interviews, they believed that if Wilcrest was open enough to accept racial diversity, it might also be open to accept them. They found this to be the case. "I'm messed up," one woman told me, "but here people only want to help me. I don't feel rejected for the mistakes I've made. I feel supported to overcome them." Rodney Woo reflects on this aspect of the congregation:

> As a congregation, it is difficult to maintain integrity if we accept all races and cultures, but dismiss others who come to the church with their lives fragmented and in need of God's grace. Acceptance of individuals who are different, then, becomes a permeating norm of our multiracial congregation. We do not stop believing in right and wrong. Rather we accept that we are all fallen people who need the support of each other and of God to grow. I love what one of our deacons proposed concerning a slight alteration to a portion of our vision statement: Wilcrest Baptist Church is God's multiethnic, multiracial, multicultural, multi-economic, multi-social, multi-educational, multi-mental bridge!

One other reason seems to make the diversity of Wilcrest attractive. Dr. Woo calls it the rise-in-status reason. Attending an interracial congregation can mean a rise in economic or social status. Such congregations can provide safe places to adapt to a new nation or region, create and expand social networks, gain access to resources not otherwise easily attainable (such as contacts with people well placed in the marketplace), and enhance educational and employment opportunities. According to Dr. Woo, "many in our congregation develop relationships with believers from other cultures that eventually help them search for jobs, negotiate the immigration system, get medical treatment, or pursue education." For example, David Adcock, one of the members we met in chapter 3, has used his connections as a professor to help members continue with their schooling. Lisa Adcock, his wife and a medical doctor, has more than once helped members get medical treatment they otherwise would not know how to obtain or could not afford. Fernando Medina, whom we also met in Chapter Three, has spent a great deal of time helping people get immigration papers and helping Spanish-speaking immigrants navigate an English-speaking nation. He has taught English classes, accompanied people to government offices to translate, and hosted free health clinics at Wilcrest in Spanish for people to get basic medical treatment.

This rise in status goes both ways, affecting not only those looking to rise in status, but others in the congregation as well. Partly to aid this process, Dr. Woo emphasizes going on mission trips to other countries, but not to just any other countries. His goal is to have the congregation go to every nation from which a member of Wilcrest has come. Using Hispanic immigrants for his example, he outlines why:

> A number of our Hispanic members have lower paying jobs and little formal education, but they are transformed to leaders when Wilcrest goes on mission trips to their home countries. We rely on them to make contacts, arrangements, and serve as liaisons during the entire trip. They are needed by the congregation. They become the mouths and the voices for the rest of the church body as ministry takes place in their country and in their language. Their spiritual status exponentially increases not only in their own eyes, but also in the eyes of the rest of the members as well.

By shifting the context, this method places those who are minorities into the place of the majority. Just as important, majority members become minorities. According to Dr. Woo, this has a powerful impact on the life of the congregation, as members come to understand and appreciate that social position is contextual, changeable, and does not correlate with spiritual worth.

As we explore why people come to Wilcrest, an important counter-influence must be noted. Because multiracial congregations are unusual, congregants at Wilcrest sometimes talked about the cost of being there. Their same-race friends and family at times question their motives and their loyalty. Some people have left Wilcrest for this reason. Others stay, but it is an issue with which they must struggle.

Why People Come to Interracial Congregations

Before we examine why people come to interracial congregations, we must ask what proportion of people are in interracial congregations simply because racially different others came to their congregation, which, like Wilcrest, was previously uniracial. My colleagues and I asked our survey respondents in interracial congregations whether their congregation was racially mixed when they first began attending. For a little less than half of the whites, a little less than a third of the blacks, and a few Hispanics and Asians, they said this was the case. For such people, their story is not about why they came to such congregations, but why they stayed in diversifying congregations. And, importantly, their story is also how they came to adapt to the changes. This is not always easy, as we heard many references in our interviews to the difficulty of adapting to new musical styles, new leadership styles, and simply different ways of doing things. For such people, they were not originally Sixth Americans, but the experience of being part of a racially diversifying congregation often changes them. Certainly in the context of congregations becoming racially diverse, people leave. But those who stay must adapt, often making new friends of racially different backgrounds, and coming to view things differently. As this white man who had been at his congregation before it became demographically multiracial and who has stayed through all the changes said:

> By associating with people in church, worshiping with each other, you interact on such a different level. I take that experience into the larger world and I don't have those fears or stereotypes that I once did. That is not to say they are completely erased. But I am better equipped now, to not prejudge people just because of their skin color or their ethnic background.

An Asian woman in southern California reflected on her congregation's change from all Korean to ethnically and racially mixed:

> I didn't want our church to change. I liked that it was Korean. It felt safe, comfortable. But despite my thoughts, it did change. I am so thankful, because I have changed, for the better. I cannot believe how I used to think. I didn't know what I was missing. I have so many new friends that I never would have had, and I see a God who is wider and higher and deeper and more powerful than I ever thought was possible.

A white male from Houston put it even more succinctly: "We are never going to be the same once we have encountered the truly interracial experience. It is experiencing God in such a bigger way."

For most people in interracial congregations, however, the congregation was already interracial when they first came. Interestingly, just as we see at Wilcrest, only a minority of people originally come to interracial congregations primarily because the congregations are interracial.[4] Rather, people often are more likely to come for reasons similar to why people would go to any congregation—friends or family invite them, the location is convenient, the people are friendly, they appreciate or are moved by the worship, or they are attracted by the available programs. Most people come to interracial congregations not out of commitment to some abstract concept like diversity or improved race relations, but because they have connections with someone already there and end up feeling at home in the congregation. This is vital. As sociologists Charles Moskos and John Sibley Butler conclude in their fascinating study of the racial diversification of the army, and as is consistent with a long-standing principle of contact theory, for racial diversification and improved race relations to occur, the central focus of the organization or program cannot be racial diversification and improved race relations.[5]

The army has become the most racially diverse institution in the United States. The percentage of non-white leaders far exceeds that in other major institutions; the army is one of the very few places where whites are routinely under the authority of non-whites, and the number of racial incidents is exceedingly small. In fact, in the last three wars or conflicts the United States has been involved in, not a single complaint of racial bias was filed.[6]

The army has not always been this way. It was riddled with racial bias and inequity for most of its existence. The leaders of the army

[4] In chapter 3 I claimed that a key path that congregations took to become multiracial was to make racial diversity a part of their mission, a part of their emphasis, and a part of their organizational fabric. Although people often are not originally drawn to a congregation for its racial diversity, those who stay often do so because of the diversity. See for example the work of Christerson, Edwards, and Emerson (2005). Also, as congregations become known for being multiracial, the percentage of people who come because it is multiracial tends to rise. But as I discuss in the upcoming text, being multiracial cannot be the sole or typically even the main focus if congregations are to succeed in being multiracial. It must be the means to an end.

[5] Moskos and Butler, *All That We Can Be* (1996). Charles Foster, in his research on education in mainline Protestant multiracial congregations, concluded that the primary focus must be on service to the community (however that is defined by the congregation) rather than on becoming or being racially diverse. See his two books, *We Are the Church Together: Cultural Diversity in Congregational Life*, with Theodore Brelsford (1996), and *Embracing Diversity: Leadership in Multiracial Congregations* (1997).

[6] Moskos and Butler 1996.

viewed the issues as so bad that they were hindering the effective-
ness of its ability to operate and defend the nation. The leaders decided something had to be done. They did not institute racial sensi-
tivity training or teach people to think better about others. Rather,
they made the following changes: they did what was necessary to increase the supply of qualified minority candidates for officer positions, and then aggressively promoted qualified minority candidates;
they made treating others free of racial bias an absolute requirement
for advancement in one's career (they did not care how people
thought of others, but rather how they treated others); they stressed
that these factors were necessary to reach the army's goal to defend
the nation. In short, to achieve its ongoing goal, racial diversification
and improved race relations were made a necessary means.

Though in a radically different context, Wilcrest and many of the
congregations in our study did much the same thing. Midwest St.
Anne's Catholic Church, Strong Tower Community Church in Ten-
nessee, New York Mainline, Bridgeway Community Church, Los Angeles Catholic Church, Minnesota Baptist, Northeast Alliance, Houston Presbyterian, and the other study congregations that were
multiracial throughout this study did not have a vision to become
multiracial for the sake of becoming multiracial. If that had been the
sole motivation for becoming multiracial, it is doubtful that these
congregations would have experienced much success. Rather, a congregation must have a higher goal that, to be met, requires being multiracial.[7] For these congregations the higher goal is a focus on worshiping, serving the supernatural, serving the community, and
attempting to live in a manner which is consistent with their beliefs.
But, according to the congregations' vision statement and teachings,
this can only happen in the multiracial context. It can only happen
when people of all cultures are welcomed and feel at home. Given
human limitations (see for example, the next chapter), this goal is
never fully attained, so the striving never ends. Wilcrest and other
congregations like it move toward changing their worship, the racial
composition of their leadership, and their very nature in ways that
lead people of a variety of backgrounds to feel at home, all in an effort to reach their broader goal. Thus, 60 percent of the congregation
of Wilcrest said on a survey that Wilcrest should become more multiracial (even though, as we saw in chapter 2, it was already more
racially diverse than 99.5 percent of U.S. congregations). This was

---

[7] See the work of George Yancey, especially *One Body, One Spirit* (2003a). We had
one congregation in our study that did seek to be multiracial for the sake of being multiracial. It failed.

not for the mere sake of becoming multiracial but because the majority in the congregation has come to view the reaching of its vision as requiring racial diversity.

Interestingly, as Wilcrest becomes more diverse, more people are drawn to it because of its racial diversity. While just about 10 percent of those who have been at Wilcrest five to ten years (all years in which Wilcrest had its vision statement and was growing more diverse) said they were first attracted to Wilcrest because of its racial diversity, a full 25 percent of those who have been at Wilcrest less than five years say they were attracted by the racial diversity. Typically people wrote, along with "racial diversity," something like, "the friendliness here," "the strong emphasis on Biblical preaching," "the love of the people," or "I felt welcomed and accepted."

As people come to feel at home, as they come to view the congregation as their own, they adopt the vision. If they were not already, as many were not, they become Sixth Americans, as their social ties come to be thoroughly infused with racial diversity and common goals, as Martin Luther King said was part of authentic integration.

INTEGRATION VERSUS ASSIMILATION

But there is more to authentic integration. It does not mean assimilation, the quite reasonable objection many people make when the concept of integration is discussed. We must take a closer look at how people in interracial congregations think. Do they support assimilation? Are they themselves assimilating to one culture or another? Do they think differently than those of their same race but in uniracial congregations?

We asked both a nationwide random sample of Americans, and the people with whom we conducted personal interviews, the following question:

A. Some people say that we are better off if the races maintain their cultural uniqueness, even if we have limited personal relationships between races.

B. Others say that we should create a common culture and close interracial friendships, even though the races may lose their cultural uniqueness.

Which one do you prefer?

Knowing that people might say they prefer a combination of these choices, we asked the following question of those who did:

[*If they said* "combination"] Do you lean more toward the first option, the second option, or are you right in the middle?

For those who support cultural pluralism, they typically will find the first option most attractive. For those who support assimilation, or the idea of a melting pot where we all meld into one new group, they typically will find the second option most attractive. Given that these two positions have been part of American views on diversity for decades (see appendix A for a historical overview), many may wish to support both, and thus choose a combination of the two options (even though, in the telephone interviews, we did not offer this option).[8]

If people in interracial congregations are supporters of assimilation rather than authentic integration, we would expect those in interracial congregations, compared to those in uniracial congregations, to be more supportive of option 2: creating a common culture and friendships across race, even though this means losing cultural uniqueness. Given that we know those in interracial congregations have much more racially diverse social networks, they may be especially likely to select this option.

I do not find support for this position. For whites, no differences exist between those in uniracial and interracial congregations. About half of whites in both congregational contexts select the assimilation option, about 40 percent select the cultural pluralism option, and about 10 percent said they would prefer a combination of the two options. (I also found the same distribution for all other whites, that is, those not regularly involved in a congregation). I did find one difference on this question among whites. Whites who have been part of interracial congregations for more than two years are less likely to select the common culture option than are other whites.

For the African Americans, Latinos, and Asians, differences exist based on the congregational context. Whereas six out of ten African Americans and Latinos in uniracial congregations favor the assimilationist option, only four out of ten in interracial congregations do. African Americans in interracial congregations are much more likely to support a combination of the two options (about 30 percent) than are African Americans in uniracial congregations (about 8 percent). Latinos in interracial congregations are much more likely to select the cultural pluralism option (about 51 percent) than are Latinos in

---

[8] In the telephone interviews, the respondent was not offered the "combination" option. Still, 14 percent gave this response. If they did, we followed up with our second question. For the in-person interviews, we did offer the "combination" option.

uniracial congregations (about 29 percent). For both African Americans and Latinos, those not involved regularly in congregations respond almost identically to those in uniracial congregations. Something is unique, then, about African Americans and Latinos in interracial congregations, and that uniqueness is in the direction opposite what is expected if interracial congregations are assimilation machines.

Asians' responses to this question also differ by congregational context. Although there is no difference between uniracial and interracial participants in the percentage supporting the assimilationist view (two-thirds of each group support this view), the two groups do differ in the support for the cultural pluralism view. One-third of Asians in interracial congregations prefer the cultural pluralist option, compared to about 15 percent of Asians in uniracial congregations. Again, to the extent that there is a difference by congregational context, it is in the direction opposite of the assimilation expectation.[9] (See table B5.1 in appendix B for the full results.)

In our face-to-face interviews with 160 people who were part of interracial and uniracial congregations, we asked the same question, but in addition to presenting the two options, we added a third: "Or do you prefer a combination of the two options?" According to analysts George and Yancey, nearly three-quarters of people responded that they preferred a combination.[10] This is instructive. In our telephone interviews, where the third option was not offered, non-whites in interracial congregations were more likely to support cultural uniqueness than were those in uniracial congregations. But when people were given the combination option, most everyone selected it as the preferred option. From reading the interviews, it is clear that *people want a balance between having something in common and being unique.* If forced to choose, those in interracial congregations are more likely to choose cultural uniqueness. They are simply less likely to give this up. Why? The interviews suggest this is because of their experiences in interracial congregations and other interracial settings.

A prime example is a story of a man from Wilcrest. He and his wife had been attending Wilcrest for about a year when after a worship service he came up to Pastor Woo and told him that for years he had

---

[9] I should also note that over 90 percent of non-whites who said they preferred a combination of the two options said they did not lean toward one option or the other, but rather were right in the middle. Whites were evenly split between leaning toward option one, leaning toward option two, and being right in the middle.

[10] See Douglas George and George Yancey, "Taking Stock of America's Attitudes on Cultural Diversity" (2004).

been hiding that he was Hispanic. He had done everything he could to keep people from knowing—even his marriage to an Anglo could be understood as part of his camouflage. But he wanted to tell Pastor Woo that here at Wilcrest it is acceptable to be Hispanic, acceptable to be different. "I can be proud of who I am, I can be proud of my family. It is safe here."

From his participation in an interracial congregation, this man came to the conclusion that one should not give up what makes one unique. It is what gives a person identity, and helps to make a group strong. As a white man from an interracial congregation in the Midwest put it, "You come together under a common goal, but it takes people with a diversity of cultural backgrounds to make us strong and reach our goal." Many echoed the words of this woman from Los Angeles, who suggests the importance of having cultural uniqueness and allowing differences: "I don't know how you could have harmony in a church that's diverse if you don't accept others. . . . I don't think you need to sacrifice your culture unless it's an ungodly practice. That's where I would draw the line. But other than that, embrace your culture." And this was the message the Wilcrest man seemed to hear.

Embracing one's culture while at the same time being part of an organization with common goals was an issue which was discussed frequently by those we interviewed. The following discussion with a black woman from an interracial congregation in the Northeast is representative. When asked if she preferred maintaining cultural uniqueness or a common culture or a combination of both, she responded:

> I think there should be something that brings us all together but I don't think I need to leave something behind in order for me to come together with people. I need to be able to be who I am in all my culturalism and everything, all that I am, I need to continue to be that way but that doesn't mean I can't hang out with another culture and enjoy the people and have a connection with the people.

> *If we should bring the races together, what do you think should bring us together?*
> Christ absolutely. Because he's the only thing that doesn't discriminate. Anything else, there will be some type of bias.

> *If you have Christ as a common culture, where can you have your distinctiveness?*
> Our heritage, our traditions. The way we cook, the way we dance. The types of music that we like to listen to. . . . And just my blackness, no mat-

ter how black I want to be and how loud I want to be, I just want to be accepted and be proud and accentuate that.

From their involvement in attending interracial congregations, respondents often talked about cultural uniqueness as an advantage for group action and learning. According to this Hispanic male from Houston:

I believe that the races should keep their uniqueness. That's what makes it great. I think that if you have a given racial background and uniqueness and so does your [for example] coworker, you can learn to work together. It makes the overall process a lot richer than if you try to force people into one common race or culture.

And from attempting to worship together, be friends, and get things done together, respondents reiterated a common theme, that there is positive value in all cultures. A Hispanic woman from Houston said:

All cultures are good and every one of them has bad things as well as good things. You need to learn to adapt without losing the culture that you know. I guess what I am trying to say is that it is a matter of respecting the differences between cultures. It is good to maintain the values of every culture because there are very nice things in each culture.

And an Asian American man from an interracial congregation in Los Angeles goes further. Not only is there positive value in other cultures, but there is positive value in learning from other cultures, as he illustrated with a specific example:

One of the things I know when I went to [my interracial congregation], there, the Latins really like to express their love and so there would be a lot of hugs. People would come up to you and give you a hug. At the beginning I was not comfortable with that. I felt like, okay, I was hugging people but I was hugging only on the exterior not really the whole me. And so I'm comfortable with that now. I think one of the things is that when you have interaction among cultures that you have the ability to be able to take advantage of that.

This man grew up with values and practices common to many Asian cultures. In most Asian cultures, and similar to white American culture, people greet others they do not know well with restraint—a bow, a nod, or a gentle handshake. Embracing another person with a hug is something reserved for those who are well known (at least in white American culture—some Asian cultures do not use hugs), such as close family members and perhaps a few friends. But people of many other cultures find such reserved behavior inappropriate, a sign of dislike or even failing to acknowledge another's humanity. Compared to Asian and white cultures, Latin cultures stress and expect much more personal contact. Whereas the typical white American who does not know a person well will stand three to five feet away from that person during conversation, the typical Latin will stand just six to nine *inches* away. Greetings with hugs are common, as they are signs of acceptance and acknowledgment. This Asian man encountered these two very different cultural expressions of greeting—the one he was raised in and the typical Latin one. His initial reaction to this juxtaposition of cultural norms was surprise and discomfort with the typical Latin expression. Over time, however, he came to see value in such an expression, recognizing it as a way to greet people raised in cultures where hugging acquaintances is appropriate and expected.

The experience of being with people of a variety of backgrounds thus helps lead those in multiracial congregations to place a positive value on people's distinctiveness; to use those differences as part of the process of working toward a higher goal; to desire the differences, too, as a way of enriching themselves; and, under healthy conditions (we explore unhealthy conditions in chapter 6), to learn how to live in a multiracial and multicultural group. In this sense, far from integration leading to assimilation, at least in the overall context of the multiracial congregations my colleagues and I studied, *integration helped people grow more secure in and proud of their cultural identities*. This finding, at least early on in the research, seemed to me counterintuitive. But the consistent pattern, combined with other factors—for example, the generalizable principle that we are more cognizant of our uniqueness when we are with people different from us—suggests that multiracial organizations may be ideal places to work toward the balance of common goals, interracial social networks, and nourishment of cultural uniqueness.[11]

The work of sociologist Elaine Howard Ecklund helps us understand these findings.[12] In her study, she focused on second-generation Koreans in Korean congregations and in multiracial congregations. Her main interest was in how these Koreans of similar socioeconomic

[11] As stated here, this conclusion may seem Pollyannaish. In the next chapter, I explore the underside of such organizations, and their potential risks. Most human organizations and institutions are fraught with inconsistencies and inequities. Multiracial congregations are no exception.

[12] See her work, *The "Good" American: Religion and Civic Life for Korean Americans* (2004). I draw particularly but not exclusively from chapter 4 of this work. See also her article "Models of Civic Responsibility: Korean Americans in Congregations with Different Ethnic Compositions" (2005).

standing but within different congregational contexts understand their civic identity. By civic identity she means how individuals perceive what it means to be American, including how they relate to and understand their ethnic identity in relation to others. Interestingly, Koreans in Korean churches talked about being Korean relatively little, and preferred to see themselves as Americans. By American, they meant white American, in contrast to being black or Hispanic American. That is, these Korean Americans wanted to share similar values with white Americans and with the nation. In contrast, Ecklund found that Koreans in multiracial congregations were much more likely to view themselves as being Korean, as not being white, and stressed that they have differences and similarities with other racial and ethnic groups. In short, the Koreans in multiracial congregations would be less likely to see value in assimilation versus value in maintaining cultural uniqueness. In contrast to the assimilating civic identities she found among Koreans in Korean congregations, she describes the civic identities of Koreans in multiracial congregations as protean or fluid, having many sides.[13] Korean Americans in these multiracial congregational contexts were able to reconcile their American and Korean identities, and do so without discomfort. They could construct cohesive identities while living in multiple worlds.

Ecklund argues that Koreans in multiracial congregations have different views of their identities than Koreans in Korean congregations, that they are able to simultaneously be Korean and American, and that they are able to value others' ethnicities and statuses because their congregations provide a cohesive religious narrative for seeing racial and ethnic diversity as important. As she writes, these mixed congregations provided a "theology or spiritual lens through which to view the importance of diversity in America."[14] In these congregations, those in attendance learned that race and ethnicity should be openly discussed and are valuable characteristics of humans. At the same time they were taught that race and ethnicity should not form barriers between people. Instead they should be used to fulfill others, and to see the fullness of God and creation.

WHO ARE THE PEOPLE IN INTERRACIAL CONGREGATIONS?

So far we have learned some about the people in interracial congregations, and how they compare to those attending uniracial congre-

---

[13] The term *protean* is developed by Robert Jay Lifton (1993), who discusses the "protean self."

[14] Ecklund 2004, p. 111.

gations (and other Americans). We have looked at what attracts them to interracial congregations, examined their social networks, and looked at their views of assimilation versus cultural pluralism.

But there are many more questions to be answered. In chapter 4, I used what is called a multivariate model to predict which factors most matter for attending an interracial as opposed to uniracial congregation. This method reports the net effect — each variable's influence after removing the effect of other variables. The method allows us to see whether income, for example, matters after we account for differences by age. Here, I look at how those in multiracial congregations differ from other Americans demographically (both those in uniracial congregations and those not attending a congregation), one variable at a time. This is the gross effect of the variable. As in chapter 4, I have found it necessary to categorize people by race, because there are often differences. Also as in chapter 4, most often the meaningful categories are white and non-white. When more specific racial categories tell us something unique, I report those.[15]

Whites in interracial congregations are, on average, younger than those in uniracial congregations, and, on average, about the same age as white Americans who do not regularly attend religious services.[16] The age difference is driven most strongly by the percentage of people over age 65. The senior population in multiracial congregations is only half that found in uniracial congregations (13 percent compared to 28 percent). Either those over 65 do not stay in interracial congregations (for example, they may retire and move to primarily white communities), or the contemporary interracial congregations are relatively new, full of younger people. Given that the founding dates of multiracial congregations average are more recent than for other congregations (see chapter 2), this latter possibility seems the better explanation. I also should note that the whites in these congregations are primarily people aged 31–64 and their children. However, as my colleagues and I noted in an earlier book, teenage white children are scarce.[17]

For non-whites, no average age difference exists between those in interracial and uniracial congregations. This is in part due to the younger overall age of non-whites compared to whites. Both the non-whites who attend interracial congregations and the non-whites who

[15] See appendix B for full results.

[16] This difference disappears when other factors, such as education, are controlled for, as reported in chapter 4.

[17] Christerson, Edwards, and Emerson 2005. See chapter 8 of that book for an explanation of why this is.

attend uniracial congregations are, however, on average about five years older than non-whites who do not regularly attend religious services.

Previous research on black Catholics and black Mormons has suggested that they have higher average class standing (measured by income, education, or occupation) than do other black Americans.[18] Dr. Woo noted earlier in this chapter that among others, one reason he sees some non-whites coming to Wilcrest is for social advancement. When considering the national data, I find that non-whites in interracial congregations indeed do have higher income and education than their counterparts in uniracial congregations, and also higher than their counterparts who are not in congregations. Measuring income in ten-thousand-dollar categories, the average income for non-whites in interracial congregations in our survey is $40,000–49,000. For non-whites not regularly attending a congregation, that average drops to $30,000–39,000, and non-whites in uniracial congregations average about $5,000 less than non-attendees.[19] The same pattern exists for education. Non-whites in interracial congregations, on average, have 13.5 years of formal education, or high school plus a year-and-a-half of additional education. The other two groups of non-whites average 12 years of education, or a high school degree. The question of causality once again needs to be asked. Are more highly educated and higher-income people more likely to choose interracial congregations, or are those in interracial congregations more likely to then obtain higher education and income?

At Wilcrest, there is clearly a mix. Keeping in mind that Wilcrest members are best described economically as lower middle class, many non-whites come to Wilcrest with little education and income. Through their involvement in the congregation and the connections they make, they return to school, and find better paying jobs. Other non-whites who come already have at least some college and solid incomes. Nationally, in most interracial congregations that my colleagues and I studied, this mix of causality appears to be similar. The exceptions we found were in the cases of congregations that were largely filled with professional people. In such cases, people had to a

[18] Cavendish, Welch, and Leege 1998; Embry 1994; Feagin 1968; Feigelman, Gorman, and Varacalli 1991; Hunt 1978, 1996, 1998; Nelson and Dickson 1972.

[19] All reported differences are statistically significant at the .05 level of probability. That is, there are less than five chances out of one hundred that the reported differences are due to sampling error instead of being actual differences in the population. Depending on the level of measurement of the dependent variable, t-tests, ANOVAs, and chi-square tests were used to test for statistical difference. See appendix B for full statistical results.

great extent achieved their class standing before coming to the congregation. Also, generally speaking, the less diverse the congregation, the higher the average class standing of the non-whites in the congregation. This certainly held true at Wilcrest. The first non-whites who came were often college educated and in well-paying jobs. As the racial diversity has grown, this is no longer the case.

Whites are a different story. No average income differences exist between whites in interracial congregations, in uniracial congregations, and not in congregations. When I turn to education, I find that the only difference is that whites not in congregations have less formal education than those in congregations, but there is no difference between those in interracial and uniracial congregations. These findings make sense in light of the national backdrop of racial history. For whites to be part of an interracial congregation does not represent class climbing, so there is no reason to expect higher income and education. Most interracial congregations are like Wilcrest, that is, formerly white congregations that have become racially diverse. But that pattern is by no means the only one. Some black, Latino, Asian, or American Indian congregations become racially diverse, and some congregations begin racially diverse. In these cases, it seems that two main types of whites belong: those who are highly educated and committed to being part of mixed-race congregations for ideological reasons, and poorer whites who are either spatially or socially more closely connected to the congregation. For the latter group, they often are not there out of a commitment to racially diverse congregations, but because the congregation is close by or because they have social connections there. Yet, whatever there initial reason for being there, they typically develop social ties across racial lines.

I find a few other demographic differences. Both whites and blacks in interracial congregations are more likely to have been divorced than whites and blacks in uniracial congregations. The percentage of those in interracial congregations who have gone through divorce is about the same level as those not involved in congregations. People we interviewed that had been divorced and were in interracial congregations often said one of the attractions of the congregation was that it was supportive of them in their time of need, and given the racial diversity, they felt that their "difference" was not so out of place.

Whites in interracial congregations are more likely to live in cities than are other whites, though even in this group, less than half do. Conversely, blacks and Hispanics in interracial congregations (but not Asians) are more likely to live in suburban areas than other blacks and Hispanics. Again, though, less than half of blacks and Hispanics in interracial congregations live in suburban areas.

Regionally, there also are racial differences, with whites in inter-racial congregations only half as likely to live in the Midwest and twice as likely to live in the West as whites in uniracial congregations. For Hispanics and Asians, I found no regional differences. African Americans in interracial congregations are less than half as likely to live in the South, and more than twice as likely to live in the West, as African Americans in uniracial congregations. As Dr. Woo communicated earlier in the chapter, the group that traditionally has been the least likely to come to Wilcrest has been American-born blacks, in part because of the strong tradition of black churches in the area, a feature more common in the South than anywhere else in the country.

ATTITUDES

Above we explored the major demographic differences. Once we account for these differences, do people in interracial congregations have different social attitudes than other Americans? I have data on social, political, racial, and religious attitudes to make these comparisons.[20]

I compared white and non-white Americans in interracial and uni-racial congregations, on 36 different measures of attitudes. Whites by congregational context differed on five of these measures, and non-whites by congregational context differed on six of these measures. The measures and significant differences are summarized in table 5.2. What stands out most is that few differences exist between people in interracial and uniracial congregations. The one significant exception to this pattern is in the race and immigration measures. Given that the basis of comparison is participation in interracial versus uniracial congregations, it makes sense that to the extent that there are differences, they occur in measures of racial issues.

Compared to whites in uniracial congregations, whites in interracial congregations are less supportive of the statement that the number of immigrants should be reduced, less supportive of the statement that there is too much talk today in the United States about racial issues, less likely to be upset if their child were to marry someone of another race, and less likely to prefer living in a neighborhood that is 75 percent their own race and 25 percent of other racial groups.

---

[20] The reported differences are statistically significant ($p < 05$), after controlling for age, being male, education, region of residence, immigrant status, and religious affiliation.

TABLE 5.2
Attitude Measures Used to Compare Those in Interracial to Uniracial
Congregations

	Multiracial Congregation Whites	Multiracial Congregation Non-Whites
Social (8 measures)		
The best way to improve the United States is to change individuals	– – –	
It is important to protect the environment, even if it hurts local business		
It is too easy to buy guns in America today		
Able-bodied people should not receive welfare		
We need a program of parental school choice		– – –
The pill is an acceptable form of birth control		
We should spend more money on prisons so that we can put criminals away		
Abortion during the first three months of pregnancy should be legal in all cases		
Government and Economic (7 measures)		
It is America's responsibility to promote democracy around the world		
I support affirmative action policies		
Too much of our federal budget goes to national defense		
The federal government income tax should be cut		
The economy is better today than it was a year ago		
How would you describe yourself politically? (1 = liberal, 7 = conservative)		
When you decide whom to vote for, which issue is most important to you?		
Gender and Family (4 measures)		
A mom of young children should work outside the home only if financially necessary	– – –	
Homosexuality should be an acceptable lifestyle		

(continued)

TABLE 5.2 *Continued*

	Multiracial Congregation Whites	Multiracial Congregation Non-Whites
The husband should be the head of the family		
Women face more discrimination in the workplace than men do		
Religion (12 measures)		
Religion is a private issue that should not influence social and political issues		
What is morally right and morally wrong should be the same for all persons		
My religious beliefs should direct my behavior in every area of life		
The Bible is the inspired word of God		
The Bible should be read literally, word for word		
Is Christ the only hope for salvation?		
Women should be allowed to be head pastors/priests		– – –
If enough people became Christians, social problems would naturally disappear		
I like the style of music at my church		
I feel like I belong at my church		
I am satisfied with the leadership at my church		
Do you think services are too long, too short, just about right, or time doesn't matter	No matter	Just right
Race and Immigration (5 measures)		
The number of immigrants who can legally enter the U.S. should be reduced	– – –	– – –
There is too much talk today in the United States about racial issues	– – –*	
Religious congregations should actively seek to become racially interrated		+++
I would be upset if my child wanted to marry someone of another race	– – –	
Prefer a neighborhood that is 75% own race and 25% other race, or 25% of 4 racial groups	– – –	

+++ Those attending interracial congregations are significantly *more* supportive of the statement than are those attending uniracial congregations.

– – – Those attending interracial congregations are significantly *less* supportive of the statement than are those attending uniracial congregations. See table B5.3 in appendix B for full statistical details.

*For white sample, significant at $p = .07$. For whites in congregations five years or less, significant at $p = .01$.

Source: Lilly Survey of Attitudes and Social Networks, 1999–2000

Non-whites in interracial congregations are more supportive of the statement that religious congregations should actively seek to be become racially integrated than are those in uniracial congregations, and like whites, less likely to prefer living in a majority "own race" neighborhood. Given that Latinos and Asians are highly supportive of immigration regardless of the congregational context, I looked at African Americans separately. Like whites in interracial congregations, blacks in interracial congregations are less supportive of the statement that the number of immigrants should be reduced, compared to their counterparts in black congregations.

Clearly, then, racial attitudes are different for those in interracial congregations compared to those in uniracial congregations. The causality problem again rears its head. The answer appears the same as before. Some people have different attitudes before they come, and this is in part why they find a home in interracial congregations. For many others, their attitudes changed because they were a part of interracial congregations. In our interviews, we heard about this change of views often. As contact theory suggests, the increased contact with racial others under relatively equal conditions leads to attitude change.[21]

A few other differences are noted in table 5.2. Whites in interracial congregations are less likely to believe that the best way to improve the United States is to change individuals than are whites in uniracial congregations. As Christian Smith and I argued elsewhere, whites overwhelmingly take an individualistic perspective to social change, and this perspective appears to be nourished in homogenous congregations and social networks.[22] As we have seen, those in interracial congregations have substantially more racially diverse social networks, in addition to their racially diverse congregational context. This appears to provide, on average, a different perspective to social change than for whites in white congregations, at least as indicated with this measure.

Compared to those in same-race congregations, whites in interracial congregations agree less strongly with the statement that mothers of young children should work outside the home only if financially necessary. In fact, while whites in same-race congregations support this statement, the average response of those in interracial congregations is "neither agree nor disagree." Perhaps for those in interra-

[21] Yancey, "An Examination of Effects of Residential and Church Integration upon Racial Attitudes of Whites" (1999).
[22] Emerson and Smith 2000.

cial congregations, whites' exposure to other cultures with a history of mothers working partly explains this difference.

For whites, worship services in interracial congregations tend to last longer than do those of their counterparts in white congregations. Conversely, for non-whites, especially for blacks and Hispanics, worship services tend to be shorter than are those of their counterparts in uniracial congregations. When whites were asked about the length of worship services, those in interracial congregations were less likely than their counterparts in uniracial congregations to say the services were just right, and much more likely to say that the length of the worship service does not matter. For non-whites, less than half of those in uniracial congregations said the worship service length was just right. But for those in interracial congregations, a full two-thirds said the worship service length was just right.

No other differences were found for whites. For non-whites, three other differences emerged. Compared to non-whites in uniracial congregations, non-whites in interracial congregations were less certain that a program of parental school choice is useful. This may be due to the perceived saliency of arguments that parental school choice will lead to greater racial segregation in schools. Somewhat surprisingly, for non-whites, those in interracial congregations are less supportive of women serving as head pastors or as priests. This finding does not hold for non-blacks.

Also important are which variables are not significantly different. No matter which congregational context—interracial, homogenous, or no congregation—whites give the same average response to statement, "I support affirmative action policies." Across the board they average somewhere between weak support and "neither agree nor disagree." For non-whites, the story is both the same—no difference by congregational context—and different—significantly more likely to say they support affirmative action policies than whites. As race and stratification scholars have identified for some time, whites, regardless of their attitudes about other racial groups, are highly resistant to government programs and policies, like affirmative action, which may change the economic structure.[23] From Fredrick Douglass to Malcolm X and Stokely Carmichael to contemporary commentators, one charge against whites is that they draw the line at giving up power, including supporting policies designed to reduce inequality. This charge seems to garner some support from my data. Although whites in interracial context have significantly more interracial contact, and are supportive of such contact, these facts do not

[23] For example, see Bonilla-Silva 2003, Feagin 2000, Jackman 1994, Kleugel 1990.

appear to lead to support for policies such as affirmative action. What is more, participation in interracial contact does not seem to reduce the gap between whites and non-whites in support for such policies. The gap between these two groups is statistically identical no matter the congregational context.[24] My anecdotal evidence from studying many multiracial congregations would support this finding. With the exception of a few congregations, almost never was there talk about issues such as affirmative action, whether from clergy to the congregation, or between individuals in the congregation. Still, we must be careful in making any strong claims. I have but one main measure, and it is sufficiently vague that is leaves room for doubt about its interpretation. Rather than providing us an answer, the findings point to the need for further study of this vital issue of support for change in the status quo.

CONCLUSION

The goal of this chapter was to understand why people come to interracial congregations, how they are demographically similar to or different from others, and how their attitudes are similar to or different from others. The answers to these questions cannot be easily summarized, but I found in brief that people in interracial congregations tend to vary in their attitudes in one primary area—race and immigration issues. The individuals that populate interracial congregations do not appear to be "race traitors" in the sense of wanting nothing to do with their racial culture. For non-whites, those in interracial congregations appear to be less supportive of assimilation than their counterparts in uniracial congregations, and proponents of cultural uniqueness. They do differ in that they want to be unique while at the same time being with people of other cultures. As one member of an interracial congregation in the Midwest said, "I love different ideas, different mindsets, different ways that people think, different beliefs. I love diversity. I love learning about people."

This and previous chapters have given a somewhat rosy picture of multiracial congregations and their members. The possible exception found in this chapter, from a political and economic perspective, is

---

[24] Mary Jackman's 1994 book, *The Velvet Glove*, plus several of her articles (e.g., with Marie Crane, 1986), demonstrate empirically the lack of effect that contact has on support for inequality-reducing policies. Her book develops a theory to explain why this is so. In fact, she argues that under certain conditions, those in power develop close interpersonal relationships with minorities to aid in retaining their power.

important. Although I found that members in interracial congregations help each other in finding jobs, getting into schools, and the like, I did not find that whites in such congregations are more supportive of national policies meant to reduce inequality, namely affirmative action programs. For some, this is not a significant issue. For many non-white leaders (and some whites too), this is a disappointing (if unsurprising) finding. Perhaps all is not rosy. In the next chapter, I take a careful look at the underside of multiracial congregations.

Chapter 6 · Shadows

> *"The dilemma was if this dream was so right, why were so many of our key people moving away?"*
> — Rodney Woo

> *"An integrating church is characterized by the need to be content with less than total satisfaction with everything."*
> — James Forbes, senior pastor of Riverside Church in New York City

> *"Nobody knows the troubles I've seen."*
> — Latino Roman Catholic priest, commenting on the complexities of leading his multiracial congregation, borrowing a well-known phrase

> *"This interracial church thing is wearing me out."*
> — An African American pastor reflecting on the difficulties of leading a racially diverse congregation

AFTER Wilcrest had been demographically a multiracial congregation for about eight years, a special service was held to ordain seven new deacons.[1] This service was special because new deacons had been ordained only twice before in the past eight years, and because this was the most racially diverse group of new deacons ever at Wilcrest.

During the planning of the service, the staff wanted to communicate the importance of the ordination through reverent and sacred worship. The ordering of the service was planned, and the music was carefully selected. During this worship service, an African American woman by the name of Lashawn visited the church. While the congregation was 40 percent non-white at the time of her visit, only about 10 percent of the congregation was black, mostly immigrants from the Caribbean and West Africa. Asked for her opinion of how Wilcrest was doing in its mission to be multiracial, Lashawn's written reply was direct, and piercing:

---

[1] Deacons at Wilcrest are the main lay leaders of the congregation, chosen for their faith maturity and record of service to the congregation.

I was surprised the church was only about half "Anglo." I realize this is probably because many Latinos appear white, but it is relevant that without any further investigation the church appears to a newcomer to be a predominately white church, culturally at the very least.

The choir was diverse. It looked to me to be about ⅓ to ½ non-white. But, the music was not only "white" but rather slow and traditional. I wondered why the non-white people are a part of the choir. Who selects the music? Are there non-whites who have input into the song and music selection?

The worship style is not the least bit charismatic. There was very little clapping or raising of the hands. Frankly, I could hardly hear people singing, outside of the choir. I did notice a black woman in the choir holding up her hands (to about waist level) and closing her eyes during one of the worship songs. It struck me that it probably took some courage to do even that, considering what, from my perspective, was a very rigid and conservative style.

The church also seems to have a number of older people who attend (50s plus). Is the church trying to be sensitive to the senior white people? Does this explain the conservative traditional white worship style? Do they have the most power, limiting what changes can be made?

Overall, the church struck me as a WHITE church! Except for the pastor and recently ordained deacons making a note of the church being a multiracial church, thereby telling me the church identifies as a multiracial church, I would not have considered it a multiracial church. Otherwise, I would consider it a white church that has some non-white people that attend the church. This makes me wonder why the non-white people attend the church. I am quite curious about this because there is really not much of anything that attracts me to the church and I cannot imagine what attracts Latinos.

Personally, I was disappointed, even sad about the disconnect that I saw between what the church claims to be and what, from my visit, it was. People who are non-white are welcome, I am sure, but they don't seem to be appreciated for what they can uniquely bring to the church or really included at every level. Given what I saw and experienced, I would not be able to invite other African Americans to Wilcrest.

Despite great changes at Wilcrest, Lashawn's assessment of the congregation and its worship was that Wilcrest remained largely a white congregation. She was reminded that she did not attend a typical energetic Wilcrest service, but one meant to express reverence and sacredness to communicate the importance of the ordination. Her response to this explanation was that it was further evidence that Wilcrest remained culturally a white church. Why did reverent and sacred mean slow, European music? Why were black gospel songs or Latin rhythms not considered reverent and sacred? Many in the staff did not agree, and found her assessment unfair and even judgmental. Some said that African Americans seem especially difficult to please.

What is happening here? The question of this chapter is not which side is right in its interpretation. The question is why there are often seemingly intractable differences in interpretation. In this chapter, I explore conflicts, difficulties, and power misused to dehumanize people, all the shadow side of social life. Conflict, difficulties, and power are found in nearly every social relationship and organization, and they influence actions, meanings, and interpretations. Shadows—and sometimes full-blown nightmares—are present at Wilcrest and every congregation my colleagues and I studied. As social analyst Mary Jackman writes, having people share an organization or institution and proclaiming love for one another does not preclude conflict and the misuse of power.[2] In fact, it can fuel these processes. For instance, power is present in marriages and spouses can use the bond of love to misuse that power in ways otherwise not possible. Husbands can be patriarchal, doing what they want but in the guise of loving and helping their spouses. If their wives question their motives, they can point out that they do what they do out of love. They need not be sinister in their motives. They truly may want what they think is best for their spouses, but the key is that *they* define what is best for their spouses.

It can work the same in congregations and all organizations. Power, distributed unequally across groups, is one reason uniracial congregations often make sense. Why be part of another congregation where one's culture, worship style, and faith are devalued, simply ignored, or thought not to exist?

This chapter's exploration of shadows begins with a necessary look at U.S. culture. It is not fully possible to understand the processes in multiracial congregations without this knowledge. We then turn to an examination of the types of conflicts that arise, the limits to people from multiple cultures sharing the same organizations, and the misuse of power. Finally, to help make sense of these shadows, I place them in the larger contexts of spiritual and racial formation.

Two Indigenous and Often Oppositional U.S. Cultures

To help understand the disagreement over the interpretation of the Wilcrest deacon ordination service and the many other shadows dis-

---

[2] Jackman, *Velvet Glove* (1994).

cussed in this chapter, we must start from the beginning. *In the United States there are two indigenous American cultures.*[3] One is associated primarily with white Americans (and "honorary whites," such as light-skinned, assimilated Mexicans), and the other is associated primarily with black Americans (and "honorary blacks," such as darker skinned, assimilated Puerto Ricans). The United States always has had people and groups who are neither white nor black. What of their cultures? American Indian cultures predate the United States. It would be incorrect to label these cultures U.S. cultures. The same can be said for Mexican culture. More indigenous U.S. cultures may develop in time, but it is too early to tell. The United States has many immigrant cultures, but they are not indigenous U.S. cultures. Immigrants, after a generation or two, typically adopt many aspects of one or the other indigenous U.S. culture, even though racially they are to meld into one of the five "Americas," that is one of the five major racial groups.[4] This can produce unique problems. As an Asian man from the Northeast reflected, "I think Asian Americans feel kind of disenfranchised from society. . . . And a lot of people have difficulty living in America and not being white or black." Non-blacks and non-whites can feel a sense of alienation as they attempt to assimilate or carve out a separate cultural space unique from the two indigenous American cultures. Importantly, if they assimilate to one or the other American culture, they help shape what those cultures look like.[5]

[3] The word "indigenous" in America is usually associated with Native Americans. They are indigenous people, and their culture is indigenous to the land. I speak here not of land but of the political entity called the United States. There are two "homegrown" cultures raised up within the political entity called the United States. It is in this respect that I use the term indigenous to refer to black and white culture. In some ways, race and ethnic scholars putting forth the segmented assimilation model of immigrant adaptation implicitly work from the model of two indigenous U.S. cultures to which immigrants may acculturate (for example, see Portes and Rumbaut 2001, and Zhou and Bankston 1998). Others would not agree with this position. For example, Alba and Nee (2003) imply that there is one mainstream which continually expands and is remade as new groups join it.

[4] See chapter 4 of this book, and Hollinger 1995.

[5] Race and ethnic scholars have much debated the coming structure of race and race relations. The debate ranges from a movement to a black/non-black United States (Yancey 2003b) to a Latin Americanization of U.S. racial categories, where there will be an expanded white category, an expanded black category, and then a middle category for persons who do not quite fit in either (Bonilla-Silva 2002). It is unlikely that a trans–Asian American culture (as opposed to Asian immigrant cultures) will develop in the near future, because of (1) the much smaller proportion of Asians in the United States, (2) the vast diversity of backgrounds and national origins of Asians in the United States, (3) the higher average socioeconomic class ranking of many Asian

American black and white cultures were developed in the United States, and are unique to this specific country. They are the product of multiple ethnic groups "melding" into racial groups. Due to the centuries-long separation of and inequality between these created races, separate cultures were developed, nourished, and institutionalized. Often these cultures develop *in opposition to one another* — to "act white" is to not "act black," and vice versa. Both cultures have their main ways of interacting, their unique forms of music, their own institutions, their own unique problems, and their own value systems and ways of looking at the world; people in both interact predominately with people in their own racial group.

At the risk of overgeneralization, it is useful to illustrate a few differences here. I borrow from the work of scholars such as Ronald Takaki and Thomas Kochman.[6] We are wise to keep in mind that in addition to race, class, region, age, and other factors shape people's cultures, and that we can always find exceptions. With these caveats in mind, white culture tends to separate intellect and passion, often described as separating mind and body. In a democracy where non-elite white men could vote, the white founders of the United States were concerned that such people be ruled by reason apart from feelings and passions. They thus stressed that a good white American is one who separates mind and body and places the mind over the body. They often made this point by placing the good white American *in opposition to* the black and the Indian, whom they viewed as ruled by their passions.[7]

Black American culture does not split mind and body. The two components are viewed as important and intertwined, and it would be artificial to separate them and rank one over the other. This difference in views leads to a number of cultural differences. For example, communications professor Thomas Kochman identifies the different cultural understandings of public debate. Within white culture, public debate should be characterized by presenting facts and

---

Americans (which traditionally has been associated with assimilation), and (4) the lack of strong Asian American lobby groups. This does not mean, however, that Asian Americans will not continue to be seen as racially different, and suffer consequences from that. Rather, it means the racialization process works in different ways for different groups (Alumkal 2004).

[6] See Ronald Takaki's book, *Iron Cages* (2000), and Thomas Kochman's book, *Black and White Styles in Conflict* (1981).

[7] Ronald Takaki's *Iron Cages* (2000) develops these ideas much more completely than I do here. Of course, the founders often did not use the term *white*, but would contrast the "American" to blacks and Native Americans, who they did not view as Americans.

citing experts. It should be dispassionate, impersonal, calm, without affect. In short, effective public debate is low-keyed and emphasizes cognition to the exclusion of affect. Being emotional or personal during a debate is a sign of losing one's cool, or trying to win a debate by deception, that is, by more than just the facts.

For many raised in black culture, the white version of debating is hardly debate at all. Within black culture, public debate should test the validity of ideas through animated, interpersonal, confrontational discussion. It is acceptable to grow heated, raise one's voice, and display affect. To do so shows concern for the topic, allows false ideas to be exposed, and truth to survive. Those raised in white culture are often intimidated by such a style, seeing it as angry argumentation rather than debate, overly aggressive and too personal.

White worship styles and musical forms typically reflect the ascendancy of mind over body. Sermons, homilies, and other forms of presenting religious messages are expected to be cerebral. The truths should speak for themselves, so the emphasis is less on style and more on the evidence and the logic of the presentation. Although some affect is allowed, if one goes too far those raised in white culture will feel uncomfortable, perhaps assume the speaker does not have much to say and so is resorting to emotion, and in extreme cases, will wonder why the speaker is "acting black."[8] Music styles that derive from white culture are many and varied, but they tend to share in common an emphasis on melody over beat and rhythm. They may be played at a slow or fast pace, quietly or loudly, but these forms tend to have in common the ascendancy of melody. Those understanding or appreciating white culture would consider the best of such music "beautiful," "soaring," able to lift one's mind above the humdrum everyday life to another realm of existence. At its finest, many would describe it as a religious experience.

Black worship styles and musical forms typically reflect the intertwining of mind and body. Sermons, homilies, and other forms of presenting religious messages are expected to be an experience, to bring people into the presence of a higher power. Messages should be communicated in their fullness, by multiple means. Thus the speaker must be concerned both with style and with facts. To simply be cerebral would not produce an experience, could be seen as presenting

[8] There are some white congregations and some white denominations which emphasize experience over or equal to cerebral value. These are typically viewed with disdain by other whites as being lower class, ethnic, "black-like," and even artificial or a fake, shallow faith. Often when these congregations or denominations want to gain respect among the white hierarchy, they attempt to downplay the experiential, emotive side of their faith.

partial truths, perhaps communicate that the speaker does not truly believe in the message, or even be viewed as "acting white." For those steeped in black culture, white music can seem flat, unmoving, and even lifeless. This is in good part because whatever else black music is, it tends to emphasize beat, rhythm, a groove. Music and words are most satisfactory when performed rhythmically, with the depth of a groove, something your body naturally moves to and which has soul. Those understanding or appreciating black culture would consider the best of such music energizing, moving, an affective "out of body" experience able to connect one to others and a higher power. At its finest, many would describe it as a religious experience. For those steeped in white culture, such music may be interesting, but may seem repetitive, and lacking melody or beauty.[9]

The culture associated with white Americans often is mistakenly viewed as American culture. It certainly has been the most dominant U.S. culture, because there have been more white Americans than other Americans, and because white Americans have held the main centers of power throughout U.S. history. But white U.S. culture is no more American than black U.S. culture. Both have been present since the nation's founding. Both have contributed immeasurably to the nation's development. Both have developed numerous subcultures within them. Both have developed unique religious cultures. And both share and contribute to the American political, educational, economic, and entertainment systems. To whatever extent there is a single overarching American culture, it is, as scholar Cornel West and others have said, the blending of black and white cultural aspects.

To understand multiracial congregations—their formation, their development, their conflicts—it is essential that we work from the

[9] Many people within a culture appreciate the musical forms of other cultures, even if their cultural toolkit makes it difficult for them to conceive of and produce the music themselves. For example, it is difficult to imagine that hip hop music could originate within white culture, just as it is difficult to imagine that country music could originate within black culture. The building blocks of the musical styles of each culture are largely foreign to the other culture. For readers interested in learning more on this topic, a classic book that examines the different cultural forms is *Variations in Value Orientations* (1961) by Florence Kluckhohn and Fred Strodbeck. Humans, they write, must solve problems for living with each other and nature. The authors see cultures developing different value orientations in five key areas, with possible responses falling along a continuum: human orientation to activity (continuum from being to doing), the relationship of humans to each other (collectivistic to individualistic), the perceived nature of human beings (evil to good), the relationship of human beings to nature (subjugation to harmony with to mastering nature), and the orientation of humans to time (past to future). American blacks and whites differ on many of these orientations. Another useful perspective on this topic is Edward Hall's 1977 book, *Beyond Culture*.

understanding that there are two indigenous U.S. cultures and, at any given time, a variety of nonindigenous cultures.[10] For congregations in the United States, then, when significant percentages of blacks and whites are members of the same congregation, I will call them *Mixed American Culture congregations*, or *MAC congregations* for short. Based on the National Congregations Survey, of the 7 percent of U.S. congregations that are racially mixed (no one racial group is 80 percent or more of the congregation), about 34 percent are MAC congregations (that is, having at least 20 percent black and at least 20 percent white in the congregation).[11] If we consider all congregations together, whether they are racially mixed or not, just 2.5 percent are MAC congregations. Even this small figure of 2.5 percent is likely an overestimate. Because the National Congregations Survey did not ask the ethnic makeup of the congregation, I cannot know if, for example, a congregation that is 30 percent black is mostly American-born black, immigrant black, or some combination. Undoubtedly, some congregations with a significant black presence are not comprised primarily of American blacks who adhere to black American cultural styles. I have studied such congregations. Wilcrest is an example. Although it is 20 percent black at the time of this writing, only about a third of that is American-born black. The percentage of congregations that combine the two American cultures, then, likely is smaller than the 2.5 percent estimated here.

Bringing different racial and cultural groups together is almost always difficult, with heightened potential for misunderstandings and conflict.[12] Having two indigenous U.S. cultures, often defined in opposition to each other, leads to the potential for unique and height-

[10] Author and multiracial church pastor David Anderson describes blacks and whites as the "bookends" of U.S. life, with others in between, closer to one end or the other, in his book, *Multicultural Ministry: Finding Your Church's Unique Rhythm* (2004).

[11] To be classified as a white/honorary white congregation, a congregation must be less than 20 percent black; to be classified as a black/honorary black congregation, less than 20 percent white. To be classified as a MAC congregation, 20 percent or more of the congregation must be black and 20 percent or more of the congregation must be white. The 20 percent figure is chosen in keeping with our understanding of the proportion needed to have influence in an organization (see chapter 2). Percentages of the three types of congregations do not add to 100 percent because a small proportion (about 2 percent) of multiracial congregations are primarily Asians and Latinos, with neither blacks nor whites comprising 20 percent or more.

[12] In actuality, as measured by survey data on reports of disagreements in the past two years, multiracial congregations do not often report significantly more disagreements than other congregations (Yancey and Emerson 2003). Our interview data suggests the conflicts that do occur more often seem to take leaders by surprise and can often be deeper.

ened conflict in MAC congregations. Most Americans seem unaware that there are two indigenous American cultures. Non-blacks especially view white culture as American, and black culture as a subculture or simply as the culture of blacks. To illustrate, at least from the perspective of whites, African Americans who were raised in and are comfortable in white American culture often are said to be assimilated or Americanized. Whites raised in black culture, however, are not said to be assimilated or Americanized, but rather, are people who are "trying to act black."

Such views and the presence of two cultures have important implications for multiracial congregations in the United States. For example, because of the heightened difficulty and social energy expended (discussed in greater detail in the following sections), we can predict that multiracial congregations are less likely to bridge the two indigenous American cultures than to be comprised of one indigenous American culture and immigrants and their offspring. From the data presented above, this appears to be the case. About two-thirds of multiracial congregations are not MAC congregations.[13] We can also predict that conflict will be most frequent and severe in multiracial congregations when the congregation is one that contains people of both indigenous American cultures, that is, when it is a MAC congregation. These two predictions follow from the facts that people of both indigenous U.S. cultures believe they have, at the very least, an equal right to practice their culturel; have little interest in giving it up; have oppositional cultures, so that adopting one may be seen as denying the other; have cultures that have been institutionalized through, among others, separate denominations and congregations; and have centuries of racial wounds. Conversely, those in immigrant cultures typically come to the United States expecting to adapt to an American culture, and to make sacrifices to succeed economically. They also may want to become American culturally (or their children will want to), so they or their children are open to acculturating. We saw evidence for these assertions in chapter 5 when discussing why Latinos and Asians come to Wilcrest. We also saw it statistically in chapter 4. A full 50 percent of churchgoing nonimmigrant Latinos and Asian Americans are in multiracial congregations, a stunning percentage in light of the current racial segregation of U.S. religious congregations.

[13] To make this claim I am conflating group presence with cultural styles. For my national sample data, I know the racial composition of the congregations, but not the cultural styles. Congregations with at least 20 percent white and 20 percent black could be assimilating, unicultural congregations. For example, from my congregational data, whereas in 80 percent or more of black congregations, choirs regularly sing black gospel music, this is true for less than half of MAC congregations.

MAC congregations are more difficult to sustain than other types of multiracial congregations. One congregation my colleagues and I studied was Mosaic, a multiracial, multiethnic congregation in the Los Angeles area. This growing congregation has been racially diverse for decades and has been much studied. At about one-third Asian, one-third Latino, and one-third white, its racial diversity is impressive. The congregation is strongly oriented toward the creative arts, and this includes writing and performing its own Mosaic music, an eclectic style meant to speak to the diversity of people in the congregation. As I was told by one of the staff members, the music is organized around modified rock beats, which they viewed as the universal musical language, being used around the world. Great attention is given to making sure that those who appear at the front of the church during worship services represent the diversity of the congregation. The staff itself, headed by a Salvadorian immigrant, is racially and ethnically diverse. This congregation is looked to by many other congregations hoping to become multiracial as a leader to be emulated. Mosaic hosts conferences to teach leaders of other congregations its philosophy of multiethnic ministry. Its lead pastor has published books. While I was interviewing staff at this congregation, no less than four calls from representatives of other congregations were received, asking for advice on becoming multiracial, or asking if they could come to observe how they operate at Mosaic. Two years prior to this writing, even Rodney Woo and his associate pastor of music, Monty Jones, came to Mosaic to learn how multiracial ministry is done there.

Despite its esteemed position and extensive diversity, Mosaic is not a MAC congregation. Gerardo Marti, a sociologist and former pastor at Mosaic, wrote that "Mosaic does not provide an ethnic haven for African Americans. It does not mean that there are no African Americans at Mosaic; it means that they do not relate to Mosaic on the basis of ethnic affinity. African Americans equate Mosaic as being the assimilated 'white' culture."[14] Among the many issues identified by African Americans at Mosaic, music was certainly near the top. As one African American woman told Marti during an interview, there is a wide chasm between Mosaic music and black music:

> If someone is used to black music and black culture, then it's tough to make a shift into a church like this because the music is basically pop-ish. We call it "Vineyard music" [after a white contemporary music style and

[14] Gerardo Marti, *A Mosaic of Believers: Diversity and Religious Innovation in a Multi-Ethnic Church* (2005), p. 161.

publishing house]. It's not gospel. It's not real soulful. You can sing it that way; we just don't sing it that way. It's uphill for a person who likes or is used to hearing a soulful gospel sound.[15]

Marti goes on to describe other African Americans views of the music at Mosaic — they do not identify with it, and find it difficult to worship.

African Americans have other struggles at Mosaic. Marti details a discussion with an African American woman who came to his office at Mosaic to tell him that she was leaving the church. Gracious in her conversation, she identified the overly white focus on individualism and the lack of focus on issues of justice. She did not view Mosaic as a place conducive to racial reconciliation between blacks and whites. I met this same woman at a conference, and she talked to me about her experiences at Mosaic. Again gracious in her demeanor, she told me of instances that lead African Americans to feel like outsiders in the congregation, from the musical forms to being told by a congregational leader that blacks complain too much and that they need to get beyond the past and be part of society like everybody else.

Marti says that some African Americans can find a place at Mosaic, if they have been raised in white culture. Mosaic, then, is a racially diverse congregation, one of the most diverse in the nation, but it is not a MAC congregation. It may be best termed a white/honorary white congregation.

The same is true of Wilcrest, at least at the time of this writing. I do not wish to communicate that only MAC congregations are authentically multiracial. That is not true. Rather, there are different types of multiracial congregations, and they can have their own dynamics. Non-MAC multiracial congregations often will not resonate with Americans who are part of the other American culture. This helps us understand the divergence in interpretation over the meaning of the Wilcrest ordination service discussed at the opening of this chapter. It also helps us understand why Lashawn, raised in black culture, did not perceive Wilcrest to be a multiracial congregation. It was to her a white/honorary white church where people of a variety of backgrounds who were willing to worship in primarily white and immigrant cultural styles would feel welcomed, but those steeped in black cultural styles would often feel excluded.

Wilcrest, like all multiracial congregations — whether they are MAC congregations or not — continuously faces difficulties and conflicts. Issues which to an outsider may seem small and relatively triv-

---

[15] Ibid., p. 162.

ial easily take on magnified meanings in a multiracial context. I explore why these shadows loom so large in the next section.

DIFFICULTIES AND CONFLICTS: WHY SMALL DIFFERENCES ARE SO BIG

At a Catholic church in the Midwest, the congregation consisted of whites, blacks, and Latinos in roughly equal numbers. Great care was taken by the diocese to ensure that this congregation flourished. They allowed the congregation to have much say in who their pastor would be, in appointing assistants, how committees would be structured, and how specific aspects of the Mass would be run.

Despite the great care taken to ensure equal voices, conflicts continually emerged, even over issues that may seem minor to an outsider. Groups often felt slighted, felt like they were not heard, or believed their voices were not fully considered. One conflict centered around what statue to place in the new courtyard of the church. At a planning meeting, members of the congregation came with their suggestions. Although they each wanted to place a statue of a saint, they soon realized they did not have any agreement as to which saint. Some also realized the saint that each member suggested was the same racial background as the person making the suggestion. Selecting a saint of the same racial background usually was not a conscious choice. Rather, each was presenting whoever they felt was the most meaningful saint to represent the congregation. But the members of different racial groups, focusing on the race of the saints, felt they were being excluded if they agreed to a saint being proposed by a member of another group.

The Latino members argued that because their commitment to their chosen saints was so deep and long-standing, they ought to be given preference in selecting the saint statue, and would be willing to give up say on other issues to have their chosen saint statue in the courtyard. The other members did not agree. Some white members of the congregation asked more than once why this was turning into a racial discussion. "Can't we just select the saint who best represents who we aim to be?" Representatives from the black congregation pointed out that the "best" seems to mean only white saints to the white members.

Try as they might, they could not come to agreement. Tempers flared, often followed by apologies for losing one's cool and acting in an unchristian manner. After multiple meetings, it was clear the debate was not resolvable. With few options left, they decided that despite the extra cost and required space, they would place three saint statues in the courtyard instead of one. Some were uneasy about this decision, as they felt three statues communicated three separate groups rather than one united congregation. Still, they agreed, this seemed the only way to move on to other issues. When the vote was taken, nearly all members voted in favor of three separate statues, one each to be selected by each respective group.

Problem solved. Well, not quite. There was that nagging question of whose statue should be placed in the center of the courtyard. . . .

At a MAC congregation in the Northeast (which consisted only of blacks and whites), a conscious attempt was made to have music typically heard in black churches and in white churches in equal proportions. This seemed to be the fair and equitable thing to do. But when I interviewed members of the congregation, this was not the common perception. Many of the white members expressed to me the frustration with so much gospel music, pointing out that the church was to be for whites as well. When I interviewed African American members, many said they were glad the music was diverse, but they so wished there was more gospel music. Members of each group, while committed to worshiping together, felt like their musical forms were getting the short end of the stick. Over time, some people actually left the congregation out of frustration from this and other perceived slights.

Back in Houston, communication at Wilcrest, as my colleagues and I detailed in an earlier book, can be problematic:

> Non-Whites and whites alike said communicating could be more difficult. More than one told of struggles communicating across language barriers, or trying to tell a joke but it was not interpreted as such. The issue of time came up often. Particularly for Latinos, but also for some blacks, they talked about struggling to see time as rigidly as whites and Asians in the church see it. "For them, something starting at 10:45 means 10:45 exactly, as if we all could have watches with exactly the same time!" "I am learning how important time is to the whites and Asians in our church. They take it very literally, and very seriously. They seem hurt if I don't come very close to the stated time. I am really having to learn to be 'on time."
>
> Some of the whites we talked to communicated hurt, or at least frustration, with different conceptions of time. They thought some people were not taking things seriously enough, and this was especially frustrating given that the issues at hand were learning about God. One white man, a teacher of an adult Sunday School class, felt his frustration build week after week as people came to the class fifteen, twenty, even thirty minutes

after the hour-long class began. He actually talked to some of the Latinos about his frustration. Some told him "that if you show up on time all the time, that in their culture that is equated with thinking you are very important and have to be there for things to work. That's not a very Christian trait." So, he mused with some befuddlement, "one culture thinks it offensive not to be on time, the other thinks it offensive to be on time. No easy solution there!"[16]

As one considers the work of a religious congregation, its aim to uplift its members, to nurture their spiritual lives, and to serve the surrounding community, it is hard to imagine instead that people are having conflict over what statue to place in their courtyard, what forms of music are played most often, or what coming on time means. In light of congregations' larger tasks and goals, these conflicts seem rather trivial.

This is a mistaken view, however. To understand why this is so, we can employ the concept of habitus, developed by Pierre Bourdieu, a French sociologist.[17] All groups have a habitus, a deeply seated, all-encompassing set of preferred tastes, smells, feelings, emotions, and ways of doing things. Habitus goes beyond and is deeper than cognition. It is learned dispositions, which are so thoroughly and completely infused in people that they struggle to communicate them. Habitus is developed through the childhood and young adult years. It can be changed, as when people attempting to be social climbers change their tastes (say from beer to rare wines), but a person has to want the change and even then, it comes through great struggle. People are not always successful in making such changes. Bourdieau spends much time in his writings analyzing the differences in habitus that develop by social class in France. In the United States, in addition to class, race and ethnicity are powerful factors shaping habitus, as early socialization experiences by racial group are often quite different.

How does the habitus concept help us understand racial and ethnic conflict in racially diverse congregations? It allows us to see that what seem like trivial differences to outsiders are in fact loaded with deep meanings, producing high stakes for those involved. What saint statue to place in the courtyard, what styles of music are used (and in what proportions), what time to show up for Sunday school class, are in no way simply about these seemingly minor issues.

[16] Brad Christerson, Korie Edwards, and Michael O. Emerson (2005). This book features six case studies of racially diverse religious organizations (four congregations, a religious university group, and a religious college). Wilcrest is discussed in chapter 3 of this book.

[17] For example, see his 1984 book, *Distinction*.

They are about a group's habitus, about how they view, understand, and experience the world. Insofar as people choose to attend congregations, they do so because the good can only be obtained through social interaction, through social activity (otherwise they could simply sit at home and "do religion" by themselves exactly as they want religion done). They must rely on others to obtain that which they seek, according to a view called social exchange theory. Goods are obtained in and through social interaction and exchange. This fact compounds conflict, for people are put in difficult situations. Each person and group must rely on the others in the organization for some good—such as uplifting music, social identity, or explanations of truth—but if the organization does not go about achieving the good in a way that resonates with people's habitus, they will grow frustrated, feel cheated, and find it difficult to experience meaning and belonging. One consequence, illustrated with this chapter's opening quote from Rodney Woo, is that people simply leave.

Because the habitus lies deeper than mental cognition, because it consists of feelings, emotions, history, tastes, and preferences, it is often beyond a person's or group's ability to communicate or accurately grasp the sources of frustration, or why the issue feels so important. Thus well-intentioned people committed to ideas of love for all people—and for most multiracial congregations studied here, committed to coming together across racial lines—end up conflicting over seemingly minor issues. They do so because these seemingly minor issues represent whole views of the world, of what is right and wrong, what is beautiful, and what is meaningful.

Building on the work of R. Stephen Warner and others, cultural sociologist Penny Edgell identifies two main types of conflict.[18] The first she calls within-frame conflict. Within-frame conflict is conflict that arises between people and groups sharing the same expectations and a similar habitus. It is resolved by routine processes that enforce compliance with the agreed-upon expectations. Americans typically share the expectation that you should get what you pay for. If someone buys an air conditioner, for example, it should cool the air. When conflict arises because one party or another perceives that expectation has been violated, routine steps are available to resolve the conflict, including taking the matter to the courts. These steps are ac-

---

[18] For a fascinating look at conflicts arising from different groups of people within the same congregation, R. Stephen Warner's book, *New Wine in Old Wineskins: Evangelicals and Liberals in a Small-Town Church* (1988) is probably the most in-depth, complete, and insightful work written. Penny Edgell Becker (1999) builds on his work with a book analyzing conflict in over twenty congregations in one community near Chicago. See also the work of Fred Kniss, especially "Ideas and Symbols as Resources in Intrareligious Conflict" (1996).

cepted, and the decision (perhaps a court decision) usually abided by. Likewise, in congregational conflicts that are within the same frame, standard procedures typically are employed, and when enacted, resolve the conflict.

The same is not the case for the other type of conflict Edgell identifies: between-frame conflict. Between-frame conflict is much more difficult to resolve, and often is more intense, because it stems from divergent habituses, divergent standards of what is right, or different expectations about how things ought to be done. Edgell says that such conflicts often become questions (and even battles) over identity, who we are, and "how we do things here." Clearly, in such conflicts, much is at stake.

What also is clear from studying congregations is that while conflicts of both types—within and between frames—arise in all congregations, between-frame conflict is more common in multiracial congregations than in uniracial congregations. Such congregations nearly guarantee the bringing together of divergent habituses and expectations into the same volunteer organization, and do so both at the individual and group levels. Interestingly, if I merely look at survey data, racially mixed and homogenous congregations do not seem to differ in the amount of reported conflict or in the frequency with which the conflict leads to a congregational split. But the survey data do not capture the depth of conflict as expressed in our interviews with pastors and in our observations of congregations. In almost every case, the clergy of multiracial congregations my colleagues and I talked to said that the congregation has more conflict and difficulties because it is a multiracial congregation, and that they would be lying if they said they have never thought how much easier it would be if the congregation was uniracial.

The day before writing this section, I sat in on a roundtable discussion of multiracial congregation leaders. They talked about the many benefits of such congregations, about the joy of leading such congregations, and about practical issues. During a portion of the discussion, the topic of difficulties and conflicts arose. One of the leaders said, "I hate to admit it, but honestly, from a purely practical view, sometimes I think it would be so much easier to have a single race congregation. There would be less intractable conflict, less confusion over what the conflict is really about." This leader's comment was met with all heads nodding in agreement, and was followed by several other leaders sharing the same sentiments. They were clear they would not give up leading such a congregation, to be sure. But they seemed to find some healing salve in discussing their common understanding that multiracial congregations, more so than uniracial congregations, generate conflict and complexities.

I asked Pastor Woo if heightened conflict and complexities matched his experience as Wilcrest diversified. He did not hesitate in his response. Not only have there been many positive outcomes, but their have been many more difficulties. "It can be exhausting. From people leaving, to hurt feelings, to disagreements over how to handle a ministry, to how long services should last. All of these issues have increased and become more complicated as we have become more diverse."

Multiracial congregations typically experience the shadows of conflict generated by racial and ethnic groups having different expectations, different tastes, different patterns, different experiences, different feelings and interpretations, or in short, different habitus. Without the understanding that conflicts of seemingly small issues are about much deeper meanings and identities, frustration and confusion can and do set in. Anthropologist Larry Naylor summarizes this point:

> As culture represents truth, when people of different cultures come together, the consequence must always be some conflict, for it is more than people coming into contact. It really means that truths come into contact and that means conflict. Each group tends to believe that its beliefs and practices are the right or more correct ones. They judge others by it and being convinced of its correctness, each group makes every effort to impose their truth on everybody else. As everybody does the same thing, cultural contact will always mean conflict.[19]

THE NIGHTMARE OF MISUSED POWER

Difficulties and conflicts do not just arise out of innocent misunderstandings or divergent habituses. They also arise from the misuse of power. Power can be defined as the capacity of some people or groups to produce intended and foreseen effects on others. The misuse of power is the use of power for the gain of one group against the wishes of another group. In many if not most of the multiracial congregations my colleagues and I studied, to varying degrees power was misused. The temptation to misuse power is great. How can between-frame conflict be solved when negotiation does not seem to be working? How can a person encounter the sacred through worship when others want to conduct worship in a way that one is not familiar or comfortable with? Often the easiest way is for the most powerful people and group(s) to misuse their power. Typically, and not the

---

[19] Naylor 1999.

least bit surprisingly, people use their power for their own advantage. How so?

After returning from a summer traveling to multiracial congregations, spending a few weeks in each of them, I sat down to summarize my observations. Having just witnessed a particularly egregious misuse of power in a congregation, I wrote out all the ways I had observed the misuse of power. Not all of these misuses of power apply to all congregations (for example, some congregations do not determine at the local level parts of their worship or Mass, and not all of these types of activities are present in all congregations, varying by religion and faith tradition). But all of these misuses of power were observed in at least some congregations. Dominant people and groups used power to:

- declare what styles of music will and will not be used
- determine what historical religious leaders looked like racially
- decide which teachings to emphasize, and which to downplay
- determine what religious education literature to use
- decide which pictures or other art goes on the walls
- declare who the spiritual heroes are and why
- decide which aspects of history to remember and how to interpret the past
- decide who is mature in their faith, and who is not
- determine how much race and ethnicity will be talked about
- declare that race is not important and will not be discussed
- declare that the race of those in leadership does not matter
- look at and treat the non-majority groups with paternalism
- force others to assimilate or leave the congregation
- determine the culture through which the faith will be interpreted
- determine the culture through which faith will be practiced
- make others feel powerless
- remain ignorant about other cultures
- determine if change will happen and the pace of change (almost always, *slowly*)
- make people feel small, unimportant, like outsiders
- deny having power

Although in a congregation where people share a similar habitus, many of these issues would not involve the misuse of power, they often do in multiracial congregations. In exercising power in the above issues, the goal was rarely to exclude, but to do things the right or comfortable way. However, because of divergent habituses, these examples can have racially based implications. All can have the impact of including some people and excluding others.

For example, in most congregations, pictures of people from scriptural history, prophets, and depictions of supreme beings are put on the walls, modeled with statues, or found in religious education materials. In uniracial congregations, these representations often look like the people in the congregation. But what should they look like in multiracial congregations? If the actual appearance of the representations is not known—for example, no one really knows what Jesus or Buddha looked like—perhaps it is most equitable to use racially ambiguous representations or multiple racial representations, or even avoid representations altogether. When the representations represent people, it would seem fair and equitable they should be a racial diverse group of people. But many of the congregations we visited did not do this. They continued to have their representations look like they all came from one racial group, usually the racial group with the most power in the congregation. Stained glass windows, artwork, photographs, manger scenes, magazines, religious study materials, individuals selected to represent the spiritual heroes in plays, and so on all would appear as if there were only one racial group. The group with power could and often did proclaim that such representations are not that important, and that people who found the racial homogeneity of the representations troubling were "too sensitive." A black woman in the Northeast who attends a multiracial congregation in which whites were the most powerful group told me,

> I asked [a staff member] why all of the pictures on the walls of our congregation have only white people in them. He said that they didn't consciously intend for that to be the case, and wanted to know why I thought it was important. I told them this was a church of many groups, so we should all be represented. [The staff person] told me perhaps I was making too much of this issue. There were more important things to be concerned about.

A congregation in the Midwest only allows music to be played that is not deemed overly emotional or unholy. The worship leader and the senior pastor make the final decisions about which music meets these qualifications and which does not. In practice, this musical selection requirement has meant that overwhelmingly the music comes from a white cultural style. Most black and Latin music is deemed too rhythmic and thus too emotional and unholy. Although Hispanics in the congregation may miss other forms of music, they do not seem to bring it up with the staff. On the other hand, occasionally African Americans have requested music that comes from a non-white cultural style, but are told their choices do not meet the qualifications. Occasionally, I was told, people are questioned for suggesting such music when they should know it is not fit for church.

In a congregation in the Midwest, and another in the South, Hispanic immigrants came to be part of the congregations. When the immigrants conversed with each other, they often spoke in Spanish, their first and most proficient language. The non-Hispanics in both of these congregations were displeased with this use of Spanish. A member of the southern congregation told me that "we don't know what they are saying, but they laugh a lot, which makes many of us think they are talking behind our backs." In this congregation, they passed a resolution that Spanish should not be spoken on church grounds.

In the midwestern congregation, the Hispanic members asked the congregational leaders if they could have the sermons translated into Spanish, so they could better understand what was being said. This so upset some non-Hispanic parishioners that a congregation-wide meeting was called to discuss the issue. A Hispanic man presented the formal request for translation. He explained that several of the Mexicans and Central Americans were recent immigrants whose English language skills were not yet advanced enough to follow the sermons in English. He also explained that they had other family members and friends they wanted to bring to the church, but currently could not because they understood little English. Several of the non-Hispanic members were incredulous. They said they were offended by the request. If translation were allowed, one woman explained, people would have even less incentive to learn English, and before you knew it, this would be a Spanish-speaking congregation with English translation. The meeting went on for some time. Ultimately, the translation service was voted down. So hurt by the events of this meeting were the Hispanic members that within a month all but two had left the congregation.

Power can be misused in all social settings. It can and is misused in uniracial congregations. But its effects can be deeper in multiracial congregations. The sheer power to proclaim a group's way of life and views to be nonexistent or wrong is a great risk of multiracial congregations. As my colleagues and I have detailed elsewhere,[20] one model of multiracial congregations that we found was the assimilated model. In such congregations, everyone was welcome, as long as they thought and acted much like the majority already there. No attention was given to representing different groups in leadership, and the suggestion of doing so was taken by the majority group to be political correctness or oversensitivity by the congregational minority groups.

[20] See DeYoung et al., *United by Faith* (2003), chapter 10, and Christerson, Edwards, and Emerson, *Against All Odds* (2005).

South African theologian David Chidester describes this orientation as *religious hegemony*, which he defines as "explanations of otherness by which plural religious beliefs, practices and experiences are forcibly re-explained in terms enforced by the singular ideology of the dominant group."[21]

In the U.S. context, such congregations use the older American model of the melting pot, where all are to become one (see appendix A for a fuller discussion), and that one should look much like the dominant group. The United States differs from many other nations in that one is a good American not by birth but by supporting the American ideology of individualism, pursuit of profit, and freedom.[22] Paradoxically, the necessity of sharing this ideology creates a strong push toward conformity.[23] Multiracial congregations, especially if headed by U.S.-born persons, at times adopt this view. One is a good member of the congregation by sharing the same views and accepting the same practices as the dominant group. Interestingly, congregations which most strongly employ this perspective can have less overt conflict, as issues are simply not open for debate. Although this type of multiracial congregation can have high turnover (the only way people can express their views), if they are able to continually bring in new people, they can maintain being multiracial even while being unicultural and maintaining the status quo. In the words of the Reverend Frank Reid, pastor of the historic Bethel A.M.E. Church in Baltimore, spoken during an interview, *assimilating* multiracial congregations mistakenly "are about the obliteration of cultural differences instead of about overcoming racial divisions."

The potential—and at times actual—nightmare of multiracial congregations is that they create situations in which power imbalances may be taken advantage of. Bringing people together in local congregations can actually create the opportunity to exploit power imbalances.[24] This is one reason people concerned with racial group rights may oppose such congregations, especially if they were to become the norm. Although uniracial congregations have their problems, they

[21] David Chidester, "Religious Studies as Political Practice" (1987).

[22] Seymour Lipset, *Continental Divide: The Values and Institutions of the United States and Canada* (1990, chapter 2.

[23] Larry Naylor discusses American ideals, and the manner in which they contradict one another, in his essay, "Introduction to American Cultural Diversity: Unresolved Questions, Issues, and Problems" (1999).

[24] See Mary Jackman's *Velvet Glove* (1994) for an outstanding study on this topic, including a fine discussion of why it is to the benefit of people in power to treat others nicely and with paternalistic care. Doing so increases their power, and makes it more difficult to challenge.

can provide a shield against power imbalances between racial groups, be a place to develop skills and resources such as leadership training, and serve as an organizational base to reduce racial power imbalances in the larger society. If multiracial congregations do not do the same — and in the ones my colleagues and I studied, at least some did not — they can actually thwart progress toward racial equality.

Indeed, for the group(s) in power in multiracial congregations, especially in multiracial congregations where the leaders had an assimilationist bent, a common refrain I heard was that congregations should have nothing to do with such "worldly" issues as power or discussing racial inequality. "We are about coming together in unity to grow in our faith" is what they said in various ways. And for the people taking such positions, to consider issues of power or empowering groups of people was viewed as divisive.

This was a common misuse of power that I observed in multiracial congregations — the power to declare that power imbalances do not exist, are off-limits, or will not be addressed. Let me be clear that rarely was power misused in a vindictive, calculating fashion with the intent to keep people down. Rather, power was misused because of the following factors working together: (1) power imbalances, (2) powerful people and groups operating from the frame of reference that made it difficult to see the power imbalance (when a group is in charge, most commonly they do not see that they are in charge), (3) operating from different habituses so that (4) they do what they view as right and honorable. For example, a not uncommon misuse of power that I observed was leaders of congregations declaring that race will not be used as a consideration in hiring staff or appointing congregational leaders. Rather, the best person for the position, regardless of race or ethnicity, will be appointed. But because "best" comes to be defined in their terms, it is usually the case that the "best" person ends up being the same race as those already in such positions. Power is not being maliciously misused here. Time and time again, these leaders were trying to do what is right, to focus on faith issues, and to appoint people that they honestly felt would serve the congregation most fully.

But despite good intentions, power is misused in at least two ways in such cases. First, power is misused to declare that race does not matter, without consulting members of other racial groups in the congregation to see if they have the same view. When I consulted members of other racial groups in these congregations, they commonly had a different view. They wanted to see themselves (members of their racial group) represented in leadership. That way, they would have a better chance of having their voices heard. To not see themselves in leadership communicated a powerful message of exclusion and left them feeling vulnerable. Second, power is misused to define what "best" means, rather than having a multiracial team define what "best" means. To combat misuses of power, then, multiracial congregations need to create structures that require input from people of a variety of backgrounds. This input should not be proportional to the size of each group, but proportional to the number of groups. If a congregation has three groups of unequal size, one third of the input should come from each group (to see why, see the paragraph below). Otherwise, well-intentioned people will often unknowingly squelch and silence the very people they call their friends.

Power imbalances in the larger society can translate into power imbalances within multiracial congregations. In the United States, white Americans have held and hold the greatest power. They are used to being in such a position. Within the congregations, this reality means that whites always seem to have greater power than their demographic size and time in the congregation would suggest. Their influence is disproportionate to what would be expected. At the same time, when whites are not the most powerful group in multiracial congregations, they seemed to struggle the most with this reality, be the most upset by the power imbalances, have the least ability to deal with such situations, and be the most likely to leave.[25] These reactions are to be expected, as whites in the larger society rarely are placed in such situations. As a black pastor of a multiracial congregation in the Northeast, whose congregation had transitioned from 60 percent white and 40 percent black to the reverse, matter-of-factly said in our interview:

> I would say that whites in the United States, as the majority people, do not find it easy to be comfortable in places where they are not in majority, where they are not in power, where they are not determining the values, and where they are not defining reality. It's their God-given responsibility. In their view, I think they believe they let God down if they don't do that. They earnestly want to serve God, and their role in the larger society has unconsciously led them to this view.

In many of the congregations we studied, whites expected things to be done in a certain way, and if they were not, the whites attempted to change the way things were done. If they were not successful, they often would leave, and other whites would not come. Sociologist Korie Edwards, based on her research on multiracial congregations, goes so far as to say that multiracial congregations can only include

---

[25] See Christerson, Edwards, and Emerson 2005, chapter 8, for a summary.

whites if they are more like "white churches" than other forms. She concluded that it did not matter so much the color of the clergy members, or the length of the service, but *how* things were done. The music must be sung is certain styles, the youth programs must be in line with whites' definitions of a good youth program, and the clergy—regardless of color—must preach in ways culturally acceptable to the white members. Whites exercise their power—often unknowingly—by placing these expectations above or as a requirement for being multiracial or engaging in reconciliation.[26]

Finally, perhaps because so little is yet known about multiracial congregations, perhaps because there are not clear-cut models of how such congregations should do things, leaders in the congregations we studied often inadvertently misused their power.[27] At Wilcrest, Rodney Woo is valued for his dedication to the Wilcrest congregation, his commitment to his faith, his advanced training and knowledge, his length of time at Wilcrest, his leading the congregation through difficult times, and his position as senior pastor. As a result, he has a good deal of power. More than once in our interviews he has lamented that he feels he and his staff must go it alone in the journey to becoming fully multiracial, and this was tied for him to the inadvertent use of power:

> It feels like we have to cut a path ourselves every step of the way. It would be so much easier if there were already well-worn routes. There are no clear cut models out there for how to do church in a multiracial context. Because of that, I can tell you in all honestly we have made more mistakes than I could have imagined. People's feelings have been hurt, and people have interpreted some of my actions and that of other leaders as devaluing them. We have lost people, good good people because we unintentionally had blinders on and made mistakes. The key for a leader in a church like ours is one must maintain a sense of humbleness. I tell my staff we must learn from these mistakes and correct them. We must constantly question ourselves and how we do things. Are we serving all of our people or just some of our people? Does everyone have a place at the table? Do we constantly seek input from the variety of Wilcrest people?

Misused power is the closest thing I observed to a nightmare in multiracial congregations. Congregations that seemed able to reduce such

[26] See ibid., chapter 8, for a summary.

[27] I of course am using a generous view of human nature. Time will tell if the misuse of power in multiracial congregations is due to lack of knowledge or to self- and group interest. It would be naïve to assume it is only the former. But perhaps the sum total of misused power will be reduced as knowledge is gained in ways to counteract its misuse.

problems had clear-cut standards that were institutionalized, such that the voices of all groups were included. Not having standards for such inclusiveness eventually led to the misuse of power that adversely affected members of some groups more than members of other groups.

PUTTING THE SHADOWS INTO CONTEXT:
SPIRITUAL AND RACIAL FORMATION

Congregations serve many functions in U.S. society. They help provide a highly mobile people a sense of rootedness and home. They are the nation's preeminent arena for obtaining and organizing volunteers, both within and outside the congregation. They are the backbone of a safety net that meets survival needs, including food pantries, health fairs, homeless shelters, and soup kitchens.[28] But whatever else congregations do, religion scholar Nancy Ammerman has found that all congregations are about worship and spiritual formation.[29] These are viewed by members and staff alike across faith traditions as the primary tasks of local congregations. Spiritual formation, at its base, provides responses to fundamental questions of human existence: Who am I? What am I doing here? How should I view others? Is there right and wrong, and if so, what is it? Worship is the collective encounter with some higher power, and greatly aids in spiritual formation, helping to define a person's place relative to others and the higher power.[30]

These key functions of congregations are deeply important and meaningful to the people involved (which helps us understand why such people forgo doing something else, such as sleeping, to attend a house of worship). When I interviewed religious people for an earlier research study, one of the questions I asked is what people felt they would lose if they decided to give up on their faith and quit attending their religious congregation. The most common response? "Everything." Some people were even brought to tears at the mere thought of giving up these things.

The point to be taken from this discussion is that what goes on in congregations is the stuff of high stakes. Identities are sought and shaped, people's places in the world (and beyond) are being defined,

---

[28] Ram Cnaan et al. in their 2002 book.

[29] Nancy Ammerman 2005. See also Chaves 2004.

[30] In some religions, and in some branches of a particular faith, the higher power may be defined as nature or even the good of humanity.

social networks are being created, encounters with a higher power are a major goal, and truths are being established. The work of a congregation, like that of any social group or organization, addresses these high stakes through cooperation and conflict, through mutual interaction, through power, and through authority structures and participants.

Most congregations have competition at some level to define truth and the manner in which its main goals will be achieved. When we add race and ethnicity to the congregational equation, we get something else as well. Congregations—whether they are uniracial or multiracial—are places that generate, sustain, remake, or eliminate racial identity and meaning.[31]

Race theorists Michael Omi and Howard Winant have labeled this continual process *racial formation*. Racial formation occurs through competing racial projects that seek to define and interpret racial dynamics and distribute resources along racial lines.

At first glance, it may appear that congregations are not engaged in racial projects. After all, as I just discussed, congregations are focused on providing worship and spiritual formation. But in so doing, they participate in racial projects that contribute to racial as well as spiritual formation. The racial composition of a congregation is itself a racial project. This racial project says much about the meaning of race: race is important or it is not; people of different racial groups ought to be together, ought to be separate, or it simply does not matter; and so on. Congregations either talk about and act on racial issues or they ignore them, thus explicitly or implicitly defining the role of race. Multiracial congregations often combine competing racial projects. Does the racial composition of leadership matter or does it not? Which styles of music will be performed and which will not be? How long will the service last? Does the congregation care about racial equality? Beyond skin color, are we all the same or do our cultural backgrounds make us different? Congregations continually engage in racial projects, even though most people do not view themselves as doing so, and in the negotiation of these projects, participate in the nation's racial formation process. They contribute to or break down racial division, they help reify separation between groups or bring them together. They contribute to the acculturation of immigrants to black or white American culture, or encourage the development of new U.S. cultures.

Given the fundamental role race has always played in the United States, and the continued existence of racial division, we would do

---

[31] See for example Emerson and Smith 2000, chapter 8.

well to recognize the roles that congregations play in racial formation. And given that they cannot avoid participating in them, congregations would do well to give thought to which racial projects they wish to engage in. For multiracial congregations, doing so may help direct the use of power for better ends.

SUMMARY

Against the backdrop of U.S. race realities, multiracial congregations are complex entities. They operate in the context of a racially unequal society, multiple immigrant streams, and divergent habituses. Not surprisingly, despite the fact that such congregations are filled with Sixth Americans, difficulties and conflicts are part of the scene. No matter how trivial these issues may look to the outside observer, they are often deep-seated, confusing, and of much importance to the people involved. People can get tired in such contexts, and many leaders spoke of wishing they had directions on how to proceed. At times out of a lack of knowledge, those in multiracial congregations did not give enough attention to the unique dynamics that result from multiple racial groups in the same organization. One result is the misuse of power that favors certain spiritual and racial projects over others, which can have the effect of marginalizing people and groups, and reproducing racial inequality. Despite much that is positive about multiracial congregations, these are the very real shadows that multiracial congregations face.

CHAPTER 7 ▪ Momentum

THE THREE years at Wilcrest leading up to Dr. Woo's tenth anniversary as senior pastor were covered with shadows. Except for Dr. Woo, for one reason or another, all the staff members left. As the congregation searched for replacements, Dr. Woo and the Wilcrest members attempted to do the work of multiple staff members. This was draining for Dr. Woo. He felt abandoned and confused. It had been an uphill battle to realize Wilcrest's vision, and the growth of Wilcrest's racial diversity had seemed to stall. Finding the right staff replacements who had the commitment and ability to serve in a multiracial context was proving difficult. There just were not many qualified people available. Troubles mounted, financial giving had not kept pace with the congregational growth, and many people in the congregation were experiencing financial, familial, social, and spiritual problems. In truth, there were too many problems for any one staff member and a few lay leaders to handle fully. Some people questioned whether Wilcrest had changed enough to fully include non-whites. At the same time, other people felt that Wilcrest had changed more than enough.

Dr. Woo wrote of this time, "These were blue days. I was exhausted. I questioned the possibility of realizing the dream to become a dynamic church of all peoples. I felt abandoned, isolated." But his faith would not allow him to stay in such a state. "In my time of prayer, I realized that we were climbing the mountain, and of course it would be difficult to climb. What mattered is that we kept climbing. We needed to press on."

In a shocking turn of events a few months later, one of the former staff members called from his new congregation in Alabama and asked if he could come back. He missed Wilcrest and was reenergized to lead music in a multiracial context. He found he no longer could be in a uniracial congregation. Upon his return, the lay leaders gave Dr. Woo two six-week sabbaticals, to visit other multiracial congregations on the West and East Coasts, to observe, to talk with leaders of these congregations, to study, to write, to rest, and to recharge. And then came the surprise service planned by the Wilcrest members to commemorate his ten years as the senior pastor of the congregation.

The congregation wanted to share with the Woos what Wilcrest meant to them. Members came up and read the vision statement, one by one, in their native language: a Haitian man in his French dialect, another immigrant in German, another in Cantonese, in Spanish, in African languages, and in different dialects of English. A spiritual mariachi band was introduced and played a special Spanish religious song, one of Rodney and Sasha Woo's favorites. A praise song was then sung in English and Spanish. Later, the worship leader asked people to stand as he announced their country. This took about ten minutes. For those in attendance, the visual illustration was a moving and powerful statement of how much Wilcrest had changed in ten years.

For Dr. Woo, the combination of being granted a sabbatical by the congregation and the moving service was emotionally and spiritually uplifting.

> When I began this exciting journey ten years earlier, I never imagined how emotionally and spiritually draining it would be to cross racial barriers in a local church context. The combination of the sabbatical and the anniversary celebration injected me with a renewed sense of hope that I am not alone on this journey. Having gained the much needed rest, and having seen how the congregation had made the vision their own, my focus was restored. We were becoming the people of the dream.

Since that time, further changes have been made to more fully realize that dream. The staff and congregation have become more racially diverse. No longer is one racial group the majority. The worship has continued to diversify, including the addition of conga player from the Cameroon. A fellowship called "Dinners of 8" has been instituted as a structural arrangement to encourage the development of cross-race friendships. Assigned to a racially mixed group of eight people, Wilcrest members meet with their group once a month for dinner at the home of someone in the group. They talk about their backgrounds, their families, church, faith, work, and a host of other topics. They meet for four to six months, and then new groups are formed.

This fellowship and other programs like it build an increasing network of cross-race relationships among Wilcrest members. As I reported elsewhere, the parishioners increasingly view Wilcrest as their community.[1] An African American woman, who talked about carrying deep scars of white racism and who viewed the Bible as God's story of freeing people, said of the racial diversity, "It makes Wilcrest a place where my family and I feel included, welcomed, involved. I love to learn from other cultures, and to see how we come together to help each other. We are like a quilt being sewn together." A white

---

[1] Christerson, Edwards, and Emerson 2005, chapter 3.

man noted that "Wilcrest is my family and my home. . . . This is where my closest friends are. Like any family, we have our differences, but we care for each other here." A Mexican immigrant, known throughout the congregation for her bubbly personality and her many works of service, communicated similar sentiments during a worship service. Praying both in English and Spanish, in front of the congregation she thanked God for her Wilcrest family, and then prayed, "At Wilcrest, Lord, you have given us a place to call home!"

This chapter considers the findings of the previous chapters, then discusses what stages U.S. multiracial churches are in to assess which dream—the American dream, Martin Luther King's dream, or Malcolm X's nightmare—these congregations represent currently, and their direction for the future. Along the way, I consider what we learn about U.S. race relations and the possible impacts such congregations are making. Key to this chapter is the perspective of movement and growth. Multiracial congregations in the United States, despite hundreds of years of attempts (forced and otherwise), are really in a toddler stage in the post–civil rights period of the nation. Like all toddlers, they have many attractive qualities. But also like toddlers, they make mistakes, are just learning how to interact with others, and are busy learning how to make a way in the world.

WAIT FOR THE MOVIE

One finding is clear. At the time of this writing, multiracial congregations are rare. Congregations have long been assumed to be highly segregated by race. Chapter 2 establishes exactly how segregated. Defining a multiracial congregation as one in which no single racial group is 80 percent or more of the congregation, only 7 percent of the approximately 350,000 U.S. congregations are estimated to be multiracial. And as further researched has revealed, even this small figure is an overestimate, as some congregations are merely transitioning from one group to another, or in the process of failing. Based on the statistical evidence, I labeled U.S. congregations *hypersegregated*. The segregation levels of congregations approach the theoretical limits, and are amazingly high given the absence of a central body requiring racial separation. I also found that the larger a faith tradition, the more racially segregated are its local bodies. Finally, as noted in chapter 6, only about one-third of multiracial congregations are MAC congregations, congregations with at least 20 percent white and at least 20 percent black. Given the racial history of the United States and the presence of two American cultures, this is an important type of multiracial congregation.

A number of factors are associated with a congregation being racially diverse. These factors include being a part of a non-Christian or Catholic faith tradition, having a charismatic worship style, residing in a racially diverse neighborhood, being in an urban area, and residing in neighborhoods with higher median incomes. Factors that are associated with reduced racial diversity in congregations include the percentage of the congregation that is over sixty years of age, and interestingly, the percentage white and black in the neighborhood. Once these factors are accounted for, several factors were *not* associated with differences in racial diversity of congregations, including the size of the congregation, its theology, the percentage of immigrants in the neighborhood, the percentage of single parents in the neighborhood, and the average age of the neighborhood. Region of the country also did not predict the racial diversity of congregations.

Turning to the in-depth study of twenty-two multiracial congregations, I identified seven pathways to becoming a racially diverse congregation. Two key underlying factors shaped the paths: the primary impetus for change (mission, resource calculation, or external authority) and the source of racial diversification (the local neighborhood, purpose and culture, or a preexisting organizational package). The more the impetus for change came from a congregation's mission (that is, its very identity) and the broader the geographic area from which racial diversity is drawn, the greater the likelihood that the congregation, it appears, will remain multiracial over time.

When we turn the focus to the individuals in multiracial congregations, we find that Asians and Latinos are more likely to be in multiracial congregations than are whites and blacks (I did not have enough American Indians in my samples to make reliable estimates). The percentage of people in multiracial congregations varies widely by racial group, immigration status, and faith tradition, from just 5 percent of white Protestants to the majority of Asian Catholics and non-immigrant Asian and Latino Protestants. Generally, the larger the group within the faith tradition, the less likely members of that group were to be in multiracial congregations, although even when accounting for this size factor, whites and blacks still appeared to be more segregated than Asians and Latinos.

In chapter 4 I discussed why this may be the case, including the lower residential segregation of Asians and Latinos compared to whites and blacks, the absence of historically separate denominations based on race, the complicated factors discussed in chapter 6 surrounding the two American cultures, and the three main types of congregations in U.S. society.

Although there is individual variation, taken as a whole the people of multiracial congregations are different than other Americans. As with congregations, I began this exploration of the individual by examining which factors predicted attendance in an interracial congregation (a congregation in which those of the person's racial group were not 80 percent or more).

Factors predicting attendance in an interracial congregation differed for whites and non-whites. For whites, the main factors included any other form of interracial contact, including having lived in an interracial neighborhood or having attended an interracial school, being interracially married, and having attended an interracial congregation in the past. Sociodemographic factors, such as age, gender, and socioeconomic status, are not associated with a greater likelihood of attending an interracial congregation.

For non-whites, factors associated with an increased likelihood of being in a multiracial congregation included other forms of interracial interaction. However, there was an exception: whereas for whites, prior living in an interracial neighborhood or attendance at interracial schools was associated with a greater likelihood of attending an interracial congregation, there was no such association for non-whites. Also different from whites, higher socioeconomic status was associated with a greater likelihood of attending an interracial congregation. Part of this higher socioeconomic effect seemed to be due to rising socioeconomic status after coming to the congregation. Factors associated with a decreased likelihood of being in an interracial congregation included being an immigrant, being black, and living in the South.

I argued that multiracial congregations are bridge organizations that gather and facilitate cross-race social ties. Looking at the rings of social relations, from strong to weak ties (spouse, two closest friends, friends in the congregation, circle of friends, and overall social networks), I found strong and consistent support for this claim, for each racial group. Americans in interracial congregations have substantially more racially diverse social ties at every level measured than do (1) Americans who do not regularly attend a religious congregation and (2) Americans who attend uniracial congregations. This also is the case for each racial group examined separately. I consider people in multiracial congregations to be harbingers of future race relations in the United States (see the last section of this chapter for more explanation). The people in these congregations, on average, are far less constrained to one of the five U.S. racial melting pots in their social networks. For this reason, I have labeled them Sixth Americans. I also found that whether these Sixth Americans had extensive racially diverse social ties before they came to be in interracial congregations or not, being part of an interracial congregation increased the racial diversity of their social ties.

It is difficult to quantify the impact that Sixth Americans and multiracial congregations have on reducing racial inequality, but one issue seems apparent. Given their extensive interracial social ties, Sixth Americans and multiracial congregations are building considerable bridging capital, that is, resources that accrue from cross-racial social ties. This bridging capital can be used for gaining access to better schools, higher education, health care, neighborhoods, jobs, and access to many other forms of information and action. Without resources gained from these cross-race ties, such access would likely be curtailed. I certainly saw evidence of the benefits of cross-race social ties at Wilcrest, and in many other multiracial congregations.

But, as discussed at the end of chapter 5, there is evidence that whites in interracial congregations are no different from other whites in their lack of support for potentially inequality-reducing national policies. Admittedly, I have limited data on this topic. The exact effects remain open to question. Most certainly, this is an area in need of further research, as the implications are of great importance.

In chapter 5 I examined why some people are attracted to interracial congregations and, comparing them to those in uniracial congregations, how they think about social, religious, and racial issues. Some people are in interracial congregations because their homogenous congregation has became more racially diverse, and they stayed through the changes. They often, but not always, become Sixth Americans through the process. Others came to congregations that are in the process of becoming or have already become diverse. It appears that people are attracted to multiracial congregations because they like the worship, feel comfortable there, feel a sense of family, and feel welcomed. These reasons are more commonly given than is racial diversity itself. Although racial diversity is often mentioned as a reason for staying in the congregation, or as something they most appreciate and value about the congregation, it frequently is not the main focus for first attracting people. As chapter 5 discusses, there must be a unifying nonracial focus that attracts a racially diverse set of people. In short, they must have something in common, and that is usually worship, a shared sense of mission, or a family atmosphere.

People in multiracial congregations are not more supportive of assimilation than are other Americans, and evidence seems to suggest that they do not have weaker racial identities (though more work must be done on this topic). Whites in multiracial congregations do not differ from their counterparts who are not in congregations and those who are in uniracial congregations. Non-whites are actually less supportive, overall, of assimilation than their counterparts in other contexts. I explored why the multiracial context can actually help develop a sense of racial identity, as it helps a person or group gain uniqueness and status within the congregation.

I compared people in multiracial and uniracial congregations across a wide array of attitudes. The two groups differ only in one major area: race and immigration. Compared to those in uniracial congregations, people in interracial congregations — overall and compared to others of their same race in the uniracial context — are more supportive of immigration, and express more support for racially egalitarian principles and racially diverse settings.

Despite the many positives that seem to describe multiracial congregations, shadows, some of which are outlined in chapter 6, also accompany such organizations. Conflicts, setbacks, difficulties, people leaving, and misuses of power continually lurk. These shadows are present to one degree or another in all organizations, but they loom larger in the multiracial settings, given the meaning and importance of race in the United States. These shadows are very real, and ever present. If they are not carefully addressed, they threaten multiracial congregations, as well as positive and equality-benefiting race relations in general.

WHICH DREAM?

Chapter 1 outlined three types of dreams: the American dream of upward mobility, Martin Luther King's dream of a beloved community where there is authentic integration and cooperation, and Malcolm X's bad dream, a nightmare that results from continued misuse of power and domination of some people — in the U.S. context, usually whites — over others. A key goal of this book is to closely examine multiracial congregations in the United States to answer the question, "People of which dream?"

The answer appears to be all three types of dreams. Some people come to multiracial congregations as a way to "become American" without the complete culture shock of joining a congregation full of people of a different race. Some others come to climb socioeconomically or to signify their climb. Through the strong and weak ties that people form in these congregations across race, chances for upward economic mobility are enhanced. Through respect given to them for their individual, cultural, and spiritual uniqueness, their status often rises in the eyes of others, and in their own eyes.

As chapter 6 outlined, shadows accompany multiracial congregations. Included among these shadows are the misuse of power, and the domination of one group over others, exactly Malcolm X's nightmare. Multiracial congregations are yet in the toddler stage. When for another book my colleagues and I set out to write a chapter on four congregations that had been multiracial for more than the tenure of one senior clergy person, we had to look hard to find four such cases.[2] All of those that we found were white congregations that had become racially diverse. We simply could not find other models. In part because of the continued inequities in the larger society, and in part because of a lack of knowledge about how to structure and navigate in multiracial settings, too many mistakes are made, and too many instances of misused power can be found. Sometimes by conscious intent, more often by the unconscious assumption that one worldview is normal and right and others are either wrong or do not exist, multiracial congregations can be places that reproduce inequality. When the shadows dominate, multiracial congregations are harmful to racial equality and race relations. In such cases, they indeed are a bad dream.

Despite the shadows and the bad dreams, however, perhaps the most dominate dream among multiracial congregations is Martin Luther King's beloved community dream. Within these congregations, very different peoples voluntarily come together for common goals. To achieve their common goals, they must learn to work together. Like a family, they disagree with each other, yell at each other sometimes, and even walk out. But also like a well-functioning family, they become closer to one another, they care for one another when they are sick, jobless, feeling depressed, or struggling with their faith. As they grow, they develop shared understandings, they work in the community together, they introduce each other to their worlds, they come to rely on each other, and they form extensively racially diverse social ties. As Martin Luther King dreamed, they often come to talk and walk as if they "are tied together in the single garment of destiny, caught in an inescapable network of mutuality."[3] Often without knowing they are doing so, the people of multiracial congregations break down racial barriers and help reduce racial inequality.

---

[2] DeYoung et al. 2003.

[3] Smith and Zepp, *Search for the Beloved Community* (1998), p. 131.

Common Principles

This research indicates that it takes more effort, and often comes with more conflict, to have an organization change from uniracial to multiracial than it is to begin multiracial. Perhaps this seems an obvious conclusion, but it is one that is often overlooked, or at the least, is not easily overcome. Most multiracial congregations that my colleagues and I studied were once uniracial congregations. To change a congregation with an identity, a history, an established structure, well defined networks, and a unique culture requires immense effort and excellent leadership skills, and involves a continual effort to gain the support of the congregation. This book has followed this process in detail for Wilcrest, and has done so primarily but not exclusively through the eyes and words of the senior pastor. To begin a new congregation is risky (as with business, many fail in the first few years) and hard work too, but it allows the founders freedom to define the mission, identity, and structures from the outset.

Bridgeway Community Church is a good case in point. It began in 1992, the same year that Dr. Woo came to Wilcrest, and both senior pastors are about the same age. The Reverend David Anderson was interning on staff in a white congregation in a suburb of Chicago and working in a Chicago housing project at the same time. Like Rodney Woo, his background and his current experiences led him to the dream of a multiracial congregation. He committed to starting a new congregation, a multiracial congregation.

But where? Having grown up in the Baltimore area, he identified what he saw as a city of the future, Columbia, Maryland. This community of about 100,000 in Howard County is situated between Baltimore and Washington, DC, and is interracial. This seemed like a good spot. Pastor Anderson knew the area and the location was excellent, but at the same time there were almost no multiracial congregations in the area.

The core group he started with, just six people, was intentionally interracial. Pastor Anderson is African American, his wife is Korean American, a white couple followed from Chicago, and another white couple from the area rounded out the team. All were committed to developing a vibrant multiracial congregation. They laid out their mission statement — to be a "multicultural army of fully devoted followers of Christ" — and laid out the principles by which they would grow. They even named the church — Bridgeway — to reflect who they intended to be (note the similarity to Wilcrest's "multiethnic bridge" metaphor). They started slowly, and had few resources. Pastor Anderson had to work another job to survive for the first two years.

But at the price of starting something new was gained the freedom to define Bridgeway from the outset as multiracial. To help reduce the communication gaps that can occur in mixed-race congregations (see chapter 6) Pastor Anderson and his team decided to make Bridgeway a performing arts church, one that would use dance, song, skits, and multimedia to communicate. And what of its musical styles? Pastor Anderson summarized Bridgeway's approach using analogy: if you invite someone of another culture to your home, you shouldn't serve as the main course your strongest, most ethnic food — for example, Norwegians should not serve lutefisk (cod soaked in lye) — as the main course. Rather, it would be best to expose others to such food as a side dish. Bridgeway committed to using this approach in music. Its styles would follow the principles of serving a main course that was palatable across cultures, a soulful and mildly upbeat contemporary style. Side dishes of traditional white hymns and choruses, traditional black gospel, and other forms would be served as well. These side dishes would allow people to worship in cultural styles not their own, and help expand their knowledge and appreciation of other ways of worship.[4]

Because Bridgeway's multiracial principles were established at the outset, they defined the church as wholly multiracial from the beginning. Unlike Dr. Woo, Dr. Anderson did not have to engage in a long and continuous process of attempting to make changes necessary to becoming multiracial in the face of opposition, criticism, and questioning about the approach, speed of change, and a host of other issues. He did not have to encounter the very real issues of people feeling like their house of worship was being taken away from them. In the process of diversifying, he did not have to battle against a reputation as a uniracial congregation. He also did not have to attempt to work within an already established system set up by one racial group with an already established culture.

Thus, though shadows are ever present, Bridgeway was multiracial at its inception and has remained so throughout its history. At the time of this writing, the congregation has grown to over 1,500 people. It is about 55 percent black (mostly African American, but some African as well), 25 percent white, and the remaining 15 percent or so a fairly even mix of Latinos and Asians. It now has a history, a culture, institutionalized practices, and an identity that are all defined in part by their multiracial character. At this point, Bridgeway would have to put in much effort and make many changes to become uniracial.

---

[4] For a fuller description, see chapter 9 of David Anderson's 2004 book, *Multicultural Ministry: Finding Your Church's Unique Rhythm*.

Bridgeway and Wilcrest are among the most racially diverse congregations in the nation, but they had divergent starting points. Their experiences and issues were different because of these dissimilar starting points. Despite these differences, they did some things very much the same way. From this research on multiracial congregations, I can identify several commonalities. For people of multiracial congregations to limit the shadows, fight off nightmares, and create healthy congregations, the following seven principles are vital:[5]

1. *An institutional commitment to racial equity, clearly stated.*[6] Wilcrest clearly stated its intent to be multiracial by institutionalizing this in its mission statement. Bridgeway did the same. This principle suggests that congregations go beyond stating they will be multiracial by also stating their commitment to equity. The principle of racial equity (or justice) squares directly with the teachings of most religious traditions. Congregations need to become convinced that they cannot be fully mature in their faith and reach their goals apart from racial equity. For at least some of the multiracial congregations I studied, the motivating force was not "we ought to reduce racial injustice," or "we ought to better understand our faith by coming together." Rather, it was simply "we ought to come together" either to survive, or because it was believed the congregation ought to be for everyone. As sociologists Penny Becker and Korie Edwards find in their case studies, this set of motivations means that in the end, such congregations try to avoid racial conflict and fail to address issues of equity.[7] For this reason, it is essential to institutionalize the commitment to racial justice.

2. *Leaders who are personally deeply committed to racial equity.* Without this personal commitment, multiracial congregations will fall short. Wilcrest and Bridgeway succeeded in becoming multiracial in good part because of the resolve and faith commitment of Rodney Woo and David Anderson, and other key leaders.

3. *A common purpose that supercedes racial equity.* As discussed in chapter 5, racial cooperation and equity are typically best achieved not by making them the central focus, but rather a means to a common purpose. Both Wilcrest and Bridgeway communicate this directly in their mission statements. Their statements do not say, "Be multiracial" or

---

[5] For a somewhat different set of principles, and for much more detail about each, see George Yancey, *One Body, One Spirit* (2003).

[6] The wording for some of these principles comes from Si Kahn, "Multiracial Organizations: Theory and Practice" (1991). For proposed ways to address racial inequity at the national level, see Asante 2003. For addressing this issue specifically within congregations and faith traditions, see works such as Barndt 1991, Davies and Hennessee 1998, Woodley 2001, and Perry 2002.

[7] Becker 1999 and Edwards 2004.

"Obtain racial equity," but rather they say they will be multiracial communities to live out their faith.

4. *Structures to ensure racial equity.* The specific structures (e.g., committees) will vary depending on the faith tradition, but there must be accountability to live up to the institutional commitment to racial justice. A key goal of these structures is to ensure that outsiders come to be and feel like insiders, that they belong and have a voice.

5. *Internal forums, education, and groups.* There must be a space where issues can be talked about, people can learn about race issues, and misuses of power can be discussed. This is a delicate balancing act. Too much emphasis on such meetings can be counterproductive. They work best if they are periodic components of regular meetings with larger purposes, such as education hours. Just as often there are separate men's and women's groups within congregations, freedom must be given for separate racial group meetings if desired by any group.

6. *Be a DJ.*[8] DJs must constantly adjust the volume, bass level, and treble level depending on the size of the room, the acoustics, and the number of people in the room. Leaders of multiracial congregations must view what they do in a similar light. Adjustments are normal, made often, and with a larger purpose in mind. What works today cannot be assumed to work tomorrow.

7. *Recognize that people are at different places, and help them move forward one step at a time.* Sociologist Korie Edwards, in her case study of a multiracial congregation in the Chicago area, found that parishioners are at different levels of commitment to being multiracial. Rodney Woo and David Anderson have identified this phenomenon as well. Dr. Woo summarizes the different stages of multiracial commitment using the model of a hand. When it comes to valuing racial diversity and equity, some people are the pinky finger. They are antagonists to racial diversity and equity. Moving to the ring finger, some people are seekers, wanting to know about the issue but not committed. The next finger represents the converted, those who come to see the importance of and are committed to racial diversity and equity. The pointer finger represents the fully integrated. They have moved beyond conversion to living racially integrated lives. Finally, a few make the leap to the thumb and become proselytizers for racial diversity and equity. These people typically are leaders in multiracial congregations. Rodney Woo notes that people can move only one finger at a time; they do not jump fingers.[9]

[8] This analogy was used by David Anderson in my interview with him, July 15, 2004. A much fuller discussion of this topic can be found in his book, *Multicultural Ministry* (2004).

[9] On page 97 of *Multicultural Ministry* (2004), David Anderson graphs his ten-stage

CONSIDERING THE FUTURE

What does the future hold for Wilcrest? And what does it hold for multiracial congregations in general? Wilcrest shows no signs of slowing down on its path to becoming a wholly integrated, multiracial congregation. Each time I return to the congregation, it appears more racially diverse than the time before. It also appears on its way to becoming a MAC congregation in the coming years. Worship continues to change, incorporating more elements of the many cultures at Wilcrest. Leadership continues to diversify. Whites at Wilcrest, unlike some multiracial congregations, continue to join. People are coming from farther away than before, because they have heard about multiracial, "multimental" Wilcrest as a place for everyone. At the time of this writing, Wilcrest is beginning to implement Rodney Woo's goal of becoming a training center for those who want to work in a multiracial congregational context. Any given snapshot of Wilcrest will reveal shadows. But the movie of Wilcrest reveals substantial movement from the uniracial congregation it once was. The journey has had its share of setbacks, mistakes, and disappointments, but Wilcrest continues to move forward on the path of becoming a fully functioning multiracial congregation.

In the seven years I have been studying multiracial congregations, I sense a swelling momentum around multiracial congregations. What I experience as momentum could be a fad, merely short-lived interest. But I do not think it is. When I first began this research, multiracial congregations seemed rather isolated. I heard over and over again from congregational leaders that they felt they were going it alone. They talked about the need to set up a network of some kind to help each other on their journeys. A few of those networks began, but leaders did not seem to know that other such networks were operating in different parts of the country. The number of those networks and their interlinkages are growing, coverage in magazines, web pages, and in books seems to have increased from almost nothing when I began this research to semi-regular discussion. Leaders of these congregations are beginning to meet and dialogue with one another, theologies are being developed around the concept, and seminary students are beginning to be trained for work in multiracial congregations, often taught by the present leaders of current multiracial congregations. This is a good deal of change in a relatively

---

"racial reconciliation continuum." Related to the hand model, but with a somewhat different focus, this model is discussed in detail in chapter 8 of Anderson (2004).

short period of time. Although multiracial congregations remain rare and sometimes have severe limitations,[10] the available evidence of demographic, cultural, and religious trends all point to a growth trajectory for these types of congregations. It will take time, but today's multiracial congregations may give birth to a new and improved generation of them—more numerous, more advanced, better checks and balances against the misuse of power, stronger, more sensitive, more intelligent.

Some recent work suggests this may happen. Alan Parker carefully followed the development of three multiracial congregations in South Africa, examining the stages they went through in changing from uniracial congregations. He identified five stages.

1. *Status Quo.* In this early stage, demographic change occurs but has little impact on church narrative, identity, and practices. New groups either tolerate this lack of reaction or remain quiet at this early stage, not trying to change things or voice concerns.

2. *Assimilation and Hegemony.* As diversity grows, so too does awareness of it by everyone. The congregation makes room for diversity, but the racially different newcomers are expected to be passionate about whatever the original congregation is passionate about, and to operate within the same culture.

3. *Limited Integration.* Over time diverse others begin to move into positions of leadership. New groups begin to feel they have some cultural space. But this time of integration also can generate real culture shock. Some original members express concerns, feel like the church is changing, or even a bit out of control, and some leave.

4. *Integration and Disintegration.* The original group may have declined in size, the future of the congregation is somewhat uncertain (will it remain diverse?), the congregation begins to find new narratives, structures, and rituals to bring the diverse components together. Hegemony breaks down as things are up for redefinition.

5. *Stabilization and Reorganization.* The congregation reestablishes itself with a new narrative, structures, power relations, and rituals. It reorganizes a new narrative and identity as a multiracial congregation. Not all multiracial congregations reach this stage, and if they do not, they rarely remain multiracial.

These stages of multiracial congregations identified by Parker in South Africa seem to capture what happens in the United States (and

---

[10] The biggest challenge will continue to be counteracting white dominance. Multiracial congregations must continually fight against being places that reinforce white normativity and racial inequality. See Edwards 2004 for an excellent study of how this process works in subtle and not so subtle ways.

perhaps elsewhere) as well. My colleagues and I found multiracial congregations in each of these five stages. Many of the shadows discussed in the previous chapter describe issues that congregations in stages 1 through 4 encounter. If they are able to overcome the stage's shadows, they move to the next stage in their development as a multiracial congregation.[11]

As with multiracial congregations, race relations must be understood as a series of steps, a process. Oppressed peoples, robbed of agency and personhood for generations, must have freedom. They must then use the freedom to work for justice and regain their identity, agency, culture, and personhood. The oppressors will not usually be of much help in this process, and so minority power movements and multiculturalism are necessary developments along the path. At the same time, oppressors must come to terms with their unfairly gained positions, and learn to share. But the groups cannot stop there. Within a nation, equality will not be achieved, injustices will never fully be faced, and healing will not take place until diverse peoples can live with each other, in the same spaces. The Sixth Americans in the multiracial congregations studied here are a different kind of American. And their congregations, where they gather together to worship and serve and support one another, despite their failures along the way, may be harbingers of what is to come.

---

[11] These stages are discussed in much more detail in chapter 9 of Parker's work, *Towards Heterogeneous Faith Communities* (2005). Chapters 6 through 8 describe the three congregations he studied. Other models of stages, with somewhat different foci, are also useful. Norman Peart (2000) describes five stages that congregations may be in, from uniracial to "differentiated" congregations built around linguistic or cultural distinctions, to "assimilated" congregations which welcome minority group members but mistake their mere presence as evidence of being a fully multiracial congregation, to "intentional but irrational," where congregations are desegregated but prejudice and discrimination are not addressed, to "integrated," where congregations are intentionally diverse and represent that diversity at all levels, and also create a common bond across differences. See also the work of Sheryl Kujawa-Holbrook (2002), who discusses six stages of congregations in terms of how they deal with and counteract racism. Reducing shadows that result from multiple groups in a congregation is perhaps most fully addressed in the works of Eric H. F. Law (1996, 2000, 2002).

APPENDIX A · Shifting Visions

*A Brief History of Metaphors
for U.S. Race and Ethnic Relations*

How to relate to one another within racial and ethnic diversity is an issue the United States has struggled to define, name, and negotiate for its entire history. And that history so very much matters for what the United States is today, and for how its people think about such issues.

The United States has been diverse since its founding—multiple states, regions, ethnic and cultural groups. The official motto of the United States—*e pluribus unum*, out of many, one—reveals both an early recognition of diversity and the hope, vision, and value of unity arising from this diversity. Most Americans of most eras have agreed with this motto. But even while agreeing, they are often mired in debate, conflict, and confusion as they try to put this motto into practice. Does the motto mean "Americanization," wherein successive waves of immigrants are "Anglocized"? Does it mean the United States is a melting pot, where diverse racial and ethnic groups meld into one new group and culture (and is this what the term "melting pot" really means)? Does the motto mean the United States is a stew, where each group contributes to the savor of the others while maintaining its own identity? Does it mean the United States is a tossed salad, a combination of many cultures mixed together, but remaining distinct? Or does it mean, in today's most common metaphor, a mosaic? A mosaic is the most static of all these metaphors, implying that cultures are fixed, stationary, and each make a unique, beautifying contribution to the whole, but do so while remaining distinct and separate from other cultures.

SMALL TENSIONS: EARLY VIEWS OF DIVERSITY

Just six years after the founding of the United States, a French-born American farmer with a long name, J. Hector St. John de Crèvecoeur, published a book which contained a series of letters to a friend back in France. The letters were in response to his friend's questions about life in the United States. On one occasion, the friend wanted to know what makes a person an American. Crèvecoeur's response is telling:

What then is the American, this new man? He is either an European, or the descendant of an European, hence that strange mixture of blood, which you will find in no other country. I could point out to you a family whose grandfather was an Englishman, whose wife was Dutch, whose son married a French woman, and whose present four sons have now four wives of different nations. . . . Here individuals of all nations are melted into a new race of men, whose labours and posterity will one day cause great changes in the world. . . . they will finish the great circle. The Americans were once scattered all over Europe; here they are incorporated into one . . .[1]

At this early date, we already see the idea that America is a melting pot, even though the term is not explicitly used. An American is a mixture of diverse peoples, producing something new and something nearly divine. In the United States what was once separated was now, finally, being brought together. Let the old divisions fall away; this was a new and chosen people. Such a perspective has been common throughout American history.

But from today's perspective, it is quite clear that this melting pot is painfully exclusionary. To Crèvecoeur, an American is a mixture of white people. The definition does not include, for example, Native peoples or African Americans. We also see that cultural and ethnic diversity is not an end it self, but simply what goes into creating the final product. In short, Group A + Group B = new group C.

Whereas for Crèvecoeur America was yet to be determined by the mixing of European peoples, George Washington communicated another continuous strain of thought in the United States (often called Americanization)—that Group A + Group B should equal Group A, for the American already exists. "The bosom of America," President George Washington said, "is open . . . to the oppressed and persecuted of all Nations and Religions." But he encouraged immigrants to shed the "Language, habits and principles (good or bad) which they bring with them." Let them come not in clannish groups but as individuals, prepared for "intermixture with our people." Then they would be "assimilated to our customs, measures and laws: in a word, soon become one people."[2]

As these two early perspectives illustrate, just what an American is, and how people in the United States should relate to each other, has always been open for debate and negotiation. But one perspective of this time is clear. "Americans" were European. Clearly, other groups

---

[1] *Letters from an American Farmer*, p. 39.
[2] Quoted in Schlesinger 1992, p. 30.

lived in the United States, but they were not, originally, defined as Americans. When the United States seceded from Great Britain, they attempted what was at the time an amazingly bold experiment. The nation would be run as a democracy, not by a ruler. Here the king would not be the law; the law would be king.[3] But how could a people govern a nation? What would be required of people for them not to run the new nation into the ground? The leaders of the time determined that for the nation to succeed, the people must be virtuous. As John Adams wrote, "The only foundation of a free constitution is pure virtue."[4]

According to historian Ronald Takaki in his book *Iron Cages*, by virtue these leaders meant the opposite of luxury and vice. To be virtuous, one must move away from the instinctual life, away from the base passions. Instead, rationality must be in control, for self-sacrifice, delayed gratification, and dedication to abstract principles were all necessary to be "civilized," that is, to be virtuous. Woven into the founding of the nation, then, was the idea that the mind must rule over the body. But this concept had important implications for the meaning of race in the new nation — then and now.

The Europeans (white Americans) saw blacks and native peoples as wild, childish, savage-like, driven by their passions, controlled by the body rather than the mind. If this new nation, this bold experiment in democracy and freedom, was to survive and thrive, it must have virtuous people. Blacks and Indians (and in many cases, women) were believed by those in power to be controlled by their passions, and thus not virtuous.

To be an "American" thus came in significant ways to be defined as being the opposite of blacks and Indians. The definition of virtue as mind over body, and of non-whites as being dominated by the body, had important implications for the new nation. First, non-whites were originally excluded from becoming American — the 1790 Naturalization Law was open only to whites who had lived in the United States for a set time period and had demonstrated "virtue." Second, when non-whites were allowed to become officially American, they were viewed as second-class Americans by whites. And third, strong justification for whites to rule over others was built into the functioning of the United States. Reflecting on the meaning of race in the United States, the French observer of U.S. life Alexis de Tocqueville wrote in 1835, "The European [white American] is to the other races of mankind what man himself is to lower animals: he makes them

[3] Ronald Takaki 2000, p. 8.
[4] Quoted in ibid., p. 10.

subservient to his use, and when he cannot subdue them he destroys them."[5]

In the mid-1800s Ralph Waldo Emerson (no relation) expanded the amalgamation of American culture and explicitly introduced the term smelting pot: "in this continent, — asylum of all nations, — the energy of Irish, Germans, Swedes, Poles, and Cossacks, and all the European tribes, — of the Africans, and of the Polynesians, — will construct a new race, a new religion, a new state, a new literature, which will be as vigorous as the new Europe which came out of the smelting-pot of the Dark Ages."[6]

For Emerson, like Crèvecoeur, the American was a new creature created from the smelting process, and this primarily involved Europeans. Unlike Crèvecoeur, he also mentioned Africans and Polynesians, undoubtedly radical for his time. But the fact that Africans and Polynesians were the last mentioned, separated from the European groups, may suggest that Ralph Waldo Emerson too, like most white Americans of his time, believed non-whites to be second-class Americans. Non-whites contributed to the development of the Europeanized United States, but they were not themselves core Americans.

Americans not of European origin held a different view. Principally using the U.S. Constitution and Christianity as the buttresses for his arguments, abolitionist Fredrick Douglass argued that Americans of all colors were to be participating in the same freedoms, together as equals — the same institutions. As he wrote in 1865, "I expect to see the colored people of this country enjoying the same freedoms [as whites], voting at the same ballot-box . . . , going to the same schools, attending the same churches, traveling the same street cars, in the same railroad cars, . . . proud of the same country, fighting the same foe, and enjoying the same peace, and all its advantages."[7]

Also strongly supporting the integration of different races were, somewhat ironically, many prominent pastors of black churches. These pastors insisted "that the integration of blacks and whites into one community was the demand of the Christian faith."[8]

Meanwhile, the overriding portrait painted by whites was that America was the fullest expression of human unity ever witnessed by the world. As historian George Bancroft wrote in 1855, "Annihilate the past of any leading nation of the world, and our destiny would

---

[5] Tocqueville, *Democracy in America* (2000 [1835]), volume I, p. 303.

[6] Taken from Ralph Waldo Emerson, *Journals of Ralph Waldo Emerson* (1909–14), pp. 115–16.

[7] *Fredrick Douglass: Selections from His Writings* (1964), p. 57.

[8] James H. Cone, *Martin and Malcolm and America: A Dream or a Nightmare?* (1991), p. 7.

have been changed. . . . Our country stands, therefore, more than any other, as the realization of the unity of the race."[9] Given the stark realities of Indian massacres, the long-term forced movement to reservations, slavery, the "coolie" class of Chinese immigrants, and the conquering of Mexican lands, "the unity of the race" here clearly excluded non-Europeans.

What is most striking about pre–twentieth-century writings, but perfectly in line with the meaning of race built into the United States at its founding, is how little concern was given by whites to issues of ethnic and racial pluralism, to assimilation, to whether or how non-Europeans should be incorporated into the nation. Successful assimilation of white groups, or Americanization as it was often called, was simply taken for granted. And the non-assimilation of non-whites was also taken for granted. As in the previous century, most nineteenth-century whites viewed non-whites as wholly inferior, not capable of living as equals with whites. The great American experiment did not apply to them. The respected historian, John Higham, puts it well:

> To speak of assimilation as a problem in nineteenth-century America is, in an important sense, to indulge in anachronism. That is because nineteenth-century Americans seemed for the most part curiously undaunted by, and generally insensitive to, the numerous and sometimes tragic divisions in their society along racial and ethnic lines. . . . Assimilation was either taken for granted or viewed as inconceivable. For European peoples it was thought to be the natural, almost inevitable, outcome of life in America. For other races assimilation was believed to be largely unattainable and therefore not a source of concern.[10]

One result of this overriding view of non-whites by whites is that non-whites largely could not immigrate to the United States, or when they did, could not become citizens. Labor pools from places like China and Mexico entered the United States to provide needed workers. But they were not welcome to stay as citizens. In 1882 the first restrictive immigration law was passed, the Chinese Exclusion Act. In subsequent years, as employers turned to other Asian nations for workers, more laws restricting Asian immigration were passed. Mexican migrant workers were welcomed during times of need, but were to be temporary, going home for much of the year, and if they stayed, to be expelled during economic downturns.[11]

---

[9] Cited in Schlesinger 1992, pp. 16–17. Originally from Bancroft's *Literary and Historical Miscellanies* (1855), p. 508.

[10] John Higham, *Send These to Me: Immigrants in Urban America* (1984), p. 175.

[11] For example, see Ronald Takaki, *Iron Cages* (2000), chapters 7 and 10.

A NEW CENTURY AND GROWING TENSIONS

The lack of concern over assimilation changed dramatically as the United States entered the 1900s. Immigration flows, always relatively modest, had been overwhelmingly from northern and western Europe. But beginning about 1880 and reaching full force at the turn of the last century, immigrants started coming in much larger numbers. Whereas in the first sixty years of recorded immigration, an average of about one and a half million immigrants came per decade, that exploded to nearly six million per decade from 1880 to 1920 — at the crest of the immigration wave in 1901–10 there were nearly nine million immigrants. What is more, these teeming masses pouring into United States entry ports were now coming overwhelmingly from southern and eastern Europe, bringing their different languages, Catholicism, and poverty. Most were rural peasants, migrating to the cities of the United States, especially in the North.

This new migration suddenly and forcefully reentered the question of "Americanization" into the national dialogue. Could, for example, peasant southern Italians and Sicilians, people viewed by American whites of the time as a swarthy, downtrodden, crime-ridden race, really become Americanized? Could they be part of the great American experiment? Could this vast new migration of people concentrating into neighborhoods of northern cities be trusted to serve the United States in times of war, or would they fight for their home nations from within? To the white majority of the time, these were serious concerns.

It is at this time, then, that the debates which we are in currently began taking shape. Because the focus was on the new European immigrants and because the question of assimilation for non-whites had long been answered by whites (their answer was no), the concern for the integration of "races" was really a debate over whether new European immigrant groups could become people of the mind, people of virtue, dedicated Americans equal to those of northern and western European descent.

A major work appeared on the scene, addressing the growing concern over what America was to be: *The Melting Pot* by Israel Zangwill. It was first a hit play (the hit of New York's 1908 season), and also played in Washington, DC, before President Theodore Roosevelt, who loved the performance. It was then published in book form in 1909. Zangwill, who is credited as the originator of the term "melting pot," was English-born, of Russian Jewish descent. The central figure in his play is David Quixano, a Russian Jewish composer, who desires to write a symphony expressing the melting pot of America, the blend of all that is good. On an even more personal level, David hopes to overcome religious and ethnic barriers to marry Vera, a white Christian whom he loves. As he says, "America is God's crucible, the great Melting-Pot where all races of Europe are melting and reforming! . . . Here you stand in your fifty groups, with your fifty languages . . . and your fifty blood hatreds. . . . A fig for your feuds and vendettas! Germans and Frenchmen, Irishmen and Englishmen, Jews and Russians — into the Crucible with you all! God is making the American."[12] At the end of the book, in the climactic scene, David Quixano is standing atop a Manhattan building with Vera, overlooking the harbor and the Statue of Liberty. Pointing to the harbor, he says to Vera, "Ah, what a stirring and a seething! Celt and Latin, Slav and Teuton, Greek and Syrian, — black and yellow — ."[13] In this quote, he briefly expands the definition, at least of those who are involved in the stirring and seething, but as with Ralph Waldo Emerson's version, non-whites groups are set apart, and last.

It is important to note that the melting pot metaphor can and does have at least two interpretations. People could and did interpret what came to be the United States' dominant metaphor in at least two ways — assimilation into an already existing mold, group A + group B = group A (like Washington more than 100 years earlier), or the creation of something new, group A + group B = new group C (like Crèvecoeur). "'We Americans are children of the crucible,' Teddy Roosevelt said. 'The crucible does not do its work unless it turns out those cast into it in one national mold.'"[14] For those favoring assimilation, that mold was already precast. For those favoring the creation of something new, that mold was determined by the particular groups in the country. Because the melting pot metaphor had such flexibility and captured both major streams of thought in previous centuries, it became the dominant metaphor among whites until at least the 1960s, and it continues to enjoy much support among segments of Americans.

In 1915, a radical new perspective — the precursor to today's' multiculturalism — was fully outlined by philosopher and Jewish immigrant Horace Kallen. He published an article in *The Nation*,"Democracy versus the Melting-Pot." Presenting a major break with the past, he argued that the melting pot was valid neither in reality nor in the ideal. What stands out about the United States, he wrote, was the persistence of ethnic groups. Immigrant groups, Kallen argued, go through distinct phases in the United States. When they first arrive, they are economically eager. Because external difference is a hin-

[12] Israel Zangwill, *The Melting Pot* (1910), p. 37.
[13] Ibid., p. 199.
[14] Taken from Schlesinger 1992, p. 41.

drance to economic success, immigrants attempt to assimilate and minimize their difference. They do much as my maternal grandparents did when they arrived from their native Italy—they learned English, attempted to learn "American ways" (the ways of those they knew at work or through the media), translated their names into English (John instead of Giovanni), and refused to teach their children Italian. As they would say to my mother, "This is America. We must act American."

But they said only that they must *act* American, not that they must *be* exclusively American. They never, in spirit, became American in the sense of discarding being Italian. And this was precisely Kallen's argument. Assimilation does not proceed, unhindered, until all groups are melted into one mold. Rather, assimilation takes place to the degree necessary, as dictated by the larger society, for economic advancement. Once that is achieved, and beyond that point, being in the United States actually strengthens ethnic bonds, as immigrants and their descendents reflect back on themselves and their ancestry.

> As they grow more prosperous and "Americanized," as they become free from the stigma of "foreigner," they develop group self-respect: the "wop" changes into a proud Italian, the "hunky" into an intensely nationalist Slav. They learn, or they recall, the spiritual heritage of their nationality. Their cultural abjectness gives way to cultural pride.[15]

And indeed, he argued, this occurs across generations. "Men may change their clothes, their politics, their wives, their religions, their philosophies, but to a greater or lesser extent: they cannot change their grandfathers."[16] According to Kallen, the promise of the United States lies in its hope to be a federation of nationalities, enriching each other:

> Thus "American civilization" may come to mean the perfection of the cooperative harmonies of "European civilization," the waste, the squalor, and the distress of Europe being eliminated—a multiplicity in a unity, an orchestration of mankind. As in an orchestra, every type of instrument has its specific timbre and tonality, founded in its substance and form; as every type has its appropriate theme and melody in the whole symphony, so in society each ethnic group is the natural instrument, its spirit and culture are its theme and melody, and the harmony and dissonances and discords of them all make the symphony of civilization.[17]

[15] Horace Kallen, "Democracy versus the Melting Pot" (1915), p. 217.
[16] Ibid., p. 220.
[17] Ibid., p. 220.

The tragedy in Kallen's eyes was that the "Americans of British descent" would not accept this view, were horrified by this view, and thus demanded that people fully "Americanize," by which they meant become like the people of British descent. Kallen reserved his strongest criticism for the elites among ethnic groups who seemed to "sell out" to Americans of British descent, including Zangwill: "And another Jew, Mr. Israel Zangwill . . . profitably promulgates it ['Americanization'] as a principle and an aspiration, to the admiring approval of American audiences, under the device, 'the melting pot.'"[18]

Though Kallen clearly reflected his time in excluding non-whites from his model, the model was a precursor to the language and perspective of multiculturalism. He defended the right of ethnic groups to maintain separate cohesive communities devoted to the perpetuation of ancestral religious, linguistic, and social practices.

Just a year later (1916), one of the most influential black leaders of the United States, Marcus Garvey, arrived from his native Jamaica with a bold and effective message: black nationalism. With his Universal Negro Improvement Organization (UNIA), he proclaimed that African Americans should be proud to be black, and should realize that integration with whites would never work, and was not desirable: "To be a negro is no disgrace, but an honor," he told his many followers, "and we of the Universal Negro Improvement Organization do not want to become white."[19] What they did want was for blacks to rule Africa, as whites ruled Europe and North America. "Africa for the Africans" was the rallying cry. As Garvey said, "A race without authority and power is a race without respect."[20] The UNIA strongly argued against integration with whites, viewing it as a self-defeating philosophy, one that obliterated black self-respect, cultural uniqueness, and power. His message galvanized many African Americans. Here was a confident black man clothed in elaborate and colorful military apparel, declaring his self-worth. He influenced many black Americans, including the father of Malcolm X and, indirectly, Malcolm X himself.

In the United States, however, whites had the power. The government, concerned that Garvey was too radical and becoming too influential, decided he needed to be stopped. With the help of some blacks who also found him too radical, Garvey was convicted of mail fraud and sentenced to prison. A few years later, the government

[18] Ibid., p. 192.
[19] *Philosophy and Opinions of Marcus Garvey* (1969), vol. 2, pp. 325–26.
[20] Ibid., vol. 1, p. 2.

commuted his sentence and deported him to Jamaica. Garvey never again returned to the United States.[21]

The same year that Marcus Garvey came to the United States, Randolph Bourne, living in the largely separate white world, published an essay in which he celebrated the more cosmopolitan America being produced by European immigrants. Cosmopolitan people, because they engaged the world in all its variety, saw as inadequate provincial tastes and skills. Bourne supported the autonomy of ethnic groups. But differing from Kallen, Bourne wanted a dynamic mixing that would change the immigrants and the Americans. So instead of Kallen's group A + group B = group A + group B, Bourne was closer to group A + group B = group AC + group BC. This model is sometimes called beef stew, where each ethnic group is distinct but both contributes to and absorbs the flavor of the stew.

This disagreement between Kallen and Bourne is noteworthy. As outlined by historian David Hollinger, the differences between Kallen and Bourne—what he labels as the pluralist and the cosmopolitan views—continue as points of contention among contemporary supporters of multiculturalism.[22]

THE MOVE TO AMERICANIZE, AGAIN

But it was not yet the time for multiculturalism. The social forces of the period quickly ran over such ideas. With World War I came immense concern over unity and loyalty to the United States. Three months after Kallen published his article, and just three days after the Germans sank the Lusitania, killing 123 Americans,[23] President Wilson spoke to a group of recently naturalized citizens. "You cannot become thorough Americans if you think of yourselves in groups. America does not consist of groups. A man who thinks of himself as belonging to a particular national group in America has not yet become an American."[24] A year after Bourne's article appeared, and the year the United States entered World War I, former president Teddy Roosevelt said in a speech in New York, "We can have no 'fifty-fifty' allegiance in this country. Either a man is an American and nothing

---

[21] http://www.isop.ucla.edu/africa/mgpp/, accessed March 16, 2005.

[22] See David Hollinger, *Postethnic America* (1995), especially pp. 92–94.

[23] http://members.aol.com/bry1976/lusi.htm, accessed Aug. 2, 2002.

[24] From a speech by Woodrow Wilson delivered May 10, 1915 in Philadelphia. The speech was published in *The Messages and Papers of Woodrow Wilson*, edited by Albert Shaw, vol. 1, pp. 115–16.

else, or he is not an American at all."[25] Concern that people be patriotic, and shedding old ways, reached a fever pitch. Americanization, or what might better be called Anglo-assimilation, was the model of the day, the same model that had always been. Laws were passed in communities across the country declaring English the official language. In 1918, the Carnegie Corporation commissioned a massive ten-volume study, called *Americanization Studies*, to learn of the needs and progress of immigrants as they moved toward Americanization.[26] The early 1920s witnessed the resurgence of the Ku Klux Klan, and massive changes in immigration laws, especially the Immigration Act of 1924. This act mummified the ethnic composition of the United States by setting national quotas proportional to their representation in 1890, greatly reducing the immigration from southern and eastern Europe and effectively eliminating immigration from Asia.

As a result of the Immigration Act and the Great Depression, 1930s immigration plummeted to 1830s levels. During the 1940s and World War II, immigrants only trickled in and Americanization and the melting pot ideas went relatively unchallenged. A depression and a world war were not times to successfully challenge the dominant modes of thinking. Nathan Glazer, author and retired Harvard professor, gives us an inside view of growing up in the public schools during this time. Raised in New York City, Glazer attended public schools (including the City College of New York) from 1929 to 1944. He describes the public schools he attended as two-thirds or more Italian and Jewish. No talk of Jewish or Italian culture could be found. The schools, Glazer writes, "were neither intended nor expected to contribute to the self-esteem of Italian American schoolchildren, and one doubts that they did. For Jewish students, the curriculum and the texts were a complete blank."[27] In class, they did not talk about unique groups in America, but about being an American. There was, he says, a "strong, unself-conscious, self-confident Americanization" where cultures other than American and its English antecedents were simply ignored, with no apologies. Thus the move toward multiculturalism as advocated by people like Kallen and Bourne were but a "murky prehistory, wiped out in a flood of Americanization that deposited uniform silt over our past."[28]

---

[25] As cited in Schlesinger 1992, p. 41. From a speech delivered September 10, 1917. Published in his *Works* (Memorial Edition), chapter 21, p. 38.

[26] *Americanization Studies: The Acculturation of Immigrant Groups into American Society*, republished under the editorship of William S. Bernard in 1971.

[27] Nathan Glazer, *We Are All Multiculturalists Now* (1997), p. 87.

[28] Ibid., p. 88.

In the late 1940s and early 1950s, upon the return of millions of GIs, the economy and the birthrate boomed. Cities were growing, but no longer primarily from millions of immigrants, with their strange customs, dress, religions, and languages. The United States, after decades of limited immigration, especially from southern and eastern European nations, and decades of a singular emphasis on Americanization, was racially and ethnically at its most homogeneous in its history. America had matured into the world leader, economically, militarily, and culturally. The nation was middle class. From the perspective of most whites, the Great American experiment, with its democracy, and freedom, and value of equality, was triumphing.

MAJOR CHANGES: THE UNITED STATES IS NOT JUST FOR WHITES

Lost in all of this was that this America had always been and remained only for whites. So it came as a shock to many white Americans when African Americans and the civil rights movement entered the scene with such fervor and transforming power. Many leaders and organizations emerged to prominence during this time, but two individuals—with separate visions of and for America—have come to represent the diversity in the movement for social change.

Martin Luther King is More Famous, Malcolm X is More Influential

For the first time in the nation's history, in the late 1950s and 1960s, non-white leaders rose to positions of such influence that non-white visions of how Americans should relate to each other in their diversity were seen by non-whites and whites alike. And their visions were revolutionary. Martin Luther King and Malcolm X, both thrust into national leadership roles at extremely young ages, offered dynamically divergent visions for most of their lives.[29]

Martin Luther King is now an American icon. He has a national holiday, and his speech given at the 1963 March on Washington is replayed on the national airwaves decades after it was delivered and is counted as one of the greatest orations in American history. His picture can be found in almost every school in the nation, regardless of the racial makeup of the children in the school. Every major city in

---

[29] It is the visions they offered in their initial years of leadership for which they are remembered, but in their last, most mature years, before each was gunned down at age 39, they moved closer toward each other's vision.

the nation has at least one street that bears his name. He has become an American hero, claimed by nearly everyone. This creates problems, however. To have such broad appeal, in a nation so diverse, necessarily means people shape Martin Luther King to fit their understandings of the nation, rather than the reverse.

Reared in the formally racially segregated South in a middle-class Atlanta family, Martin Luther King was a third-generation preacher. He was just beginning his first pastorate — in Montgomery, Alabama — when the Montgomery Bus Boycott began in 1955. In need of a spokesman, the boycott leadership elected twenty-six-year-old Martin Luther King as a compromise choice. He quickly proved to have extraordinary leadership abilities, and soon was in the national spotlight. In one of his very first articles, he wrote that the aim of the Montgomery Bus Boycott "is reconciliation; the end is redemption, the end is the creation of the beloved community."[30]

Desegregation can be legislated. Integration, the ultimate goal, cannot. "When segregation has been abolished and desegregation has been accomplished, blacks and whites will then have to learn to relate to each other across those nonrational, psychological barriers which have traditionally separated them in our society."[31] Desegregation creates the condition "where elbows are together and hearts apart," whereas integration will lead to true brotherhood and a complete sense of the interrelatedness of humanity. The Beloved Community was for King "the solidarity of the human family."

From this understanding, driven by his religious faith, Martin Luther King and many in the civil rights movement brilliantly linked American ideals — freedom, equality, the chosen city on the hill, justice — to their cause, broadening the definition of American to include African Americans. Given the nation's history of excluding non-whites and viewing them as inferior candidates for first-class American status, this was a revolution every bit as dramatic as a military coup. And it set off an explosion of activity by other racial and ethnic groups, demanding inclusion into the rights and privileges of the United States. It led to court decisions, acts, and laws. As American politics professor Lawrence Fuchs puts it, the nearly 200-year-old exclusionary system, seen by most whites as natural and right, cracked.[32] Non-whites entered into the American system in ways never before even thought possible.

Controversial during his lifetime, Martin Luther King has risen to

---

[30] Smith and Zepp, *Search for the Beloved Community* (1998), p. 130.
[31] Ibid., p. 131.
[32] Lawrence H. Fuchs, *The American Kaleidoscope* (1990), part III.

186 · Appendix A

mythical status, not as a person who challenged the American system, but as a person who showed the greatness of it. He asked, nonviolently, that the great American Experiment be broadened, to include a wider diversity of people. He is viewed as someone who helped the United States become more American, and for that he is celebrated by liberal and conservative, young and old, urban and rural, male and female, and all racial and ethnic groups. He is viewed by most as saying simply that the American system is honorable, and non-whites should have the right to join it.

For most of his public life, Malcolm X had a very different message, a message that resonated most directly with poor, urban African Americans. His views were born out of personal experience. Born Malcolm Little in 1925, four years before King, he grew up seeing the underside of the United States, a nation with high ideals that appeared to be nothing but empty rhetoric.

The United States he saw was not open to all who worked hard; it was a world of rejection, hate, poverty, violence, and death. The Ku Klux Klan drove his family out of Omaha, Nebraska. A white-based group burned down his family's house in Lansing, Michigan, where the Littles had moved when they were forced from Omaha. Malcolm's maternal grandmother was raped by a white man, with the result that his mother appeared "near white"; his own reddish brown skin was a constant reminder of the violence of whites. While Malcolm was still a youth, his father died (either by accident or murder — the exact cause is unknown), leaving his mother to raise eight children during the depression years of the 1930s. In dire poverty, she could not bear the responsibility, and was committed to a mental institution six years after his father's death, when Malcolm was 12. He and his siblings were split up. Malcolm was sent to live with a white family who ran a detention home, and attended nearly all-white schools. In eighth grade a teacher told him that his dream to be a lawyer was not realistic, and that he ought to consider becoming a carpenter, a more "realistic goal for a nigger." Devastated, Malcolm dropped out of formal schooling after that year, moved to Boston, entered a world of crime and drugs, was eventually sentenced to eight to ten years for burglary, and was sent to prison.

When released from prison in 1952, he came out as a dedicated member of the Nation of Islam, and soon became its leading spokesman. An orator every bit as gifted as Martin Luther King, what he preached is best expressed in his own words. As noted in chapter 1, "What is looked at as an American dream for white people has long been an American nightmare for black people."[33] "No, I am not an

---

[33] Cone, *Martin and Malcolm and America* (1991), p. 89.

American. I am one of 22 million black people who are the victims of Americanism."[34] "We didn't land on Plymouth Rock—that rock landed on us."[35] "I am not interested in being American, because America has never been interested in me."[36]

As Martin Luther King came to represent the integrationist perspective, Malcolm X represented the separatist, nationalist perspective. And he did so with flair and authority, constantly challenging the hypocrisy of whites and the American system. Though he changed over the last year or so of his life, Malcolm X is remembered for advocating that blacks separate from whites—the people who did not want them—and arguing that blacks do not need to be accepted by whites to have self-respect. Blacks were not ruled by body over mind, blacks were fully human, and black was beautiful. Stop trying to be white, he would say to African Americans, and be proud of your culture, your heritage, your looks, and your self-worth. The white devil, as he often called whites and the Western system, are bent on destroying black Americans, attempting to make you fit white stereotypes, making you into exactly what they say you are—hedonistic, crime-ridden, downtrodden, subservient, passion-inflamed imbeciles.

Both he and King wanted non-white Americans to have equality in the United States, but for different reasons, and by divergent means. "As Martin King's commitment to justice cannot be understood apart from his *faith*, Malcolm X's faith cannot be understood apart from his commitment to *justice*."[37] This, according to scholar James Cone, is the fundamental difference between these two influential leaders.

It is widely believed that he was assassinated by Nation of Islam followers for his break with that faith. Malcolm, like King, died by gunshot. His boldness, directness, and message did not win him many friends in the white world, nor, originally, even in the black world, who feared he did more harm than good by criticizing the powerful. At the time of his death in 1965, the white media proclaimed him a racist demagogue who preached a gospel of hate, a twisted man bent on inciting violence, frightening white people, and destroying the nation. Some went so far as to say the world would be a better place now that he was gone.[38]

Martin Luther King had greater impact during his life, is more famous today, and is revered by a much wider segment of Americans than Malcolm X. Yet it is remarkable that what Martin Luther King

[34] Ibid., p. 1.
[35] Ibid., p. 197, and see p. 339.
[36] Ibid., p. 38.
[37] Ibid., p. 155.
[38] Newspaper summaries gathered from Cone 1991, pp. 39–40.

stood for, called for, and died for—integration (not desegregation) and the formation of the beloved community—largely has been rejected by post–civil rights Americans.

But hindsight tells us clearly that Malcolm X has gained influence over time, becoming increasingly influential on American life since the mid-1960s. Even during the last years of Martin Luther King's life, the civil rights movement was fracturing. King's message was losing favor among younger black Americans, while Malcolm X's was gaining favor. Racial moderates, mostly white, began to feel the civil rights movement had run its course, meeting its main objectives. But most minorities, tasting progress but knowing true equality and justice remained far in the distance, were hungry for more—full equality and political power in the American system. Black and red and brown and yellow power came to dominate the youth organizations, and eventually other organizations.

Integration became synonymous with forced assimilation, with the loss of culture, heritage, and respect, and was abandoned in favor of group self-determination and separation. An influential and a representative figure in the critique of integration was Black Power advocate, former coordinator for the Student Non-violent Coordinating Committee, and former head of the Black Panther Party, Stokely Carmichael. Clearly building on the words and writing of Malcolm X, and crediting him for opening the eyes of younger blacks, Carmichael said that striving for the right to live with whites bordered on insanity:

> For too many years, black Americans marched and had their heads broken and got shot. . . . After years of this, we are at almost the same point—because we demonstrated from a position of weakness. We cannot be expected any longer to march and have our heads broken in order to say to whites: Come on, you're nice guys. For you are not nice guys. We have found you out.[39]

For Carmichael, because whites were not nice guys and because so many whites could not even see that society was racialized, the only solution to overcoming racism and achieving equality was for a totally new America to be born. Integration was not the answer, he argued, because it assumed all was basically healthy and right, and all we needed to do was welcome everyone in. But America was sick (Martin Luther King, in the last year of his life, came to a similar conclusion). Integration, in Carmichael's view, did not speak to the problems of poverty, racism, oppression, and class. Moreover, it spoke to

[39] Stokely Carmichael, *Stokely Speaks: Black Power Back to Pan-Africanism* (1971), p. 18.

non-white Americans in a condescending way, saying that the "successful" people among minority communities could leave and enter into the superior white world. Thus, built into the very definition of integration was the implied inferiority of people of color. And, Carmichael wrote, "This is why integration is a subterfuge for the maintenance of white supremacy."[40] Furthermore, the call for integration meant nothing more to whites than the call for blacks to assimilate into white ways, thus abolishing black life, "the final solution to the Negro problem."[41]

The only real answer, and the only real change, would come from people of color forming their own strong communities, apart from the inferiority-producing rule of whites. Only when people of color shed themselves of the sad sick master, and gained power and influence, would real change come. Integration must be avoided until "it can mean white people moving from Beverly Hills into Watts."[42]

Such talk horrified whites, and made them angry. From their perspective, blacks and others had equality of opportunity. They had the Civil Rights Act, the Fair Housing Act, the Voting Rights Act, and other equality-producing legislation. Perhaps minorities did not want equal opportunity; perhaps they wanted revenge. But as French philosopher Jean-Paul Sartre asked white Americans: "What then did you expect when you unbound the gag that had muted those black mouths? That they would chant your praises? Did you think that when those heads that our fathers had forcefully bowed down to the ground were raised again, you would find adoration in their eyes?"[43]

The black, red, brown, and yellow power movements, the riots of the mid- and late '60s, and the growing unrest in the nation convinced many whites what they subconsciously already thought: people of color were not people of the mind. They were ungrateful, angry, and scary. The only option was to avoid such people, their supposed culture, their ways, their attitudes, and their violence. Yes, the laws now said everyone should have the right to work where they want to, live where they want to, eat where they want to, and have the right to vote. And, grudgingly, most whites came to agree with these laws.

But togetherness, the kind Martin Luther King once talked about, was not possible, not now. It was not safe. Children must be protected, and property values must be maintained. Whites too then

[40] Ibid., p. 23.
[41] Ibid., p. 39.
[42] Ibid., p. 23.
[43] Sartre quote taken from ibid., p. 93.

moved away from serious consideration of large-scale integration. A few persons of color, if willing to assimilate into white ways of living (usually believed by whites as the American way to live) could do so, but concentrations of minorities must be avoided. Figuratively and literally, the goal was to get as far from Watts as possible.

Within this emerging context, the now idealized Martin Luther King did not look like a radical to many whites. From their perspective, he advocated that the United States was fundamentally good, and that anyone who wanted to join that goodness should have the right to do so. Carmichael and his ilk, they thought, were barking the same hate as Malcolm X, and were so very wrong.

From Nationalism to Multiculturalism

The sheer power of white America meant that black nationalists could not win. Black nationalism soon lost steam. Even Stokely Carmichael gave up hope that black Americans could muster enough power to overcome the sick giant called white America, and moved to Guinea to work for change from there.

Despite the brief period of high-visibility activity, black, brown, red, and yellow nationalism had long-lasting effects. The power movements did not disappear uneventfully, but transmuted into racial and ethnic pride, pluralism, and, eventually, multiculturalism. This move was far-reaching, not only spreading among non-whites, but leading to a resurgence of white ethnic identity.[44] Everywhere, the buzzwords were to get in touch with one's roots, to get ethnic, to appreciate and live one's unique culture. Uniqueness, not acculturation, was the goal. Culture became tightly linked to one's racial and ethnic community, trumpeting other forms of culture. A particular racial or ethnic group's food, clothes, hairstyles, music, and communication styles all came to be self-consciously defined over and against other racial and ethnic communities.

Even the names parents gave their children became more self-consciously ethnic-specific. For example, researchers Stanley Lieberson and Kelly Mikelson found that while in the first part of the twentieth century there was a high positive correlation between what black and white parents named their children, by the mid-1960s that correlation was essentially zero. And since then, they have found a negative correlation, meaning that the more likely one group is to give their child a particular name, the less likely the other group is to give

[44] Michael Novak, *Unmeltable Ethnics* (1971).

their child that same name.[45] Celebrating diversity and distinctiveness became the thing to do.

The importance of this shift was magnified by the resurgence of immigration to the United States following the 1965 changes to immigration law. The result of those changes, unintended at the time, was that the large majority of immigrants came from Latin America, Asia, and the Caribbean, greatly diversifying the number and size of ethnic groups. Entering into a context of celebrating diversity, the large growth of diverse groups has served to strengthen the move toward pluralism and the development of cultural identities.

From this context emerged multiculturalism and the mosaic model of racial and ethnic relations. Despite significant and sometimes bitter critiques by some elites,[46] the multicultural movement has been so powerful that author Nathan Glazer could write a book in 1997 entitled, "We Are All Multiculturalists Now," and historian David Hollinger could declare that "virtually no one defends monoculturalism, with the result that multiculturalism is deprived of an honest, natural opposite."[47]

The exact definition of multiculturalism, like that of any widely accepted ideal in U.S. life, is open to debate, but the general concept is that there is value to all cultures, and so they ought to be celebrated, encouraged, and nurtured. In education, it means decentering the dominance of a Eurocentric view of the world, opening the door to other ways of viewing the globe, such as Afrocentricity, and broadening courses of studies to include ethnic and international studies and languages other than western languages.[48] It is in education that multiculturalism has taken its strongest hold, and therefore also the area where the most directed critiques have been leveled. Charges of falsely rewriting history to boost the self-esteem of racial and ethnic groups, ignoring what Americans have in common, and serving only to further divide the nation are commonplace. But to date, those voices have not won the day. And given the move toward postmodernism in general, which shuns the idea that there is one scientifically observable truth, it is unlikely they ever will.

---

[45] Stanley Lieberson and Kelly S. Mikelson, "Distinctive African American Names: An Experimental, Historical, and Linguistic Analysis of Innovation" (1995).

[46] For example, Schlesinger, *The Disuniting of America* (1992); Schmidt, *The Menace of Multiculturalism* (1997); Hollinger, *Postethnic America* (1995); Miller, *The Unmaking of Americans* (1998); Barry, *Culture and Equality* (2001); Diane Ravitch, *The Great School Wars* (1974).

[47] Hollinger 1995.

[48] See, for example, Molefi Kete Asante, *The Painful Demise of Eurocentrism* (1999).

A key mantra of the multicultural era is tolerance, an ideal always held to some degree or another by Americans, but one that has now risen to an exalted status. Tolerance is viewed as the key way by which to address the diversities of cultures in the contemporary United States. To be considered intolerant is viewed by most Americans as a sin against America's civil religion.

The ideal of tolerance has important implications for how people relate and should relate to each other. Namely, they do not have to. Its critics charge tolerance as mere escapism. Rather than attempting to resolve differences and working to correct injustices, people are merely told to be tolerant. Tolerance, critics charge, has no healing power. Rather than producing understanding, it merely produces indifference.

Set within the context of tolerance, holding to the idea of nurturing cultures, and assuming that culture is best nurtured in racially homogenous private institutions, the most favored image of U.S. diversity offered currently is the mosaic model. Each ethno-racial group culture is a beautiful pane of glass. As these panes are placed side by side, distinct from each other but within the same framework of a nation, beauty and strength emerge.

Multiculturalism's singular focus on culture offers many advantages to people and groups. Identity is nurtured, political strength is heightened, people can find a primordial home amidst massive depersonalizing modern nation-states, the hegemony of western ways of understanding the world can be challenged (when I took history in junior high and high school I often wondered what people in Asia, Africa, and Latin America were doing all the while Europeans were inventing things), and it can enrich and increase understanding of different cultures and peoples.

But multiculturalism's singular focus on culture has weaknesses too. In its pluralist form (the form Kallen advocated, as opposed to the less common cosmopolitan form advocated by Bourne), it wrongly assumes that culture is static and pure, uninfluenced by other cultures, as if culture really were like a pane of colored glass. As such it does not allow for cultures to improve and be purified of their negative aspects by coming into contact with other cultures. Indeed, to suggest that cultures have negative aspects in need of purifying is considered intolerant. Many forms of multiculturalism seem to trivialize inequality. They seem to equate justice with the right to practice and live in one's own culture, and have little to say about addressing socioeconomic inequality. Clearly, multiculturalism serves valuable functions, but in and of itself it is not the answer to inequality and injustice. As such, its dominance to the exclusion of other solutions will hinder the cause of equality and justice. Multiculturalism may be a necessary step, but it is not the final step.

CONCLUSION

And so Americans stand. The present dominant model of how to relate to each other in diversity essentially advocates equal access to the public institutions of the United States, and separation in the private institutions. It comes as no surprise then that though there have been increases in the level of contact between races in the public institutions, little change has occurred in the private institutions. Again, for most people, this is quite all right. If what happens in the private institutions is at all connected with what happens in the public institutions (and many people seem to assume they are not related), people are best served in the public institutions if they are separated into their own racial and ethnic groups in the private institutions. There is disagreement around this issue to be sure, but this seems to be the dominate view among elites. Time will tell if the dominate vision shifts yet again.

Multiracial congregations do not fit well into the dominant paradigm. In fact, they are violations of it, or at best, aberrations. For some, multiracial congregations are a reminder of an older, outdated model of integration (read assimilation and control). For others such congregations simply are attempting to do the impossible. The reality, as this book tries to sketch out, is more complex. These congregations may be harbingers of a new stage of U.S. race relations.

Appendix B · Statistical Tables

TABLE B3.1
Tobit Models of the Effect of Internal and External Characteristics on the Racial Heterogeneity of Religious Congregations

	Model 1	Model 2	Model 3	Model 4	Model 5
Internal					
Traditional					
Non-Christian	.20** (.02)	.20** (.02)			.12** (.02)
Catholic	.11** (.02)	.09** (.02)			.06** (.02)
Conservative Protestant	.02 (.01)	.00 (.01)			−.01 (.01)
Pentacostal Charismatic	.03 (.02)	−.04 (.03)			−.08** (.03)
Black Protestant	−.03 (.03)	−.08** (.03)			−.09** (.03)
Not known	.18** (.06)	.17** (.06)			.06 (.05)
Cong Characteristics × 10					
# Adults, logged		.09 (.05)			−.02 (.05)
Charismatic worship		.23** (.05)			.21** (.05)
% >60 × 10		.01** (.00)			−.01** (.00)
Theo—Middle		.32* (.13)			.12 (.12)
Theo—Liberal		.08 (.19)			−.19 (.18)
Small groups		.62** (.14)			.30** (.14)
Founded last ten years		.21 (.19)			−.26 (1.7)
External					
Racial Characteristics (U.S. Census Tract)					
Heterogeneity			.28** (.04)	.24** (.04)	.22** (.04)
% Black × 10			−.04** (0.0)	−.03** (0.0)	−.04** (.00)
% White × 10			−.02** (.01)	−.01** (.00)	−.02** (.01)
Foreign Born × 10			.02** (.01)	.01 (.01)	.00 (.01)
Other Characteristics (U.S. Census Tract)					
% Urban × 10				.01** (.00)	.01** (.00)
% Renters × 10				.01 (.00)	.01 (.00)
Md HH Inc × 10,000				.03** (.01)	.02** (.01)
% Managerial or Professional				.04** (.01)	.04** (.01)
%<19 × 10				.00 (.01)	.00 (.01)
Region					
Northeast				.02 (.02)	.02 (.02)
Midwest				−.02 (.02)	−.01 (.02)
South				−.01 (.02)	.01 (.02)
Pseudo R²	.11	.18	.23	.40	.50
Log likelihood	−449	−412	−390	−302	−254
Sample size	1174	1153	173	1173	1152

*p < .05 **p < .01 Data weighed by the inverse of congregational size, as necessary because of the study design

[a]Tradition Comparison Group: Mainline Protestant congregations

Note: Standard errors are in parenthesis. Tract education level included as control variable in equations 4 and 5.

Sources: 1998 National Congregation Study and 1990 U.S. Census Tract Summary Data

TABLE B4.1
Factors Associated with Attending an Interracial as Opposed to a Uniracial
Congregation, for Whites and Non-Whites: Log Odds Ratios

Variable	Whites	Non-Whites
Other Interracial Involvement		
In past, lived in a racially mixed neighborhood or attended a racially mixed school	1.89**	1.32
Not previously part of an interracial congregation	0.32**	.03**
Married to someone of a different racial background	4.55**	12.35**
Racial homogeneity of current neighborhood	0.97**	0.99**
Religious Tradition[a]		
Protestant	0.23**	0.52[†]
Catholic	1.19	1.28
SocioDemographics		
Live in a central city	1.61	0.87
Live in a suburb	1.00	1.05
Immigrant	1.09	0.20**
Black	—	0.26**
Have children under 19 at home	1.06	1.70[†]
Male	1.30	1.06
Age	0.99	1.01
SES (income and education)[b]	1.00	1.08**
Region of Residence		
South	0.87	0.36**
Midwest	0.54	0.47[†]
−2 Log likelihood	356.73	359.41
Pseudo R^2	.315	.450
Sample size	714	420

[†]$p < .10$, *$p < .05$, **$p < .01$ (two-tailed)
[a]Comparison category is all non-Christian traditions.
[b]Measured as income category (in $10,000 intervals) plus two times the person's formal years of education. Several other measures of SES were explored, but this measure fit best and was the most economical.
[c]Comparison category is the Northeast and West, which do not differ from each other.
Source: Lilly Survey of Attitudes and Social Networks, 1999–2000.

TABLE B5.1

Percentage of Respondents Preferring That Racial Groups Maintain Their Cultural Uniqueness, Form a Common Culture, or a Combination, by Race

	Homogenous Congregation	Mixed Congregation	Statistical Results for Group
Whites			
Cultural uniqueness	38	41	
Combination	17	9	
Common culture	45	51	c^2 for White = 3.47 (2), p > .10
Blacks**			
Cultural uniqueness	35	29	
Combination	8	29	
Common culture	57	43	c^2 for Black = 9.42 (2), p < .01
Latinos*			
Cultural uniqueness	29	51	
Combination	9	10	
Common culture	62	39	c^2 for Latino = 7.04 (2), p < .05
Asians+			
Cultural uniqueness	16	33	
Combination	19	4	
Common culture	66	63	χ^2 for Asian = 4.75 (2), p < .10

Source: Lilly Survey of Attitudes and Social Networks, 1999–2000.

Table B5.2
Demographic Comparisons by Congregational Context and Race,
No Controls

	Interracial Congregations	Homogenous Congregation	Not in a Congregation
Whites (N = 1655)			
Over 65	28%*	13%	15%
Income[a]	5.5	5.2	5.1
Education	13.9	13.5	13.1*
Ever divorced	13%	6%*	13%
Live in city	45%	25%	34%
Live in Midwest	17%	32%	30%
Live in South	30%	40%	30%*
Live in West	25%	12%*	22%
Non-Whites (N = 809)			
Over 65	9%	9%	4%*
Income	4.9*	3.5*	4.1*
Education	13.5*	11.7	12.0
Ever divorced	15%*	7%	7%
Live in city	47%†	58%	56%
Live in Midwest	6%*	16%	15%
Live in South	27%	46%	29%
Live in West	36%	22%	33%

*Indicates that group differs from the other two groups, p < .05.

†Indicates that group differs from the other two groups, p < .10.

[a]Measured in $10,000 categories. 1 equals less than $10,000, 2 equals $10,000–$19,999, 3 equals $20,000–$29,999, and so on.

Source: Lilly Survey of Attitudes and Social Networks, 1999–2000.

TABLE B5.3
Attitude Measures Used to Compare Those in Interracial and Uniracial Congregations, by White and Non-White[a]

	Interracial Congregation	Homogenous Congregation
Non-Whites		
Social		
The best way to improve United States is to change individuals	–	–
We need a program of parental school choice	2.60	2.13*
Gender and Family		
Moms of young children should work outside of home only if financially needed	–	–
Religion		
What is morally right and morally wrong should be the same for all persons	–	–
Women should be allowed to be head pastors/priests	3.64	2.99*
Do you think services are too long, too short, *just about right*, or time doesn't matter?	66%	48%**
Race and Immigration		
The number of immigrants who can legally enter the U.S. should be reduced[b]	4.58	3.21*
There is too much talk today in the United States about racial issues	–	–
Religious congregations should actively seek to become racially integrated	2.43	3.36**
I would be upset if my child wanted to marry someone of another race	–	–
Prefer a neighborhood that is *75% own race and 25% other race, or 25% of 4 racial groups*	7%	17%*

Whites

Social		
The best way to improve United States is to change individuals	3.86	2.74**
We need a program of parental school choice	—	—
Gender and Family		
Moms of young children should work outside of home only if financially needed	3.09	2.48*
Religion		
What is morally right and morally wrong should be the same for all persons	3.13	2.42*
Women should be allowed to be head pastors/priests	—	—
Do you think services are too long, too short, just about right, or *time doesn't matter?*	49%	32%**
Race and Immigration		
The number of immigrants who can legally enter the U.S. should be reduced	3.85	3.16*
There is too much talk today in the United States about racial issues	—	—
Religious congregations should actively seek to become racially integrated	—	—
I would be upset if my child wanted to marry someone of another race	6.03	4.95**
Prefer a neighborhood that is *75% own race and 25% other race, or 25% or 4 racial groups*	16%	33%**

*p < .05, **p < .01 (two-tailed t-tests, except when percentages reported, than c^2 tests)

[a]Mean score reported, 1 to 7 scale, with 1 meaning Greater Agreement. The two exceptions are the length of service and neighborhood racial preference questions, which report the percentage.

[b]Reports only for African Americans (support for immigration among Asians and Latinos is high, and does not differ by congregational context).

Source: Lilly Survey of Attitudes and Social Networks, 1999–2000.

APPENDIX C ▪ Methodology

THIS BOOK is the product of nearly six years of research on multiracial congregations. With a generous grant from the Lilly Endowment, Inc., my colleagues and I embarked on several stages of research on multiracial congregations. We began with pre-research, reading all we could find on the subject, and selecting three congregations to conduct pretest interviews. These interviews with clergy and laity were largely open-ended, designed to help us begin understanding the issues, challenges, and joys of these congregations. We used this pre-test to begin learning about the people involved in the congregations, such as where they came from, why they were there, and where they were headed.

After this pre-research, we knew we needed to randomly select a large number of people, and that we needed strong comparative data—people not involved in multiracial congregations. We called the result the Lilly Survey of Attitudes and Social Networks (LSASN). I discuss the many details of this survey below, but the most important questions on the survey were those that we used to determine if a person attended an interracial congregation. As discussed in chapter 4, I defined a person as attending an interracial congregation if it was not made up of 80 percent or more of people of his or her same race. This definition is based on research in organizations, as I discuss in chapter 2.

How did we measure whether a person attends an interracial congregation? First, we did not want to include people who attend a congregation that has racially separate services, such as a Catholic church with a Mass in English and Mass in Spanish or Vietnamese. To get around this problem and measure exactly what we were after, we asked people about the racial composition of the service they attend.

Second, we needed to ask the question in a way most worship-attending people could answer. Would they know the racial composition of the service they attend? To find out, I solicited responses from people in several congregations in which I knew the racial composition of the worship service (by asking clergy, looking at official congregational data, and attending myself). People sometimes varied dramatically in their estimates of the relative size of each racial group. In short, their responses offered little encouragement in the hopes of obtaining accurate measurement.

But I did discover that people who attended at least semiregularly (defined as twice a month or more) could estimate with accuracy whether their congregation was 80 percent or more of their own race (with the caveat noted in footnote 1). Therefore, the question we asked worship-attending people in the LSASN was the following:

Though hard to know for sure, would you say that [respondent's race] make up more than 80 percent of the worship service that you normally attend at your [church/synagogue/mosque/temple]?

1) Yes
2) No
3) Don't Know
4) Refused

[If above question = 2 or 3] about what percent of the people at the worship service that you normally attend would you say are [respondent's race]?[1]

The Lilly Survey of Attitudes and Social Networks (LSASN), designed to assess individual attitudes, social networks, and involvement in religious life of congregations, consists of 2,561 American respondents. The telephone survey was conducted by the University of North Texas Survey Research Center. The survey was performed from October of 1999 through March of 2000 (excluding the last three weeks in December). The survey had ambitious aims in terms of content, experimental designs, and oversampling African Americans, Hispanic Americans, and Asian Americans (300 of each group). Using a random list of prefixes from Survey Sampling Inc., and random digit dialing for the last four digits, telephone numbers were called with the goal of speaking to the person 18 years or older who had the next birthday. In the case of no answer, up to eight callbacks were performed.

The instrument, which was programmed into the CATI system, was also translated into Spanish. Approximately one-third (94) of the interviews completed with Hispanic respondents were conducted in Spanish. Due to the variety of Asian languages, the survey represents only English-speaking Asian Americans. Thus, the survey obviously misses some immigrant Asians, and likely overestimates the degree that immigrant Asians are involved in multiracial congregations. However, given that American-born Asians nearly always speak En-

[1] Because of people's tendency to overeestimate diversity, and their strong tendency to round, anyone saying 75 or higher was classified as non-mixed congregation. This involved reclassifying 10 people who said 75 or 80 percent.

glish, the survey does a much better job estimating factors for this group.

If people originally refused to complete the survey, they were called back twice to see if they would reconsider completing it. Slightly under 6 percent of the final sample (134 respondents) were "refusal conversion" respondents. When the white quota (1660) was filled, the survey introduction was changed to request to speak to non-white respondents only. The black and Hispanic quotas were filled quickly, but at the time of their completion, only 70 Asian interviews had been completed. One more week was spent attempting to identify and interview a random sample of Asian Americans. At the conclusion of the week, approximately 100 interviews had been completed. Due to money and time constraints, the remaining 110 interviews were conducted using a surname phone number list compiled by GENESYS. This method suffers from the obvious bias of missing any Asians with unidentifiably Asian surnames. Approximately 40 percent of Asians are excluded by this method. Because we had a sufficient number of randomly selected English-speaking Asian Americans, we are in a position to estimate the impact of this sampling choice, and to make corrections for any resulting bias. I address this issue after addressing response rate issues.

Survey Representativeness and the Response Rate

The LSASN aims to represent the English- and Spanish-speaking adult population who have phones and, due the study's aims in measuring residential issues and attitudes, have lived at their current residence for at least 3 months. The response rate for the LSASN was 53 percent. According to Mangione,[2] response rates between 50 and 60 percent "need some additional information that contributes to confidence about the quality" of the data. Error from nonresponse is a function of (a) how large the nonresponse is and (b) how different the nonresponders are from the responders. According to the survey research literature, the additional information which can aid in the assessment, and, if need be, the improvement of sample representativeness, includes the following:

1. Comparing the sample to a census or sample with a much higher response rate.
2. Under the assumption that refusal conversion respondents are similar

[2] Thomas Mangione, *Mail Surveys: Improving the Quality* (1995), p. 61.

to other refusers, or at least more similar than are initial respondents (those who responded on the first call), comparing refusal conversions to initial respondents.

3. Though rare to have such data (almost by definition), comparing information of nonrespondents with respondents.

Because the research team wished the LSASN to be representative of the population it desired to cover, I undertook a careful analysis of the sample and its representativeness. I began by obtaining a file of another survey with which to compare the LSASN. The U.S. Census typically is an excellent choice, but it is best to use data collected during the same period that the LSASN was collected. Ideally, we would like to compare the LSASN to a reliable data source representing the midpoint of the LSASN survey period. Fortunately, the Department of Labor conducts a large, monthly survey called the Current Population Survey (CPS). I selected the January 2000 CPS. The CPS, with its 124,000 cases, 93 percent response rate, and elaborate weighting procedures, is an excellent, contemporary source by which to compare our sample.

Based on comparisons of sociodemographic variables, the LSAF, like most telephone surveys, underrepresents the less educated and males. To correct for this, and our oversamples of non-whites, I constructed weights for each respondent. I first generated a table from the CPS that created cells for each racial group by gender and five categories of education (less than high school, high school grad, some college or vo-tech, bachelor's degree, and post-bachelor's degree). I created the same cells for the LSASN. For each cell I calculated a weight by taking the CPS cell percentage and dividing it by the corresponding LSASN cell percentage. Before analysis on the LSASN is conducted, then, this weight must be applied to the sample. Doing so produces nearly identical percentages on the variables race, sex, and education as the CPS. And after doing this, within these categories, marital status, income, and age also closely resemble the CPS. Demographically (and at this point, only demographically), applying the weight variable renders the LSASN representative of the population.

It would be convenient to assume that, within each subcategory for which the weight corrects, those who did not respond are much like those who did respond. If this assumption were correct, we could say with confidence that the LSASN now represents the population. However, without additional information, we do not know if this assumption is justified.

For this reason, I undertook a comparative analysis of initial respondents to refusal conversion respondents. I wanted to compare these two groups not just by demographic variables, as I was forced to do with the CPS, but also by a number of attitudinal, religious, and social network variables. Comparisons were tested statistically using independent sample t-tests, and when the comparison variable was not interval level, chi-square tests of significance. Statistically comparing initial respondents and refusal conversion respondents on over 50 variables produced three clear patterns.

First, the two groups were statistically identical on about 90 percent of the comparison variables. Second, the refusal conversions respondents are shyer, as measured by the fact that they, compared to initial responders, are more likely to prefer being with people they know as opposed to meeting new people. This helps explain in part why they initially said no and had to be coaxed into agreeing to an interview.

Third, the four other differences that exist can be attributed almost exclusively to one key difference: the refusal conversion respondents were twice as likely to be over 64 years of age as the initial respondents (31 percent to 15 percent). This led to employment status difference, in that the refusal conversion respondents were also twice as likely to be retired as the initial respondents (30 percent to 15 percent). All other initial differences—racial makeup of social network, stated views that morality ought to be universal, and able-bodied people should not receive welfare—disappeared when I accounted for the age difference.

The results are instructive for assessing the representativeness of the LSASN. It is likely that non-responders are more likely to be over 64 years of age and retired. For the variables of interest in the LSASN, this fact can lead to slightly overstating the degree of interracial networks, and slightly more liberal stances on a few selected attitudinal variables. Based on the fact that when I accounted for age, these differences no longer remained, it does appear that weighting can correct for these biases. As stated earlier, when I weighted for race, sex, and education, within these categories, the age distributions of the LSASN and CPS were quite similar.

What I cannot adjust for is the fact that non-responders are likely shyer than responders. Yet, this difference did not lead to any differences between initial respondents and refusal conversion respondents. So, despite this difference, its apparent impact on the representativeness of our results is statistically zero.

CONGREGATIONAL DATA

I used two sources of congregational data. The first was the National Congregations Study.[3] As the preeminent nationally representative survey of congregations, this was my main source for comparative purposes. A good description of this survey and methods can be found in the article, "The National Congregations Study."[4] The survey used hypernetwork sampling, asking General Social Survey respondents what congregation, if any, they attended. These congregations, when inversely weighted by congregational size, produce a random sample of congregations. Most interviews were done with senior clergy persons (of all faith traditions) by telephone. The response rate was an impressive 83 percent.

My colleagues and I used the same method to produce a random sample of congregations as well. Our sample was smaller, and to ensure that we had enough multiracial congregations, we oversampled such congregations. Our survey, reprinted at the end of this appendix, was mailed to the congregations. We followed up with two more mailing and reminder cards. Our response rate was 51 percent. This survey was designed to ask questions that were not on the National Congregations Survey. Because we had so few non-Christian congregations, and because of the extra time, work, and expense needed to create separate instruments for each faith tradition, we only mailed our surveys to Christian congregations. We had two versions—one for Catholics, and one for Protestants. For comparisons with non-Christian congregations, I used the National Congregations Study. All in all, for this book, our own congregations survey was used relatively little, at least directly.

The survey was used in our research design to help us select the thirty congregations with which to do more in-depth study. We wanted to visit congregations in all four major regions of the country (Northeast, Midwest, South, and West), so we selected one metropolitan area in each region with at least four multiracial congregations. We took care to select metropolitan areas of varying size—from one of the smallest to the nation's second largest—and areas with different racial compositions. We first mailed a letter to each selected congregation—twenty-two multiracial congregations, and for comparative purposes, eight single-race congregations (two each of Asian, Black, Latino, and White). We then called and talked with the senior clergy person, explaining again the purpose of the study (as our let-

[3] Mark Chaves, *National Congregations Study* (1999).
[4] Mark Chaves et al. 1999.

ter did), and asking if we might spend a few weeks studying the congregation in person. We did not have any refusals.

In the summer of 2000, a research team of four people, composed racially to match the racial composition of the congregations we would be visiting, traveled to one area at a time. We spent two weeks in each of the four localities, spending our entire time visiting the congregations, interviewing members and clergy, attending services and other events, reading each congregation's literature, taking extensive field notes, and studying the neighborhoods and cities in which the congregations resided.

Our goal in interviewing respondents was not to gain a random sample (we already had that) but to talk to people involved in the congregation. We asked the senior clergy person to provide us a list of 10 to 12 names and contact information of people that represented the diversity of the congregation (racially, by gender, age, and time in the congregation). We then set up interviews with eight people in the congregation. We did not have any direct refusals, but some people were out of town when we were interviewing, and so we had to move further down our list of names.

The interviews with respondents lasted from a half hour to two hours. Interviewers had an interview guide, but were trained to allow the respondents to talk about issues important to them, in addition to the questions in the interview guide (see the guide in appendix D). Interviews were done wherever the respondent suggested, from place of worship, to home, to a restaurant or library.

Since 2000, I or members of the research team have had the opportunity to revisit approximately half of these congregations, sometimes multiple times. These revisits have been useful for understanding change and stability, and the issues that arise over time. This longitudinal aspect was done most systematically with Wilcrest.

WHY WILCREST?

I attended Wilcrest from August 1999 through May 2004. When I first began attending, Wilcrest was demographically a multiracial congregation, perhaps 25 percent non-white. Tremendous changes took place during the nearly five-year period that I attended. Shortly after I arrived, Wilcrest entered what Rodney Woo called his bluest days (hopefully not related to my presence!). The staff that arrived within his first year had left, and with the exception of some part-time staff, Rodney Woo was the staff. Although much change had taken place at

Wilcrest, things were changing more slowly than Dr. Woo had hoped. During the five-year period, Wilcrest's change gained a second wind, transforming to a majority minority congregation, experiencing tremendous changes in leadership, worship styles, and the breadth of its diversity.

I began talking with Dr. Woo shortly after my arrival. I talked with him about the research my colleagues and were doing. Despite the frustrations and difficult times the congregation was experiencing at the time of my arrival, Dr. Woo "opened up the doors" to me to study the transformation process. He allowed me inside access to the congregation, from attending committee meetings, to visiting members, to talking with him about the issues of the current week. I became close with many of the parishioners at Wilcrest as well.

My involvement at Wilcrest as a member had benefits and costs in writing this book. On the positive side, I knew much more about Wilcrest, its people, its staff, social relationships, and the processes involved in the diversification of the congregation than I could have known by visiting it for a few weeks. I simply could not have written what is in this book about Wilcrest without my "inside" knowledge.

A potential cost of my involvement at Wilcrest is a biased perspective. Because I was a member there, it would be in my interest to present it in a favorable light, and because I knew the people in the congregation, they might expect or even demand me to present it in a favorable light. As Dr. Woo and other members know, I had my criticisms of Wilcrest, and most are presented in this book. Wilcrest members and Dr. Woo read what I wrote. Dr. Woo and Wilcrest members helped me get dates, names, and sequencing of events correct. But in only one instance did someone suggest a substantive change.

That instance for a substantive change occurred at the opening of chapter 6. Recall that the opening of this chapter describes a particular service, and the interpretation of that service by an African American visitor. In my initial draft, I gave a value judgment of the service and where Wilcrest was in its quest to become fully multiracial. I agreed with the African American woman and suggested there was other evidence in support of her view. Dr. Woo did not ask me to change this interpretation, but suggested that he did not fully agree with the interpretation. After considering his viewpoint, and talking further with the author of the letter, I changed the opening of the chapter. The changes better introduce the spirit of the chapter — that some differences in interpretation are seemingly intractable, with a "correct" interpretation of meaning not evident.

CONCLUSION

Together, these components of the research project provided an extensive overall look at such congregations, and comparative data. No method by itself is sufficient, but when these methods are combined they provide a rich source of data from which I drew to write this book.

APPENDIX D ▪ Instruments

The Lilly Survey of Attitudes and Social Networks

TELEPHONE SURVEY OF AMERICANS, 18+ YEARS OF AGE, ENGLISH AND

SPANISH SPEAKERS

"Hello. This is _____. I'm calling from the University of North Texas. I'm not asking for money and I'm not trying to sell you anything. We are doing a national research study on Americans' values and friendships. In order to get a random person from your household, I need to speak to the person 18 or older who has the next birthday. Is that you or someone else?"

[*If asked how got number*: "Your number was drawn from a random sample of telephones in the U.S."] [If asked how long it will take: "This survey should take between 15 and 20 minutes."]

[*If person who answered is person with next birthday*] "Great. Then you are the person I need to talk to. Your answers are very important to us. Your responses will be anonymous and you may skip any question you'd rather not answer. We would really appreciate your help, and we think you will find this a very interesting survey. May I continue?"

[*If respondent is different person*] "May I speak to him or her?" [*If person with next birthday is unavailable*] "When would be a good time to call back to reach him/her? Could I get the first name so we'll know who to ask for when we call back? Thank you." [Record name and call-back time]

[*When respondent with next birthday is on line*] "Hello. This is _____ at the University of North Texas. I'm not asking for money and I'm not trying to sell you anything. We are doing a national research study on Americans' values and beliefs. Your answers are very important to us. Your answers will be completely anonymous, and you may skip any question you'd rather not answer. We would really appreciate your help, and we think you will find this a very interesting survey. May I continue?"

[*If* "yes"] Thank you. [*Go to SQ1*]

[*If general hesitation*] "This won't take much time and we'd really appreciate your opinions."

[*If* "too busy"] "This will only take a few minutes. I can call you back at a more convenient time. What would be a better time within the next few days?"

[*If respondent says they are too old, doesn't matter what they think, or otherwise discount their opinion*] "Your opinion is as important as anyone's. In order for our survey to be accurate, we need to hear from people like you."

[*If* "doesn't like surveys"] "We think this particular survey is very important because the questions we are researching will help to promote better understanding and relations between different kinds of Americans, so we would really like to have your opinion too."

[*If* "doesn't like telephone surveys"] "We do the survey by phone because it is much faster and less expensive than interviewing people in person, and it gives us a better cross-section than a mail survey.

The survey is brief, only about 15 minutes."

[*If* "sick," "bad health"] "I'm sorry to hear that. I would be happy to call back in a day or two. Would that be okay?"

[*If* "No one else's business what I think"] I can certainly understand, that's why all our interviews are anonymous. Protecting people's privacy is one of our major concerns, so when the results are released, no one will be able to know that you participated."

Could we speak with the person who is over 18 and will have the next birthday in your family? (*If* "no:" "May we interview you?")

◆ *First we'd like to ask a few questions to make sure we are talking to a wide range of Americans.*

SQ1. How long have you lived at your current residence? [If < 3 months: "Thank you for your time." Otherwise, proceed with the interview]
1) Less than 3 months
2) More than 3 months
3) Don't know
4) Refused

SQ2. In which type of area do you currently live?
1) City
2) Suburb
3) Small town
4) In the country
5) Don't know
6) Refused

Q1. Are you currently married, or are you living with someone in a marriage-like relationship, widowed, divorced, separated, or have you never been married? [If "divorced and separated," *code as* Divorced. *If* "marriage-like relationship and divorced/separated/widowed," *code as* Living with someone]
1) Married [GO TO Q2]
2) Living with someone [GO TO Q2]
3) Widowed [GO TO Q2]
4) Divorced
5) Separated [go to Q2]
6) Never married

      7) Don't know [*go to* Q2]

      8) Refused

Q2. [*If Q1=1-3, 5, or 7*] Have you ever been divorced?

      1) Yes

      2) No

      3) Don't know

      4) Refused

Q3. What race or ethnic group do you consider yourself? [*If necessary*] That is, are you white, black American, Hispanic, Asian American, Pacific Islander, American Indian, or of mixed race? [*If* "human," *ask*: "Would you mind telling us your ethnicity?"]

      1) White/Caucasian/Anglo (included Middle Eastern)

      2) Black/African American

      3) Hispanic/Latino/a

      4) Asian/Asian American

      5) Pacific Islander

      6) American Indian/Native American

      7) Mixed

      8) Other [*only if volunteered and cannot be placed in a category 1-7*]

      9) Don't know

      10) Refused

Q4. [*If Q3=1-5, or 7, read categories under appropriate racial group*]

Q4a [If say Asian]
Are you:
1) Chinese
2) Filipino
3) Japanese
4) Asian Indian
5) Korean
6) Vietnamese
7) Or something else? Other
8) Mixed (if volunteered)

Q4b [If say Hispanic]
Are you:
1) Mexican
2) Cuban
3) Puerto Rican
4) Other Caribbean

5) Or something else? Other
6) Mixed (if volunteered)

Q4c. [*If say* "Mixed"] What ethnic/racial groups are part of your heritage? _____

Q5. Do you identify with one of these more than the others? _____

Q6. [*If Q1=1-2*]: What race or ethnicity is your [spouse/partner]?

      1) White (includes European, Middle Eastern)

      2) Black (includes African American, African, Dominican, other black)

      3) Hispanic (includes Mexican, Cuban, Puerto Rican, other Latin American)

      4) Asian (includes Asian and Pacific Islander ethnicities)

      5) American Indian (includes Native American and tribes)

◆ *I am going to read you three pairs of opposites. For each set, please tell me which is closest to being true for you.*

Q7. A) I don't mind moving every once in a while
B) I would prefer to stay in one place
Which one of these comes closest to being true of you?
1) Don't mind moving
2) Stay in one location
3) In between [only if volunteered]
4) Don't know
5) Refused

Q8. A) I like trying new kinds of foods
B) I prefer eating foods I am used to eating
1) Try new foods
2) Prefer familiar foods
3) In between (only if volunteered)
4) Don't know
5) Refused

Q9. A) I enjoy getting to know people different from me
B) I enjoy meeting people who have a great deal in common with me
1) Know people different from me
2) Meet people like me
3) In between (only if volunteered)
4) Don't know
5) Refused

Q10. [*If Q1=1–2*] Do you think your [spouse/partner] would give mostly the same answers on these pairs as you, or mostly the opposite answers?
1) Mostly the same answers
2) Mostly opposite answers
3) Some of both (only if volunteered)
4) Don't know
5) Refused

◆ *Now I would like to ask you a few more background questions.*

Q11. Are you working for pay full-time or part-time, working as a home-maker, retired, a student, or something else? [*If 2 answers offered, ask which spend most time doing*]
1) Full-time
2) Part-time
3) In school
4) Unemployed
5) On leave
6) Retired
7) Keeping house
8) Other

9) Not applicable
10) Don't know
11) Refused

Q12. Do you consider yourself to be Protestant, Catholic, Jewish, Muslim, nothing in particular, or something else?
1) Protestant (includes Baptists, Methodists, Presbyterians, Mormons, Reformed)
2) Catholic
3) Jewish
4) Eastern Orthodox Christian
5) Muslim
6) Hindu-Buddhist
7) Nothing in particular/Not religious
8) "Just a Christian" [*go to Q108*]
9) Other: _____
10) Don't know
11) Refused

Q13. How often have you been attending [church/synagogue/mosque/temple] services in the last year?
1) Never
2) Less than once a month
3) Once a month
4) 2–3 times a month
5) Once a week
6) More than once a week
7) Don't know
8) Refused

Q14. Would you say your religious faith currently is not important, slightly, moderately, very, or extremely important in your own life?
1) Not important
2) Slightly important
3) Moderately important
4) Very important
5) Extremely important
6) Don't know
7) Refused

Q15. Would you say religion in your family while you were growing up was not important, slightly, moderately, very, or extremely important?
1) Not important
2) Slightly important
3) Moderately important
4) Very important
5) Extremely important
6) Don't know
7) Refused

◆ *To help us learn more about American's friendships, I want to ask you about your friends. To help guide you, I will ask you about a few specific categories. Please remember, we are not taking an inventory of you personally, but of American friendships in general.*

◆ *Think about your 2 very best friends* [if Q2=1–2: *"other than your [spouse/ partner]."*]

Q16. [*if attend once a month or more*] How many of your 2 very best friends attend the same [church/synagogue/mosque/temple] as you?

    0) 0
    1) 1
    2) 2
    3) Don't know
    4) Refused

Q17. For your 2 very best friends, how many are [respondent's race]?

    0) 0
    1) 1
    2) 2
    3) Don't know
    4) Refused

Q18a. [*if Q17=1*] What is the race of your other friend?

Q18b. [*if Q17=2*] What is the race of the friend you have known the longest?

    1) Asian/Asian American [includes any specific Asian ethnic groups]
    2) Black/African American [includes African]
    3) Hispanic/Latino [includes any specific Latin American ethnic groups]
    4) White/European/Middle Eastern
    5) American Indian/Native American [includes any specific tribes]

Q19. For your 2 very best friends, how many are female?

    1) 2
    2) 1
    3) 0
    4) Don't know
    5) Refused

◆ *Now think of your circle of friends, people that you like to do things with and have conversations with. They may be people you see often, or because they may live far away, they may be people you primarily keep in contact with by calling or writing.*

Q20. [*If attend once a month or more*] Thinking about your circle of friends, which of the following categories best describes how many attend your [church/synagogue/mosque/temple]?

1) All
2) Most
3) About half
4) Few
5) None
6) Don't know
7) Refused

Q21. DROPPED AFTER 6 RESPONDENTS, *deleted from dataset*

Q22. For your circle of friends, how many [respondent's race] are among these people?
   1) All
   2) Most
   3) About half
   4) Few
   5) None
   6) Don't know
   7) Refused

Q23. DROPPED AFTER 20 RESPONDENTS deleted from dataset

Q24. [*If* Q13 = 4-7] Now think about the people, if any, that you have frequent contact with, and enjoy being around in your [church/synagogue/mosque/temple]. With these people in mind, how many [respondent's race] are among these people?
   1) All
   2) Most
   3) About half
   4) Few
   5) None
   6) Don't know
   7) Refused

Q25. Now please think about all the people that you have frequent contact with and enjoy being around, including people in your neighborhood, [*if* Q36 = 1-4] [church/synagogue/mosque/temple], [*if* Q11 = 1-2, 5-6] [workplace], [*if* Q11 = 3] [school], any associations or clubs to which you may belong, and any other people that you have contact with and enjoy being around. With these people in mind, how many [respondent's race] are among these people?
   1) All
   2) Most
   3) About half
   4) Few
   5) None
   6) Don't know
   7) Refused

◆ *Now I am going to read you some statements about morality and America. For each, please tell me whether you agree or disagree, and if you do so strongly, moderately, or slightly.*

Q26. Religion is a private matter that should not influence social and political issues. Do you personally agree or disagree with this statement, and do you do so strongly, moderately, or slightly?
   1) Strongly agree
   2) Moderately agree
   3) Slightly agree
   4) Neither agree nor disagree, "In between" (only if volunteered)
   5) Slightly disagree
   6) Moderately disagree
   7) Strongly disagree
   8) Don't know
   9) Refused

Q27. The best way to improve America is to change individuals. [*If need to be reminded of the categories again: "Do you agree or disagree, and do you do so strongly, moderately, or slightly?"*]

Q28. What is morally right and what is morally wrong should be the same for all people.

◆ *Here are some statements about family. For each, again please tell me whether you agree or disagree, and if you do so strongly, moderately, or slightly.*

Q29. A mother of very young children should work outside the home only if financially necessary. [*If ask what* "very young" *means, say* "under 5."]

Q30. Homosexuality should be an acceptable lifestyle.

Q31. Women face more discrimination in the workplace than men do.

Q32. The husband should be the head of the family.

◆ *I am going to read you a list of about 20 statements. For each, please tell me whether you agree or disagree, and if you do so strongly, moderately, or slightly.*

Q33. I support affirmative action policies.

Q34. It is important to protect the natural environment, even if it hurts local business.

Q35. It is America's responsibility to promote democracy around the world.

Q36. It is too easy to buy guns in America today.

Q37. Too much of our federal budget goes to national defense.

Q38. The federal income tax should be cut.

Q39. The economy is better today than it was a year ago.

Q40. Abortion during the first three months of pregnancy should be legal in all cases.

Q41. Able-bodied people should not receive welfare.

Q42. The number of immigrants who can legally enter the U.S. should be reduced.

Q43. There is too much talk today in the United States about racial issues.

Q44. We need a program of parental school choice.

Q45. Religious congregations should actively seek to become racially integrated.

Q46. The pill is a morally acceptable form of birth control.

Q47. We should spend more money on prisons so that we can put criminals away for a long time.

Q48. My religious beliefs should direct my behavior in every area of my life.

Q49. We should give businesses special tax breaks for locating in largely [rotate racial group] areas.

Q50. Compared to other racial groups, [rotate racial group] on average tend to prefer to live on welfare.

Q51. Compared to other racial groups, [rotate racial group] on average tend to be patriotic to the United States.

Q52. Compared to other racial groups, [rotate racial group] on average tend to be arrogant.

Q53. I would be upset if I had a child who wanted to marry [a/an] [rotate racial group, other than respondent's own racial group].

◆ *We want to ask you a few questions about your [church/synagogue/mosque/ temple].*

[Ask of any attending church/synagogue/mosque/temple at least 2 times a month]

Q54. How long have you been attending this [church/synagogue/mosque/ temple]? _____

Q54a. What is the full name of your [church/synagogue/mosque/ temple]? _____

Q54b. And what city and state is that in? _____ _____

Q55. How many people—both adults and children—would you say typically attend services at your [church/synagogue/mosque/temple]—whether or not they are officially members? _____

Q56. About what percent of your congregation, if any, would you say are immigrants to the U.S.? _____ (if want to give number, record so we can tell difference between absolute number and percentage)

Q57. Though hard to know for sure, would you say that [respondent's race] make up more than 80 percent of the worship service that you normally attend at your [church/synagogue/mosque/temple]?
    1) Yes
    2) No
    3) Don't know
    4) Refused

Q58. [If Q57=2 or 3] About what percent of the people at the worship service that you normally attend would you say are [respondent's race]?

_____

Q59. [If Q58 < or = 80%] What other racial groups are represented in the worship service that you normally attend? [record all that are mentioned]

Q60. When you first started attending your current [church/synagogue/mosque/temple], would you say that [respondent's race] made up more than 80% of the worship service that you attend?
    1) Yes
    2) No
    3) Don't know
    4) Refused

Q61. In addition to your own ethnic group, are there any other ethnic groups represented in the worship service that you normally attend?
    1) Yes
    2) No
    3) Don't know
    4) Refused

Q62. [If Q61 = 1] Which ethnic groups? [record all that are mentioned]

Q63. As an adult, have you ever in the past been a member of a congregation in which [respondent's race] made up less than 80% of the congregation?
    1) Yes
    2) No
    3) Don't know
    4) Refused

Q64. [If Q63 = 1] In the past, were you a member of 1 of these congregations or more than 1?
    1) One
    2) More than one
    3) Don't know

4) Refused

5) Don't know

Q65a. [*If Q64 = 1*] For how long did you attend services at this [church/synagogue/mosque/temple]? _____

Q65b. [*If Q64 = 2*] For your most recent congregation that you attended before your current congregation, for how long did you attend services at this [church/synagogue/mosque/temple]? _____

Q66a. [*If Q64 = 1*] What was the most important reason for leaving?

Q66b. [*If Q64 = 2*] What was the most important reason for leaving the last mixed-race congregation you attended?

1) Moved
2) Not being spiritually fed
3) Got married
4) Had child
5) Not providing programs seeking
6) Problems with clergy/persons in congregation
7) Not biblically based/not serious about God/not committed
8) Didn't like the worship
9) Too much talk about race/too much focus on race/integration
10) Other: _____
11) Don't know
12) Refused

Q67. Is there one person who is the head or senior clergy person or religious leader of your present [church/synagogue/mosque/temple]?

1) Yes
2) No
3) Don't know
4) Refused

Q68. [*If Q67 = 1*] Is that person male or female?

Q69. [*If Q67 = 1*] What race or ethnicity is this person?

1. White
2. Black
3. Hispanic
4. Asian
5. American Indian
6. Other

Q70. How long do your worship services typically last? [*record to nearest quarter hour*] [*If say "varies" or "depends" or "I'm not sure," ask:* "Most often, how long does it last?"] _____

Q71. [*If for Q70, actual time is given*] Do you think the services are too long, too short, about right, or does it not matter?

1) Too long
2) Too short

3) About right
4) Time does not matter
5) Don't know
6) Refused

Q72. During a typical worship service, do people regularly call out "amen" or other expressions of approval?
1) Yes
2) No
3) Don't know
4). Refused

Q73. In every congregation, disagreements and conflicts can arise. Within the last two years, has your congregation experienced a conflict that led some people to leave the congregation?
1) Yes
2) No
3) Don't know

Q74. How often, if at all, do you go to congregational activities other than your main worship service, such as potlucks, Bible studies, choir practice, small groups, etc.?
1) Never
2) A few times a year
3) Once a month
4) 2–3 times a month
5) Once a week
6) 2 times a week
7) 3 or more times a week

◆ *I would like to get your thoughts on a few other questions. [Race]*

Q75. Imagine that you are looking for a new house and that you have [no, two school-aged] children. You find a house that you like much better than any other house — it has everything that you'd been looking for, it is close to work, and it is within your price range. Checking on the neighborhood, you find that [*rotate variables presented*]
A. the public schools are of [low, medium, high] quality,
B. the neighborhood is [1–100%, *randomly chosen*] [Black, Hispanic, Asian] (do not ask respondent's own race],
C. the other homes in the neighborhood are of [lower, equal, higher] value than the home you are considering,
D. property values are [declining, stable, increasing],
E. and the crime rate is [low, average, high].

How likely or unlikely do you think it is that you would buy this home?
1) Very unlikely
2) Moderately unlikely
3) Slightly unlikely

4) Slightly likely
5) Moderately likely
6) Very likely

Q76. Given a house that you very much like, would you prefer this house to be in a neighborhood that is
   1) 75% [respondent's race] and 25% [rotate Asian, Black, Hispanic, White (not respondent's own race)]
   or
   2) One that is 25% each [respondent's race] [each of the three racial groups respondent is not]?
   3) No preference
   4) Don't know
   5) Refused

Q77. In the U.S., we generally refer to 5 racial groups: Whites, Blacks, Hispanics, Asians, and American Indians. Do you personally think that any one of these groups experiences more discrimination than the other groups?
   1) Yes
   2) No

Q77a. If yes, which group?
   1) White
   2) Black
   3) Hispanic
   4) Asian
   5) American Indian

◆ We are interested in what you consider to be prejudice and what you consider to be racism. I am going to read you 3 short scenarios. For each please tell me if you think it is prejudice or not, and if it is racism or not. [Rotate order, and give only 3 of 7 to any one respondent. There are 2 questions for each of the 3 scenarios.]

Q78a, b. A foreman has a good record in hiring and promoting racial minorities. However he tells racial jokes when around his minority subordinates. These jokes make racial minorities extremely uncomfortable. Despite his hiring and promotion record, do you think that his jokes are an example of prejudice? Do you think his jokes are an example of racism?
   1) Yes
   2) No
   3) Don't know
   4) Refused

Q79a, b. A group of [black (if respondent is white, black, mixed, or no preference)]/[Asian (if Asian)]/[Hispanic (if Hispanic)]/[American Indian (if American Indian)] teenagers are angry that the school administration seems insensitive to racial concerns. Because of their frustration, some of them assault a white classmate. The individual is attacked in part because he is white. Clearly this assault is wrong, but is it also an example of prejudice? Is it an example of racism?

Q80a, b. A white teenage girl begins dating a black teenage boy. Her parents pressure her not to date him. They do not resent him for being black, but feel they must shield their daughter from social rejection they think their daughter will face. Are actions to stop their daughter from dating this boy an example of prejudice? Are they an example of racism?

Q81a, b. A black professor [if respondent is Asian, Hispanic, or American Indian, use their race] grades all of her students fairly. However, she spends extra time with her black students [if respondent is Asian, Hispanic, or American Indian, use their race] because she feels that they have a hard time relating to white professors. Some of her white students complain that this extra time is prejudice, since white students do not get this special attention. Would you agree? Others claim this is racism. Would you agree?

Q82 a, b. A white cab driver can pick up a black man in a suit and tie or a white man wearing blue jeans and a T-shirt. The driver has no ill feelings towards African-Americans but does not want to risk being asked to go to an inner-city black neighborhood, since he fears this will put him at a risk of being assaulted. Therefore the driver passes the black man and picks up the white man. Has the driver engaged in prejudice? Has the driver engaged in racism?

Q83a, b. A white homeowner decides to move out of the neighborhood, because she has noticed several racial minorities moving into the neighborhood. Even though she gets along with non-whites, she is afraid that the value of her home will decrease. Is her decision to move prejudice? Is her decision to move racist?

Q84a, b. In a certain city, most white children go to schools that are predominately white. Since they live in different neighborhoods, most black children go to schools that are predominately non-white. Standardized tests were taken 5 years in a row. While 80% of the white students passed, 80% of the black children failed. Is this an example of prejudice? Is this an example of racism?

Q85. This is a somewhat long question, so please feel free to ask me to repeat it.
   A. Some people say that we are better off if the races maintain their cultural uniqueness, even if we have limited personal relationships between races.
   B. Others say that we should create a common culture and close interracial friendships, even though the races may lose their cultural uniqueness.

Which one do you prefer?
1) A
2) B
3) combo

Q85a. [*If combo*] Do you lean more toward A or more toward B or are you right in the middle?

Q86. Not including your current neighborhood, have you ever lived in a neighborhood that was 20% or more non-[respondent's race]? YES / NO

Q87. Not including any school you may be presently attending and not including college, have you ever attended a school that was 20% or more non-[respondent's race]? YES / NO

Q88. Have you ever dated someone of another race? YES / NO

Q89. On a political scale of 1 to 7—with 1 being extremely liberal, 4 being middle of the road, and 7 being extremely conservative—how would you describe yourself politically?
1) Extremely liberal
2) Liberal
3) Slightly liberal
4) Moderate, middle of the road
5) Slightly conservative
6) Conservative
7) Extremely conservative
8) Don't know
9) Refused

◆ *When you decide who to vote for in an election, you have several issues that may concern you. On a scale from 1 to 7—with 1 being not important, 4 being moderately important, and 7 being very important—please rank the importance of each of the following issues in determining how you vote.*

Q90. Abortion. Is this issue very important, moderately important, or not important in determining how you will vote?

Q91. Affirmative action

Q92. Environmental issues

Q93. Foreign policy

Q94. Gun control

Q95. National defense

Q96. Taxes

Q97. Welfare policy

Q98. Education

Q99. Crime

Q100. Social security

Q101. Immigration

Q102. Most important issue?
1) Abortion
2) Affirmative action
3) Environment
4) Foreign policy
5) Gay rights
6) Gun control
7) Taxes
8) Welfare policy
9) Education
10) Crime
11) Social security
12) Immigration

Q103. [Discontinued after 55 respondents.]

[For Christians only—Protestant or Catholic If Q12=1-3, or Q15=1, or Q16=1-13 or 15-30] ◆ *These next few questions are questions we are asking of the Christians we are interviewing.*

Q104. Do you think that the Bible is the inspired word of God, or not?
1) Yes, inspired
2) No, not inspired
3) Don't know
4) Refused

Q105. [If Q104 = 1] I'm going to read you three views about the Bible. Please tell me which one best reflects your own view:
1) The first is: The Bible is true in all ways, and to be read literally word for word.
2) The second is: The Bible is true in all ways, but not always to be read literally.
3) The third is: The Bible is a moral guide, but should not be read literally, and may contain some errors about non-religious matters.

Q106. Do you think that the only hope for salvation is through personal faith in Jesus Christ, or are there other ways to salvation?
1) Yes, Christ only hope
2) No, other ways
3) Don't know
4) Refused

Q107. *[if Q12 = 1 and Q13 = 2-6]* [If gave denomination, code here. Otherwise ask:] What is the denomination of the church you most often attend, or is it nondenominational?

Q108. [if Q12 = 8] Would you say you are either a Catholic or Eastern Orthodox Christian?
1) Yes
2) No
3) Don't know
4) Refused

[Q109 and Q110. Dropped.]

Q111. [*If say* "Baptist"] With which Baptist group is your church associated? Is it Southern Baptist, National Baptist, American Baptist, independent Baptist, or some other Baptist group?
1) American Baptist Association
2) American Baptist USA
3) Baptist Bible Fellowship
4) Baptist General Conference
5) Baptist Missionary Association
6) Conservative Baptist Association of America
7) Free Will Baptist
8) Fundamentalist Baptist (no denominational ties)
9) General Association of Regular Baptists (GARB)
10) Independent Baptist (no denominational ties)
11) Missionary Baptist
12) National Baptist Convention America
13) National Baptist Convention USA
14) Primitive Baptists
15) Progressive National Baptist Convention
16) Southern Baptist
17) Other: _____
18) Don't know, "Just Baptist"

Q112. [If say "Methodist"] Is that the United Methodist Church, African Methodist Episcopal Church, or some other Methodist group?
1) African Methodist Episcopal
2) African Methodist Episcopal Zion
3) Christian Methodist Episcopal
4) United Methodist
5) Other: _____
6) Don't know, "Just Methodist"

Q113. [*If say* "Presbyterian"] Is that the Presbyterian Church in the USA, the Presbyterian Church in America, or some other Presbyterian group?
1) Evangelical Presbyterian Church (EPC)
2) Orthodox Presbyterian Church (OPC)
3) Presbyterian Church in America (PCA)
4) Presbyterian Church in the USA (PCUSA)
5) Other: _____
6) Don't know, "Just Presbyterian"

Q114. [*If say* "Lutheran"] Is that the Evangelical Lutheran Church in America, the Missouri Synod, the Wisconsin Synod, or some other Lutheran group?

1) Evangelical Lutheran Church in America (ELCA; formerly the Lutheran Church in America, American Lutheran Church)
2) Missouri Synod
3) Wisconsin Synod
4) Free Lutheran
5) Other: _____
6) Don't know, "Just Lutheran"

Q115. [*If say* "Christian"] When you say "Christian," does that mean the denomination called the "Christian Church (Disciples of Christ)," or some other Christian denomination, or do you mean to say "I am just a Christian"?

1) Disciples of Christ
2) "Just a Christian"
3) Other Christian denomination: _____
4) Don't know

Q116. [*If say* "Pentecostal"] What kind of church is that? What is it called exactly? Is that part of a large church or denomination?

1) Apostolic Pentecostal
2) Assemblies of God
3) Church of God (Cleveland, TN)
4) Church of God (Huntsville, AL)
5) Church of God in Christ
6) Church of God in Christ (international)
7) Church of God in Prophesy
8) Four Square Gospel
9) Full Gospel
10) Pentecostal Church of God
11) Pentecostal Holiness Church
12) Spanish Pentecostal
13) United Pentecostal Church International
14) Other: _____
15) Don't know, "Just Pentecostal"

Q117: [*If say* "Charismatic"] Is that a Charismatic church associated with any denomination, a Pentecostal church, or a nondenominational Charismatic church?

1) Associated with denomination [*return to Q14*]
2) Pentecostal [*return to Q23*]
3) Independent Charismatic
Don't know, "Just Charismatic"

Q118. [If say "Protestant"] When it comes to your religious identity, would you say you are a fundamentalist, evangelical, mainline, or theologically liberal Christian, or do none of these describe you?

1) Fundamentalist
2) Evangelical

3) Mainline
4) Theologically liberal
5) None of these
6) Other _____ [*must volunteer*]
7) Don't know
8) Refused

Q119. [If say "Catholic"] When it comes to your religious identity, would you say you are a traditional, moderate, or liberal Catholic, or do none of these describe you?
1) Traditional
2) Moderate
3) Liberal
4) None of these
5) Other _____ [*must volunteer*]
6) Don't know
7) Refused

◆ *I am going to read you a few statements. As you have done before, please tell me whether you agree or disagree, and whether strongly, moderately, or slightly.*

Q120. Women should be allowed to be [head pastors/priests (if Catholic)]. Do you strongly agree, moderately agree, slightly agree, neutral, slightly disagree, moderately disagree, or strongly disagree?

Q121. If enough people became Christians, social problems would naturally begin to disappear.

[*Asked only of those Christians attending church 2 or more times a month*]

Q122. I like the style of music at my church. 1 = Strongly Agree to 7 = Strongly Disagree

Q123. I feel like I belong at my church.

Q124. Attending my church has made me more sensitive to other racial groups.

Q125. I'm satisfied with the leadership at my church.

◆ *You are being very helpful. We are almost done. Just a couple of final background questions, and that will be it.*

Q126. [*If not sure about respondent's sex*] Are you male [1] or female [2]?

Q127. How many children do you currently live with and raise? [includes stepchildren]

Q128. Are any under 18?
1) yes
2) No
3) Don't know
4) Refused

Q129. What year were you born? _____

Q130. Were you born in the United States?   [YES/NO]

Q130a. [*If "no"*] In what country were you born? [*Code 1 Afghanistan, 2 Argentina, 3 . . .*]

Q130b. [*If "yes"*] In what state were you born? [*Code state*]

Q131. From age 8–18, in what state or country did you live the longest? [Code state or country]

Q132. [*If Q130 and Q131 = country other than U.S.*] Since you moved to the United States, in which state have you lived the longest?

Q133. In what state or country was your father born?

Q134. And in what state or country was your mother born?

Q135. Do you currently own your own house, rent an apartment, or something else?
1) Own own house
2) Rent a house
3) Rent an apartment
4) Rent a duplex
5) Own a condominium
6) Rent a condominium
7) Live in a dorm
8) Other: _____
9) Don't know
10) Refused

Q137. How many rooms do you have (for your family), not counting bathrooms?

Q138. What is the highest grade of school, year in college, or graduate degree you have completed? [In years 0–20]

Q139. And to do our statistical analysis, we need to have respondents' zip codes. We will not use this to contact you or send you anything. Your answers are totally anonymous. What is your zip code?

Q140. Now here is the last question. I am going to read you a list of income categories. Please tell me to stop when a category I read best describes your total household income before taxes.
1) <10,000
2) Between 10,000 and 20,000
3) Between 20,000–30,000
4) Between 30,000–40,000
5) Between 40,000–50,000
6) Between 50,000–60,000
7) Between 60,000–70,000
8) Between 70,000–80,000

9) Between 80,000–90,000
10) Between 90,000–100,000
11) More than 100,000
12) Don't know
13) Refused [*Prompt if necessary*: "Remember, your answers are totally anonymous, and we don't need to know your exact income, just an income bracket within ten thousand dollars. It would really help us out." *Wait for YES or NO before reading answer categories*]

Okay, thank you very much. I really appreciate your taking the time to answer our questions. You did a great job.

[*Asked of Christians attending a church at least 2 times per month*] One last thing: to learn a little more about your church, we may want to send a short mail survey to a [pastor/priest] at your church. We will not identify you or any of the information you gave us. We will not try to sell anything. Replying to the survey will be completely voluntary and completely anonymous. Could you tell us the street address of your church? Zip code? Telephone number? That's it. Thank you again for your time and cooperation.

LILLY SURVEY OF CONGREGATIONS, PROTESTANT VERSION

I. WORSHIP

1. *Worship Services*. If your congregation holds worship services less than once a week, ✔ here ❑ and answer for a typical weekend hold services.

	Friday	Saturday	Sunday before 5 pm	Sunday after 5 pm
A. How many worship services does your congregation have on each of the following days of a *typical* weekend?				
B. How many people—both adults and children—*typically* attend services held on this day? (If more than one service, report combined total.)				

If your congregation offers *multiple* worship services on a typical week-end, do they vary by any of the following? (Please ✔ all that apply)

❏ Intended for different age groups ❏ Different worship styles
❏ Different racial/ethnic groups ❏ Different languages
❏ Other: _____

2. In what language(s) does your congregation regularly conduct worship services? (Please ✔ all that apply)

❏ English ❏ Spanish ❏ Latin ❏ French ❏ Mandarin ❏ Korean
❏ Other: _____

3. Does the worship service with the largest attendance typically include a sermon?

❏ Yes ❏ No ❏ Don't know

[*If Yes to question* 3:] How frequently is the STYLE of the sermon:

	Always	Often	Sometimes	Seldom	Never
A. Scholarly, appealing to logic	❏	❏	❏	❏	❏
B. Emotionally rousing	❏	❏	❏	❏	❏
C. Quietly poignant, tugging at one's heart	❏	❏	❏	❏	❏
D. Folksy, a lot of stories from everyday life	❏	❏	❏	❏	❏

[*If YES to question* 3:] How frequently is the SUBJECT MATTER of the sermon:

	Always	Often	Sometimes	Seldom	Never
A. An exposition of Scripture or doctrine	❏	❏	❏	❏	❏
B. A discussion of a contemporary issue	❏	❏	❏	❏	❏
C. Challenging and provoking, calling attendees to change their *personal lives*	❏	❏	❏	❏	❏
D. Challenging and provoking, calling attendees to change something in the *social world*	❏	❏	❏	❏	❏
E. Comforting, reminding worshipers that God will care and provide	❏	❏	❏	❏	❏

4. How long do your worship services typically last (report to the nearest quarter hour)? _____

5. What style(s) of music are routinely sung by your choir(s)? If you do not have a choir, ✔ here ❏ and leave this question blank.

❏ Classical Church Music ❏ Traditional Anthems (free composed choir songs)
❏ Contemporary Anthems ❏ Black Gospel
❏ Spirituals ❏ Praise/Worship Anthems
❏ Southern Gospel ❏ Other _____

6. What style(s) of music are *routinely* sung by your *congregation*?

❏ Liturgical ❏ Traditional hymnody
❏ Black Gospel ❏ Traditional Praise and Worship
❏ Gen X music ❏ Contemporary Praise and Worship
❏ Other: _____

	Yes	No
7. Do congregational members ever call out "amen" or other expressions during worship?	❏	❏
8. Do congregational members ever speak in tongues during worship?	❏	❏
9. Do congregational members ever engage in quiet, meditative worship?	❏	❏
10. Are congregational members ever slain in the spirit during worship?	❏	❏
11. Do congregational members ever dance or jump for joy during worship?	❏	❏
12. Do congregational members ever engage in liturgical worship?	❏	❏

II. ORGANIZATION

13. In what year was the congregation founded? _____

14. With what denomination or movement was it associated at the time of founding, if any?
❏ none_____

15. With what denomination or movement is it associated now, if any?
❏ none _____

16. Does your congregation have cell groups or regular small-group gatherings?
❏ Yes ❏ No ❏ Don't know
[*If Yes*] About what percentage of your congregation participates in a cell group or small group? _____%

17. In practice, who would you say has the *most influence* in making decisions and implementing policies in your congregation? (Please ✔ one)

❑ The senior pastor   ❑ Assistant or Associate   ❑ The clergy
                           pastor(s)   as a group

❑ Board of lay leaders ❑ A denominational   ❑ Individual
                           body or official   members

❑ All have equal   ❑ Other: _____
   influence

18. Does your congregation have a "sister" or satellite relationship with any other congregation?

❑ Yes   ❑ No   ❑ Don't know

[*If Yes*] Is your congregation the older or the younger congregation in the relationship?

❑ Older   ❑ Younger   ❑ Don't know

19. Which, if any, are the major sources of new members/attendees for your congregation? (Please ✔ all that apply):

❑ A. Friends or relatives   ❑ E. People who have left
     of members   another congregation (of
                                     any denom.)

❑ B. People who marry   ❑ F. People who have recently
     members   moved to area

❑ C. College or university   ❑ G. Parents of children
     students   attending congregational
                                     activities

❑ D. New converts,   ❑ H. Other:_____
     unchurched

19a. [*If checked two or more*] Write the letter that corresponds to the greatest source of new members: _____

19b. What percent of the congregation has joined in the past 12 months?

_____

On average, are the new members
   racially similar to other members?   ❑
   racially different from other members?   ❑
   no new members   ❑
On average, are the new members
   economically similar to other members?   ❑
   economically poorer than other members?   ❑
   economically wealthier than other members?   ❑
   no new members   ❑

20. In the past 10 years, has your congregation undergone a split in which some members left to form or join another congregation? ❑ Yes ❑ No ❑ Don't know

21. In congregations, disagreements can arise. In the past 2 years, have disagreements in the areas listed below occurred in your congregation? If so, how serious or disruptive were the disagreements? [If more than one disagreement in the specific area, record the average level of seriousness.]

	No	Yes, Not Very Serious	Yes, Moderately Serious	Yes, Very Serious
A. Theology	❑	❑	❑	❑
B. Money/Finances/Budget	❑	❑	❑	❑
C. Worship style	❑	❑	❑	❑
D. A specific program or mission priority	❑	❑	❑	❑
E. How to or who should make decisions	❑	❑	❑	❑
F. Clergy leadership	❑	❑	❑	❑
G. Clergy behavior or lifestyle	❑	❑	❑	❑
H. Member behavior/ lifestyle	❑	❑	❑	❑

22. Does your congregation share building facilities with another congregation?

❑ Yes   ❑ No   ❑ Don't Know

[If Yes]	Yes	No	Don't know
Do you have a shared name?	❑	❑	❑
Are you under one authority structure?	❑	❑	❑
Do you share a common budget?	❑	❑	❑

III. IDENTITY AND THEOLOGY

On a seven-point scale, circle the number that best describes where your congregation *currently* stands, *1* meaning most like the characteristic on *left*, 7 meaning most like the characteristic on the *right*, and 4 meaning an *equal mix of both*. If you do not know which best describes your congregation, leave the question blank.

23. Our congregation is   1 2 3 4 5 6 7   We are more influenced more influenced by history & tradition.   by modern ideas & trends.

24. The congregation's   1 2 3 4 5 6 7   The congregation's approach approach to social issues is basically educational, leaving any action to individual conscience.   to social issues is activist. We have a history of taking institutional stands

25. Our congregation feels like a close-knit family. 1 2 3 4 5 6 7 Our congregation feels like a loosely knit association of people and groups.

26. Our congregation believes that the practice of homosexuality is sinful. 1 2 3 4 5 6 7 Our congregation believes that the practice of homosexuality is not sinful.

27. Our members tend to come from the same economic class. 1 2 3 4 5 6 7 Our members are in very different economic classes.

28. Our members socialize with with one another a great deal outside of scheduled church meetings and events. 1 2 3 4 5 6 7 Our members don't socialize much with one another outside of scheduled church meetings and events.

29. It is very important to our congregation to win people to the one, true faith. 1 2 3 4 5 6 7 It is very important to our congregation to support an ecumenical approach to faith.

For congregations that belong to a denomination

30. Our congregation gives strong expression to its denominational identity and heritage. 1 2 3 4 5 6 7 A visitor might not know to which denomination we belong.

31. According to the theology of your congregation, can women:

	Yes	No	Don't Know
A. Lead group prayer during the primary worship service?	❑	❑	❑
B. Be ushers?	❑	❑	❑
C. Teach adult classes where there are men?	❑	❑	❑
D. Serve on a lay governing body (e.g., Board of Elders)?	❑	❑	❑
E. Be a pastor who is not the senior pastor?	❑	❑	❑
F. Be the senior pastor?	❑	❑	❑

32. Theologically, which best describes your congregation?
❑ Fundamentalist ❑ Evangelical ❑ Moderate-mainline
❑ Theologically liberal ❑ Other: _____ ❑ Don't Know

33. Politically, which best describe how your congregational members vote?
❑ Mostly Republican ❑ More Republican than Democrat

❑ Equal mix ❑ Mostly Democrat
❑ More Democrat than Republican ❑ Don't know
❑ Other _____

IV. PROGRAMS AND FINANCING

34. Is tithing strongly encouraged in your congregation? ❑ Yes ❑ No
❑ Don't know

35. What was your congregation's total annual budget for 1998 and 1999 —
including standard operating costs, salaries, money sent to your denomination or other religious organizations, and all other purposes?
    1998: $_____ 1999: $_____

36. Approximately what percentage of your 1999 annual operating budget
comes from member offerings? _____%

37. Has the congregation's total annual budget increased or decreased
from 5 years ago?
❑ Increased ❑ Remained the same ❑ Decreased ❑ Don't know

38. Which, if any, of the following has your congregation sponsored or supported (financially or with volunteers) *in the past year*? [For most congregations, only one or a few will be checked.]

❑ Spiritual or psychological counseling for members
❑ Food pantry or soup kitchen
❑ Prison ministry
❑ Counseling services hotline
❑ Day care or pre-school programs
❑ Tutoring/literacy programs
❑ English as a Second Language program
❑ Health programs/clinics/ education
❑ Other _____

❑ Providing cash assistance
❑ Clothing donations or thrift store
❑ Elderly, emergency or affordable housing
❑ Programs for migrants or immigrants
❑ Before or after school programs
❑ Organized social issue advocacy
❑ Employment counseling, placement or training
❑ Voter registration or voter education
❑ None

V. DEMOGRAPHICS

39. About how many persons—both adults and children—would you say
regularly participate in the religious life of your congregation—whether or
not they are officially members of your congregation? _____
    A. Number of *regularly participating* adults (18 and over) _____
    B. What percentage of the *regularly participating adults* are
    male? _____%

40. Which *best* describes the type of area in which your congregation's primary worship building is located?

Rural or open country ❏
Town or village of < 10,000 ❏
In a metropolitan area (or city if you are not in a metro area) of:
Less than 50,000 ❏
50,000–249,999 ❏
250,000–999,999 ❏
1 million to 2 million ❏
More than 2 million ❏

A. If in a metropolitan area (or city), is your building located:
Downtown ❏
In the inner city ❏
In another part of the major city ❏
In an older suburb around the city ❏
In a newer suburb around the city ❏

B. If in a metropolitan area (or city), is your building located:
In a residential area ❏
In a mixed residential & commercial/industrial area ❏
In a commercial or industrial area ❏

41. To the best of your ability, please check the economic group(s) that have the largest representation in your congregation's neighborhood or surrounding area. Please check no more than 2 boxes.
❏ Lower Class/Poor ❏ Working Class ❏ Middle Class
❏ Upper Middle Class ❏ Upper Class

42. On average, would you say that the people in your congregation are poorer, wealthier, or have about the same income compared to residents of the surrounding neighborhood or area?
❏ Poorer ❏ Wealthier ❏ About the same ❏ Don't know

43. To the best of your ability, please check the racial group(s) that have the largest representation in your congregation's neighborhood or surrounding area. *For the groups you checked*, about what percentage of the surrounding area's people do they comprise?
❏ White, Not Hispanic _____% ❏ Black _____%
❏ Hispanic _____% ❏ Am. Indian _____%
❏ Asian/Pacific Islander _____% ❏ Other _____%

44. *At its founding*, what would you estimate was/were the racial background(s) of your congregation's members?
If not known, check here ❏ _____

45. In the *last 5 years*, has congregational attendance increased, decreased, or remained about the same?
❏ Increased ❏ Decreased ❏ Remained about the same

If you have a senior pastor, please answer questions 46–51. If not, skip to question 54. (If you have co-senior pastors, please ✔here ❏ and fill out based on the pastor who has served your congregation the longest.)

46. Age of the senior pastor:
    ❏ 21–30 ❏ 31–40 ❏ 41–50 ❏ 51–60 ❏ 61–70 ❏ 71–80 ❏ Over 80

47. Sex of the senior pastor ❏ Male ❏ Female

48. Race/ethnicity of the senior pastor (if more than 1 ethnicity, record each): _____

49. *If applicable*: Race/ethnicity of other clergy members (if more than one, summarize their ethnicities. For example, "all are white," or "3 Asians, 1 Hispanic"): _____

50. Is your senior pastor:
    ❏ Full time, paid   ❏ Part time, paid   ❏ Volunteer, unpaid
    ❏ Other

51. In what country was the senior pastor born?_____

52. In what country was the senior pastor educated mostly? _____

53. What is the senior pastor's level of formal education?
    ❏ High school graduation or less
    ❏ Two-year college degree, some college, or technical training
    ❏ Four-year college degree
    ❏ Some graduate education, but no degree
    ❏ Master's degree (including M.Div.)
    ❏ Doctoral degree (including D.Min and Th.D.)

54. Think about lay leaders who are in positions of responsibility in the congregation. What percentage of lay leaders fall into each of the following groups? If none of your leaders is in the category, write "N" for none.

Male . . . . _____	White, Not Hispanic . . . . _____
Over 50 . . . . . . _____	Hispanic . . . . _____
Black . . . . _____	Asian/Pacific Islander . . . . _____
Hispanic . . . . . _____	American Indian . . . . _____
Under 30 . . . . . _____	New Believers (last 5 years) . . . _____

55. Which racial group comprises *80% or more* of your congregation?
    ❏ American Indians/Native Americans [go to Question 56]
    ❏ Anglos/Whites [go to Question 57]
    ❏ Asians or Pacific Islanders [go to Question 58]
    ❏ Blacks/African Americans/Africans/Caribbean Black [go to Question 59]
    ❏ Hispanics/Latinos [go to Question 60]
    ❏ No one racial group comprises 80% or more [go to next page]

Answer only 1, based on your response to question 55:

56. Is there one main tribe or band (for example, Lakota, Hopi, Navajo) that comprises 80% or more of your congregation?
   ❏ Yes [go to Question 61] ❏ No [go to next page] ❏ Don't know [go to Question 61]

57. Is there any recent immigrant group (such as Russians) that comprises at least 20% but no more than 80% of your congregation?
   ❏ Yes (go to next page) ❏ No (go to Question 61) ❏ Don't know (go to Question 61)

58. Is there any ethnic group (for example, Korean, Chinese, Vietnamese) that comprises more than 80% of your congregation?
   ❏Yes (go to Question 61) ❏ No (go to next page) ❏ Don't know (go to Question 61)

59. Is there any recent immigrant group (such as Haitians) that comprises at least 20% but no more than 80% of your congregation?
   ❏Yes (go to next page) ❏ No (go to Question 61) ❏ Don't know (go to Question 61)

60. Is there any ethnic group (for example, Mexican, Cuban, Puerto Rican) that comprises more than 80% of your congregation?
   ❏Yes (go to Question 61) ❏ No (go to next page) ❏ Don't know (go to Question 61)

RESPONDENT INFORMATION

61. Your position within the congregation? _____
   Number of years you have been part of congregation _____

FOR MULTIRACIAL/ETHNIC CONGREGATIONS

Based on your response to the preceding questions, your congregation has been identified as a multiracial/ethnic congregation. By that term we mean any congregation where *no single racial or ethnic group makes up 80 percent or more of the congregation*. If this describes your congregation, please respond to the questions below.

62. Our congregation was:
   ❏ Multiracial/ethnic since its founding
   ❏ Multiracial/ethnic sometime after its founding
   ❏ Don't Know

63. For how many years has your congregation been multiracial/ethnic?
   _____ years   ❏ Don't know

64. Considering the *regularly participating adults* in your congregation, please list the two or three largest racial or ethnic groups

Group 1. _____ Approximate % of congregation _____
Group 2. _____ Approximate % of congregation _____
Group 3. _____ Approximate % of congregation _____

65. If the percentages above do not total 100%, what other racial or ethnic groups are also part of your congregation?

_____

66. For each of the 2 or 3 groups you listed in Question 64, what percent of that racial or ethnic group is in the following categories?

For example, the first category below is "Active leaders in your congregation." If the two groups you listed above were Mexicans (Group 1) and Koreans (Group 2), first estimate the percentage of Mexicans who are leaders in your congregation (perhaps 10% of all Mexicans in your congregation are involved in leadership), and then the percentage of Koreans who are leaders in your congregation (perhaps 5% of all Koreans in your congregation are involved in leadership).

You may not be able to answer all of these. For those you can't answer, please write "DK" for Don't Know.

	Group 1 %	Group 2 %	Group 3 %
A. Active leaders in your congregation	_____	_____	_____
B. Attended a year or less	_____	_____	_____
C. Female	_____	_____	_____
D. Live within 10 minutes commute to your location	_____	_____	_____
E. Over 60 years of age	_____	_____	_____
F. Born outside the U.S.	_____	_____	_____
G. College or university students	_____	_____	_____
H. College educated or more	_____	_____	_____
I. Participate in congregational activities outside of worship services (e.g., fellowship, Bible study)	_____	_____	_____

Please respond to questions 68–70 by *circling* the number that most accurately reflects your congregation *currently*.

67. Members of our congregation generally socialize within their own racial/ethnic group.

Very True		In Between		Very Untrue	
1	2	3	4	5	6	7

68. Being multiracial/ethnic is important to us.

	1	2	3	4	5	6	7

69. Being multiracial/ethnic is essential to our congregation's identity.

	1	2	3	4	5	6	7

70. Which of the following factors have led to your congregation being multiracial/ethnic? (Please ✔ all that apply)
- ❏ Just happened, people began showing up and staying
- ❏ Congregation moved to a new location in an attempt to become multiracial/ethnic
- ❏ Congregation moved to a new location for another reason
- ❏ Neighborhood became more racially or ethnically diverse
- ❏ Movement of God
- ❏ Existing clergy developed multiracial/ethnic vision
- ❏ New clergy came with multiracial/ethnic vision
- ❏ Lay leadership developed multiracial/ethnic vision
- ❏ Clergy urged congregation to make a deliberate effort
- ❏ Congregation members themselves decided to make a deliberate effort
- ❏ Part of the congregation's evangelism plan
- ❏ Part of the congregation's social outreach program
- ❏ Members married interracially/ethnically
- ❏ Friendship circles expanded multiracially/ethnically
- ❏ New student population
- ❏ Original members left church
- ❏ Changed worship styles
- ❏ Offered worship services in different languages
- ❏ Other:_____

Of those that you checked, write the letters corresponding to the top three factors, in order of importance:

Most Important	2nd Most Important	3rd Most Important
_____	_____	_____

71. [*Optional:*] We recognize that the above categories may not fully capture the real reasons you believe your congregation is multiracial/ethnic. Please feel to tell us in your own words in the space provided below:

If you hold more than 1 worship service on a typical weekend, answer Q72–Q73.

If not, please go to Q74.

72. Are each of your services racially or ethnically mixed, where "mixed" means roughly equal to the racial or ethnic makeup of your entire congregation? ❏ Yes ❏ No ❏ Don't know

73. [*If No*] Please estimate the percentages of each of the major racial/ethnic groups for each service.

Service 1 _____

Service 2 _____

Service 3 _____

Service 4 _____

74. For your congregation, please ✔ Yes or No for the following statements.

	Yes	No	Don't know
All of our worship services are held in the same building/on the same campus.	❏	❏	❏
All of our worship services share the same pastoral staff.	❏	❏	❏
All of our worship services are held under the same church name.	❏	❏	❏
Our cong. is composed of merged congregations that now form one cong.	❏	❏	❏
All services are held in the same language	❏	❏	❏
All worship services have a similar worship style.	❏	❏	❏
At least one of our worship services is multiracial (no more than 80% of any one racial/ethnic group).	❏	❏	❏

METRO INTERVIEW SCHEDULE, SUMMER 2000

Personal Background — Family, Upbringing, Religion

    1. Where did you grow up?

    2. Tell me about your upbringing and your family. [*probe for racial diversity of neighborhood — gently please*]

    3. Overall, did you have a good experience at school? Why or why not? [*probe for racial diversity of school*]

    4. Were most of your friends of your race?

    5. Did you grow up attending a church? [*probe for racial diversity of church*]

Immigration Issues [Ask only if either of interviewee's parent(s) is an immigrant]

    6. If either of your parents is an immigrant, from which country/ies did they come?

    7. Approximately what year(s) did the parent(s) come to the U.S. to live?

    8. About how old were they at the time?

    9. Growing up, did you ever speak a language other than English at home? If yes, which language? How well do you speak and read that language?

Broad Issues

    10. Is there anything that you see as uniting all Americans? Why?

    11. Is there anything that you see as dividing all Americans? What?

Networks and Friendships

> 12. Now think of your circle of friends. These are people that you like to do things with and have conversations with. They may be people that you see often, or, because they live far away, you may keep in touch with them by calling or writing. Estimate the percentage of your circle of friends that are of your race.

> 13. [*If answer to 12 is 80% or less*]: In our study so far, we have found that people in mixed-race churches are more likely to have friends and acquaintances of different races. We are interested in whether people who come to mixed-race churches had these friendships and social networks before they came to their present church or after. Which best captures your situation?

Issues Concerning Church

> 14. Tell me about your church.

> 15. [*Possible probes*] When did you join?
> > Why did you first come to this church?
> > Is this church very important to your life?
> > How often do you attend?
> > Do you do anything with people from your church outside of worshiping together?

> 16. What do you like about your church?

> 17. If you could change anything, what would you change about your church?

> 18. How much longer do you expect to stay at this church?

> 19. Are you involved in any church activities in addition to worship service/mass?

> 20. What do you think the purposes of a church should be?

Attitudes about Christians

> 21. What, if anything, do you find Christians doing today that you think they should not be doing?

> 22. What are Christians not doing that they should be doing?

Racial Attitudes

> 23.Do you think there is too much talk about racial issues in American today? Why?

> [*Possible probe*: "Have you ever given much thought to topics such as race, racism, racial conflict or racial cooperation? If so, what sorts of things have you thought about?"]

24. Some people say that we are better off if the races maintain their cultural uniqueness. Others say that we should create a common culture. Which one do you prefer, or do you prefer a combination? Why? If you prefer a combination, then what should we have in common and what should remain unique?

Children

25. Do you have any children? [*If not, skip to next section.*]

26. Where do your children go to school?

27. How did you decide on that school?

28. [*If private school*] What is the racial makeup of that school?

29. What sorts of things do you most want your children to learn from you?

Socioeconomic Status

30. Have there ever been years when your income dramatically increased?

31. If so, when did this occur, and why did your income increase?

[*If you need examples: they may have graduated from college, landed a high-paying job, or received a promotion*]

Political Attitudes

32. What are the most important political issues for you? Why?

Lifestyle

33. What would you like people to say about you at your funeral? In other words, how would you like to be remembered?

Bibliography

Alba, Richard, and Victor Nee. 2003. *Remaking the American Mainstream: Assimilation and Contemporary Immigration.* Cambridge, MA: Harvard University Press.

Aldrich, Howard. 1999. *Organizations Evolving.* Thousand Oaks, CA: Sage Publications.

Allen, Rt. Rev. Richard. 1983. *The Life Experience and Gospel Labors of the Rt. Rev. Richard Allen, to Which Is Annexed the Rise and Progress of the African Methodist Episcopal Church in the United States of America.* Nashville, TN: Abingdon Press.

Alumkal, Antony W. 2004. "American Evangelicalism in the Post-Civil Rights Era: A Racial Formation Theory Analysis." *Sociology of Religion* 65:195–213.

Ammerman, Nancy T. 2005. *Pillars of Faith.* Berkeley, CA: University of California Press.

Ammerman, Nancy T., and Arthur Farnsley II. 1997. *Congregation and Community.* New Brunswick, NJ: Rutgers University Press.

Anderson, David. 2004. *Multicultural Ministry: Finding Your Church's Unique Rhythm.* Grand Rapids, MI: Zondervan Publishing Company.

Asante, Molefi Kete. 1999. *The Painful Demise of Eurocentrism: An Afrocentric Response to Critics.* Trenton, NJ: Africa World Press.

___. 2003. *Erasing Racism: The Survival of the American Nation.* Amherst, NY: Prometheus Books.

Ayers, Edwards L. 1992. *Promise of the New South: Life after Reconstruction.* New York: Oxford University Press.

Barndt, Joseph. 1991. *Dismantling Racism: The Continuing Challenge to White America.* Minneapolis, MN: Augsburg.

Barry, Brian. 2001. *Culture and Equality: An Egalitarian Critique of Multiculturalism.* Cambridge, MA: Harvard University Press.

Beaman, Lori. 2003. "The Myth of Pluralism, Diversity, and Vigor: The Constitutional Privilege of Protestantism in the United States and Canada." *Journal for the Scientific Study of Religion* 42:311–25.

Becker, Penny Edgell. 1998. "Making Inclusive Communities: Congregations and the 'Problem' of Race." *Social Problems* 45:451–72.

___. 1999. *Congregations in Conflict: Cultural Models of Local Religious Life.* Cambridge: Cambridge University Press.

Bernard, William S. (ed.). 1971. *Americanization Studies: The Acculturation of Immigrant Groups into American Society.* Montclair, NJ: Patterson Smith.

Billig, M., and H. Tajfel. 1973. "Social Categorization and Similarity in Intergroup Behavior." *European Journal of Social Psychology* 3:27–52.

Blau, Peter M., and Joseph E. Schwartz. 1984. *Crosscutting Social Circles:*

Testing a Macrostructural Theory of Intergroup Relations. Orlando, FL: Academic Press.

Blum, Edward J. 2004. "The Soul of W.E.B. Du Bois." *Philosophia Africana* August.

___. 2005. *Reforging the White Republic: Race, Religion, and American Nationalism, 1865–1898*. Baton Rouge, LA: Louisiana State University Press.

Blum, Edward J., and W. Scott Poole. Forthcoming. *Vale of Tears: New Essays on Religion and Reconstruction. "'Oh God of Godless Land': Northern African American Challenges to White Christian Nationhood, 1865–1906."* Atlanta: Mercer University Press.

Bonilla-Silva, Eduardo. 2001. *White Supremacy and Racism in the Post-Civil Rights Era*. Boulder, CO: Lynne Reinner Publishers.

___. 2002. "We are all Americans! The Latin Americanization of Racial Stratification in the USA." *Race and Society* 5:3–16.

___. 2003. *Racism without Racists: Color Blind Racism and the Persistence of Racial Inequality in the United States*. Latham, MD: Rowman and Littlefield Publishers.

Boston, John. 2003. "At Long Last, Going to Church Finally Pays." Online [cited 7 August 2003]. Available from the http://www.the=signal.com/News/ViewStory.asp?storyID=2906.

Bourdieu, Pierre. 1983. "Ökonomisches Kapital, kulturelles Kapital, soziales Kapital." *Soziale Welt*, Supplement 2:183–98.

___. 1984. *Distinction: A Social Critique of the Judgment of Taste*. Translated by Richard Nice. Cambridge, MA: Harvard University Press.

___. 1985. In *Handbook of Theory and Research for the Sociology of Education*, edited by J. G. Richardson. New York: Greenwood.

Braddock, Jomills Henry. 1980. "The Perpetuation of Segregation across Levels of Education: A Behavioral Assessment of the Contact-Hypothesis." *Sociology of Education* 53:178–86.

Brundage, W. Fitzhugh. 1993. *Lynching in the New South: Georgia and Virginia, 1880–1930*. Urbana: University of Illinois Press.

Butler, Jon. 1990. *Awash in the Sea of Faith: Christianizing the American People*. Cambridge, MA: Harvard University Press.

Carmichael, Stokely. 1971. *Stokely Speaks: Black Power Back to Pan-Africanism*. New York: Random House.

Cavendish, J. C., M. Welch, and D. Leege. 1998. "Social Network Theory and Predictors of Religiosity for Black and White Catholics: Evidence for a 'Black Sacred Cosmos?'" *Journal for the Scientific Study of Religion* 37(3):397–410.

Chaves, Mark. 1997a. "Secularization: A Luhmannian Reflection." *Soziale System* 3:437–48, 1997.

___. 1997b. "The Symbolic Significance of Women's Ordination." *The Journal of Religion* 77:87–114.

___. 1999. The National Congregations Study. Machine-readable data file. Department of Sociology, University of Arizona, Tucson.

___. 2004. *Congregations in America*. Cambridge, MA: Harvard University Press.

Chaves, Mark, and James Cavendish. 1997. "Recent Changes in Women's Ordination Conflicts: The Effect of a Social Movement on Intraorganizational
Controversy." *Journal for the Scientific Study of Religion* 36:574–84.

Chaves, Mark, Mary Ellen Konieczny, Kraig Beyerlein, and Emily Barman.
1999. "The National Congregations Study: Background, Methods, and Selected Results." *Journal for the Scientific Study of Religion* 38:458–76.

Chidester, David. 1987. "Religious Studies as Political Practice." *Journal of
Theology for Southern Africa* 58:10–19.

Christerson, Brad, Korie Edwards, and Michael O. Emerson. 2005. *Against
All Odds: The Struggle for Racial Integration in Religious Organizations.*
New York: NYU Press.

Cleage, Albert B., Jr. 1972. *Black Christian Nationalism: New Directions for
the Black Church.* New York: William Morrow and Company, Inc.

Cnaan, Ram A. 1997. "Social and Community Involvement of Religious Congregations Housed in Historic Religious Properties: Findings from a Six-
City Study." Final Report to Panthers for Sacred Places, December 2.

Cnaan, Ram A., Stephanie C. Brody, Femida Handy, Gaynor Yancey, and
Richard Schneider. 2002. *The Invisible Caring Hand: American Congregations and the Provisions of Welfare.* New York: New York Press.

Coleman, James S. 1988. "Social Capital in the Creation of Human Capital."
American Journal of Sociology 94:95–121.

Cone, James H. 1970. *Liberation: A Black Theology of Liberation.* Philadelphia and New York: Lippincott Company.

———. 1991. *Martin and Malcolm and America: A Dream or a Nightmare?* Maryknoll, NY: Orbis Books.

Crèvecoeur, J. Hector St. John de. 1957 [1782]. *Letters from An American
Farmer.* New York: E. P. Dutton & Co., Inc.

Curtiss, J. E., E. D. Grabb, and D. E. Baer. 1992. "Voluntary Association Membership in Fifteen Counties: A Comparative Analysis." *American Sociological Review* 57:139–52.

Davies, Susan E., and Sister Paul Teresa Hennessee. 1998. *Ending Racism
in the Church.* Cleveland, OH: United Church Press.

Davis, James Hill. 1980. *Racial Transition in the Church.* Nashville, TN:
Abingdon Press.

DeYoung, Curtiss, Michael O. Emerson, George Yancey, and Karen Chai Kim.
2003. *United by Faith: The Multicultural Congregation as a Response to
the Problem of Race.* New York: Oxford University Press.

Doane, A. 1997. "White Identity and Race Relations." In *Perspectives on Current Social Problems*, edited by G. L. Carter. Boston, MA: Allyn and Bacon.

Dougherty, Kevin D., and Kimberly R. Huyser. Forthcoming. "Racially Diverse Congregations: A National Profile." *Journal for the Social Scientific
Study of Religion.*

Douglass, Frederick. 1964. *Frederick Douglass: Selections from His Writings.*
Edited by Philip S. Foner. New York: International Publishers.

———. 1968 [1855]. *My Bondage and My Freedom.* New York: Arno Press.

Dray, Philip. 2003. *At the Hands of Persons Unknown: The Lynching of Black
America.* New York: The Modern Library.

Du Bois, W.E.B. 1968. *The Autobiography of W.E.B. Du Bois: A Soliloquy on Viewing My Life from the Last Decade of Its First Century*. N.p.: International Publishers.

___. 2003 [1903]. *The Negro Church: Report of a Social Study Made under the Direction of Atlanta University; Together with the Proceedings of the Eighth Conference for the Study of the Negro Problems, Held at Atlanta University, May 26th, 1903*. Reprint, Walnut Creek, CA: Rowman & Littlefield Publishers, Inc.

___. 1996 [1899]. *The Philadelphia Negro: A Social Study*. Philadelphia: University of Pennsylvania Press.

Duster, Troy. 2001. "The 'Morphing' Properties of Whiteness." In *The Making and Unmaking of Whiteness*, edited by Birgit B. Rasmussen, Irene J. Nexica, Eric Klinenberg, and Matt Wray. Durham, NC: Duke University Press.

Dvorak, Katherine L. 1991. *An African-American Exodus: The Segregation of the Southern Churches*. New York: Carlson Publishing Inc.

Eck, Dianna L. 2001. *A New Religious America: How a "Christian Country" Has Now Become the World's Most Religiously Diverse Nation*. San Francisco: HarperSan Francisco.

Ecklund, Elaine Howard. 2004. *The "Good" American: Religion and Civic Life for Korean Americans*. Doctoral dissertation, Cornell University, Department of Sociology.

___. 2005. "Models of Civic Responsibility: Korean Americans in Congregations with Different Ethnic Compositions." *Journal for the Scientific Study of Religion* 44:15–28.

Edwards, Korie. 2004. *Beyond Segregation: Understanding How Interracial Churches Work*. Doctoral dissertation, University of Illinois at Chicago, Department of Sociology.

Embry, Jessie. 1994. *Black Saints in a White Church: Contemporary African American Mormons*. Salt Lake City, UT: Signature Books.

Emerson, Michael O. 1999–2000. Lilly Survey of Attitudes and Social Networks. Machine readable file, Rice University.

Emerson, Michael O., and Karen Chai Kim. 2003. "Multiracial Congregations: An Analysis of the Development and a Typology." *Journal for the Scientific Study of Religion* 42:217–27.

Emerson, Michael O., and Christian Smith. 2000. *Divided by Faith: Evangelical Religion and the Problem of Race in America*. New York: Oxford University Press.

Emerson, Ralph Waldo. 1909–14. *The Journals of Ralph Waldo Emerson*. Edited by Edward Waldo Emerson and Waldo Emerson Forbes. 10 vols. Boston: Houghton Mifflin.

Feagin, Joe R. 1968. "Black Catholics in the United States: An Exploratory Analysis." *Sociological Analysis* 29:186–92.

___. 1984. *Racial and Ethnic Relations*. Englewood Cliffs, NJ: Prentice-Hall.

___. 2000. *Racist America: Roots, Current Realities and Future Reparations*. NY: Routledge.

Feigelman, William, Bernard S. Gorman, and Joseph Varacalli. 1991. "The

Social Characteristics of Black Catholics." *Sociology and Social Research* 75:133–43.

Feld, Scott. 1981. "The Focused Organizations of Social Ties." *American Journal of Sociology* 86:1015–35.

———. 1982. "Social Structural Determinants of Similarity among Associates." *American Sociological Review* 47:797–801.

Findlay, James F., Jr. 1993. *Church People in the Struggle: The National Council of Churches and the Black Freedom Movement, 1950–1970.* New York: Oxford University.

Finke, R., and R. Stark. 1992. *Winners and Losers in our Religious Economy.* New Brunswick, NJ: Rutgers University Press.

Fong, Bruce W. 1996. *Racial Equality in the Church: A Critique of the Homogenous Units Principle in Light of a Practical Theology Perspective.* Lanham, MD: University Press of America.

Forman, Tyrone. 2004. "Color-Blind Racism and Racial Indifference: The Role of Racial Apathy in Facilitating Enduring Inequalities." In *Changing Terrain of Race and Ethnicity*, edited by M. Krysan and A. Lewis. New York: Russell Sage.

Foster, Charles R. 1997. *Embracing Diversity: Leadership in Multiracial Congregations.* Bethesda, MD: Alban Institute.

Foster, Charles R., and Theodore Brelsford. 1996. *We Are the Church Together: Cultural Diversity in Congregational Life.* Valley Forge, PA: Trinity Press.

Frey, Sylvia R., and Betty Wood. 1998. *Come Shouting to Zion: African American Protestantism in the American South and British Caribbean to 1830.* Chapel Hill: University of North Carolina Press.

Fuchs, Lawrence H. 1990. *The American Kaleidoscope: Race, Ethnicity and the Civic Culture.* Hanover, NH: Wesleyan University Press.

Gallagher, Charles A. 1997. "White Racial Formation: Into the Twenty-First Century." In *Critical White Studies: Looking beyond the Mirror*, edited by R. Delgado and J. Stefancic. Philadelphia: Temple University Press.

———. 2003. "Playing the White Ethnic Card: Using Ethnic Identity to Deny Contemporary Racism." In *Whiteout: The Continuing Significance of Racism*, edited by A. Doane and E. Bonilla-Silva. New York: Routledge.

Garvey, Marcus. 1969. *Philosophy and Opinions of Marcus Garvey.* Edited by Amy Jacques Garvey. New York: Arno Press/New York.

George, Douglas, and George Yancey. 2004. "Taking Stock of America's Attitudes on Cultural Diversity: An Analysis of Public Deliberation of Multiculturalism, Assimilation and Intermarriage." *Journal of Comparative Family Studies* 35:1–19.

Gilkes, Cheryl Townsend. 2001. *If It Wasn't for the Women.* Maryknoll, NY: Orbis Books.

Glazer, Nathan. 1997. *We Are All Multiculturalists Now.* Cambridge, MA: Harvard University Press.

Graetz, Robert S. 1998. *A White Preacher's Memoir: The Montgomery Bus Boycott.* Montgomery, AL: Black Belt Press.

Gratton, T. A. 1989. *Strategizing an Effective Ministry in an Urban, Evan-*

gelical, and Racially Integrated Southern Baptist Church. D. Min. dissertation, Eastern Baptist Theological Seminary.

Grettenburger, Susan and Peter Hovmand. 1997. "The Role of Churches in Human Services: United Methodist Churches in Michigan." Presented at the annual meeting of the Association for Research on Nonprofit Organizations and Voluntary Actions, Indianapolis, IN.

Hall, Edward T. 1977. *Beyond Culture*. New York: Anchor Books.

Hallinan, M. T., and R. A. Williams. 1987. "The Stability of Students' Interracial Friendships." *American Sociological Review* 52:653–64.

———. 1989. "Interracial Friendship Choices in Secondary Schools." *American Sociological Review* 54:67–78.

Hamilton, David L., and Tina K. Trolier, 1986. "Stereotype and Stereotyping: An Overview of the Cognitive Approach." In *Prejudice, Discrimination, and Racism*, eds. John F. Dovidio and Samuel L. Gaertner. Orlando, FL: Academic Press.

Hechter, Michael. 1987. *Principles of Social Solidarity*. Berkeley: University of California Press.

Hendriks, H. J. 1995. "Diversity and Pluralism in the Church: A Theory to Enhance Reconciliation and Unity." Unpublished paper presented at the annual meeting of the Religious Research Association.

Hewstone, Miles, Jos Jaspers, and Mansur Lalljee. 1982. "Social Representations, Social Attribution and Social Identity: The Intergroup Images of 'Public' and 'Comprehensive.'" *European Journal of Social Psychology* 12:241–69.

Heyrman, Christine Leigh. 1997. *Southern Cross: The Beginning of the Bible Belt*. Chapel Hill and London: University of North Carolina Press.

Higginbotham, Evelyn Brooks. 1993. *Righteous Discontent: The Women's Movement in the Black Baptist Church, 1880–1920*. Cambridge, MA: Harvard University Press.

Higham, John. 1984. *Send These to Me: Immigrants in Urban America*. Baltimore: Johns Hopkins University Press.

Hochschild, Jennifer L. 1995. *Facing up to the American Dream: Race, Class, and the Soul of the Nation*. Princeton, NJ: Princeton University Press.

Hodgkinson, Virginia A., and Murray S. Weitzman. 1993. *From Belief to Commitment: The Community Service Activities and Finances of Religious Congregations in the United States*. Washington, DC: Independent Sector.

Hogg, Michael. 1992. *The Social Psychology of Group Cohesiveness*. New York: New York University Press.

Hogg, Michael, and Dominic Abrams. 1988. *Social Identifications: A Social Psychology of Intergroup Relations and Group Processes*. London: Routledge.

Hollinger, David A. 1995. *Postethnic America: Beyond Multiculturalism*. New York: Basic Books.

Hughes, Robert. 1993. *Culture of Complaint: The Fraying of America*. New York: Oxford University Press.

Hunt, Larry L. 1978. "Black Catholicism and Occupational Status." *Social Science Quarterly* 58:657–70.

___. 1996. "Black Catholicism and Secular Status: Integration, Conversion, and Consolidation." *Social Science Quarterly* 77:842–59.

___. 1998. "Religious Affiliation among Blacks in the United States: Black Catholic Status Advantages Revisited." *Social Science Quarterly* 79:170–92.

Hunt, Larry L., and J. G. Hunt. 1976. "Black Catholicism and the Spirit of Weber." *The Sociological Quarterly* 17.

Jack, Homer A. 1947. "The Emergence of the Interracial Church." *Social Action* 13:1.

Jackman, Mary R. 1994. *The Velvet Glove: Paternalism and Conflict in Gender, Class, and Race Relations.* Berkeley: University of California Press.

Jackman, Mary R., and Marie Crane. 1986. "'Some of My Best Friends Are Black': Interracial Friendships and Whites' Racial Attitudes." *Public Opinion Quarterly* 50:459–86.

Jenkins, Kathleen. 2003. "Intimate Diversity: The Presentation of Multiculturalism and Multiracialism in a High-Boundary Religious Movement." *Journal for the Scientific Study of Religion* 42:393–409.

Kahn, Si. 1991. "Multiracial Organizations: Theory and Practice." *Liberal Education* 77:35–37.

Kallen, Horace M. 1915. "Democracy versus the Melting Pot." *The Nation*, Feb. 18, pp. 190–92, and Feb. 5, pp. 217–20.

Kanter, Rosebeth M. 1977. "Some Effects of Proportions on Group Life: Skewed Sex Ratios and Responses to Token Women." *American Journal of Sociology* 82:965–91.

King, Martin Luther, Jr. 1964. *Why We Can't Wait.* New York: Penguin Books.

Kleugel, James R. 1990. "Trends in Whites' Explanations of the Black-White Gap in Socioeconomic Status, 1977–1989." *American Sociological Review* 55:512–25.

Kluckhohn, Florence R., and Fred L. Strodbeck. 1961. *Variations in Value Orientations.* Evanston, IL: Row and Peterson.

K'Meyer, Tracy Elain. 1997. *Interracialism and Christian Community in the Postwar South: The Story of Koinonia Farm.* Charlottesville and London: University Press of Virginia.

Kniss, Fred. 1996. "Ideas and Symbols as Resources in Intrareligious Conflict: The Case of American Mennonites." *Sociology of Religion* 57:7–23.

Kochman, Thomas. 1981. *Black and White Styles in Conflict.* Chicago: University of Chicago Press.

Kujawa-Holbrook, Sheryl A. 2002. *A House of Prayer for All Peoples: Congregations Building Multiracial Community.* Bethesda, MD: The Alban Institute.

Law, Eric H. F. 1993. *The Wolf Shall Dwell with the Lamb: A Spirituality for Leadership in a Multicultural Community.* St. Louis: Chalice Press.

___. 2000. *Inclusion: Making Room for Grace.* St. Louis: Chalice Press.

___. 2002. *Sacred Acts, Holy Change: Faithful Diversity and Practical Transformation.* St. Louis: Chalice Press.

Lecky, R. S., and H. E. Wrights (eds.). 1969. *Black Manifesto: Religion, Racism, and Reparations.* New York: Sheed and Ward.

Lewis, Amanda E. 2004. "'What Group?' Studying Whites and Whiteness in the Era of 'Color-Blindness.'" *Sociological Theory* 22:623–46.

Lieberson, Stanley, and Kelly S. Mikelson. 1995. "Distinctive African American Names: An Experimental, Historical, and Linguistic Analysis of Innovation." *American Sociological Review* 60:6.

Lifton, Robert Jay. 1993. *The Protean Self: Human Resilience in an Age of Fragmentation*. New York: Basic Books.

Lipset, Seymour. 1990. *Continental Divide: The Values and Institutions of the United States and Canada*. New York: Routledge.

Lischer, Richard. 1995. *The Preacher King: Martin Luther King, Jr. and the Word That Moved America*. New York: Oxford University Press.

Loescher, Frank S. 1948. *The Protestant Church and the Negro: A Pattern of Segregation*. New York: Association Press.

Mangione, Thomas. 1995. *Mail Surveys: Improving the Quality*. Thousand Oaks, CA: Sage Publications.

Marti, Gerardo. 2005. *A Mosaic of Believers: Diversity and Religious Innovation in a Multi-Ethnic Church*. Bloomington: Indiana University Press.

Martin, William 1991. *A Prophet with Honor: The Billy Graham Story*. New York: William Morrow and Company.

___. 1996. *With God on Our Side: The Rise of the Religious Right in America*. New York: Broadway Books.

Mathews, Donald G. 1977. *Religion in the Old South*. Chicago and London: University of Chicago Press.

McPartland, James M., and Jomills Henry Braddock. 1981. "Going to College and Getting a Good Job: The Impact of Desegregation." In *Effective School Desegregation: Equity, Quality, and Feasibility*, ed. by Willis Hawley, Beverly Hills, CA: Sage Publications.

Miller, John. 1998. *The Unmaking of Americans: How Multiculturalism Has Undermined America's Assimilation Ethic*. New York: Free Press.

Moody, James. 2001. "Race, School Integration, and Friendship: Segregation in America." *American Journal of Sociology* 107: 679–716.

Morris, Aldon D. 1984. *The Origins of the Civil Rights Movement: Black Communities Organizing for Change*. New York: The Free Press.

Moskos, Charles C., and John S. Butler, 1996. *All That We Can Be: Black Leadership and Racial Integration the Army Way*. New York: Basic Books.

Naylor, Larry L. 1999. "Introduction to American Cultural Diversity: Unresolved Questions, Issues, and Problems." In *Problems and Issues of Diversity in the United States*, edited by Larry L. Naylor. Westport, CT: Bergin and Garvey.

Nelson, Hart M., and Lynda Dickson. 1972. "Attitudes of Black Catholics and Protestants: Evidence for Religious Identity." *Sociological Analysis* 33: 152–65.

Novak, Michael. 1971. *Unmeltable Ethnics*. New York: Macmillan Publishing Company.

Oldfield, J. R. (ed.). 1995. *Civilization and Black Progress: Selected Writings of Alexander Crummell on the South*. Charlottesville and London: University Press of Virginia.

Olson, Ted. 2004. "Fred Caldwell: Paying the Price for Unity." *Today's Christian*, July/August, 2004.

Ortiz, Manuel. 1996. *One New People: Models for Developing a Multiethnic Church*. Downer's Grove, IL: InterVarsity Press.

Parker, Alan. 2005. *Towards Heterogeneous Faith Communities: Understanding Transitional Processes in Seventh-Day Adventist Churches in South Africa*. Ph.D. dissertation, University of Stellenbosch.

Paxton, Pamela. 1999. "Is Social Capital Declining in the United States? A Multiple Indicator Assessment." *American Journal of Sociology* 105:88–127.

Peart, Norman A. 2000. *Separate No More: Understanding and Developing Racial Reconciliation in Your Church*. Grand Rapids, MI: Baker Books.

Perry, Dwight (ed.). 2002. *Building Unity in the Church of the New Millennium*. Chicago: Moody Publishers.

Pettigrew, Thomas F. 1975. "The Racial Integration of the Schools." In *Racial Discrimination in the United States*, edited by Thomas F. Pettigrew. New York: Harper & Row.

Pettigrew, Thomas F., and Joanne Martin. 1987. "Shaping the Organizational Context for Black American Inclusion." *Journal of Social Issues* 43:41–78.

Pocock, Michael, and Joseph Henriques. 2002. *Cultural Change and Your Church: Helping Your Church Thrive in a Diverse Society*. Grand Rapids, MI: Baker Books.

Pope, Liston. 1947a. "Caste in the Church: I. The Protestan Experience." *Survey Graphic*, no. 1, January.

———. 1947b. "A Check List of Procedures for Racial Integration." *Social Action* 13:1, January.

Portes, Alejandro. 1998. "Social Capital: Its Origins and Applications in Modern Sociology." *Annual Review of Sociology* 24:1–24.

———. 2000. "The Two Meanings of Social Capital." *Sociological Forum* 15:1–12.

Portes, Alejandro, and Rubén G. Rumbaut. 2001. *Legacies: The Story of the Immigrant Second Generation*. Berkeley and New York: University of California Press and Russell Sage.

Putnam, Robert. 2000. *Bowling Alone: The Collapse and Revival of American Community*. New York: Simon and Schuster.

Raboteau, Albert J. 1978. *Slave Religion: The "Invisible Institution" in the Antebellum South*. Oxford: Oxford University Press.

Ravitch, Diane. 1974. *The Great School Wars, New York City 1805–1973: A History of Public Schools as a Battlefield of Social Change*. New York: Basic Books.

Rhodes, Stephen A. 1998. *Where the Nations Meet: The Church in a Multicultural World*. Downers Grove, IL: InterVarsity Press.

Sagar, H., and J. Schofield. 1980. "Racial and Behavioral Cues in Black and White Children's Perceptions of Ambiguously Aggressive Acts." *Journal of Personality & Social Psychology* 39:590–98.

Schlesinger, Arthur M. 1992. *The Disuniting of America: Reflections on a Multicultural Society*. W. W. Norton & Company.

Schmidt, Alvin J. 1997. *The Menace of Multiculturalism: Trojan Horse in America*. Westport, CT: Praeger Publisher.

Shaw, Albert. 1924. *Messages and Papers of Woodrow Wilson*. Vol. 1. New York: The Review of Reviews Corporation.

Sigelman, Lee, Timothy Bledsoe, Susan Welch, and Michael W. Combs. 1996. "Making Contact? Black-White Social Interaction in an Urban Setting." *American Journal of Sociology* 101:1306–32.

Silverman, William. 2000. "The Exclusion of Clergy from Political Office in American States: An Oddity in Church-State Relations." *Sociology of Religion*, June 22.

Smith, Kenneth L., and Ira G. Zepp, Jr. 1998. *Search for the Beloved Community: The Thinking of Martin Luther King, Jr.* Valley Forge, PA: Judson Press.

Tajfel, H. 1978. *Differentiation between Social Groups*. London and New York: Academic Press.

Takaki, Ronald T. 2000. *Iron Cages: Race and Culture in Nineteenth Century America*. New York: Oxford University Press.

Taylor, D. M., and V. Jaggi. 1974. "Ethnocentrism and Causal Attribution in a South Indian Context." *Journal of Cross-Cultural Psychology* 5:2, 162–71.

Tocqueville, Alexis de. 2000 [1835]. *Democracy in America*. Translated, edited, and with an introduction by Harvey C. Mansfield and Debra Winthrop. Chicago, IL: University of Chicago Press.

Turner, V., and E.L.B. Turner. 1978. *Image and Pilgrimage in Christian Culture: Anthropological Perspectives*. New York: Columbia University Press.

Veroff, Joseph, Elizabeth Douvan, and Richard A. Kulka. 1981. *Mental Health in America*. New York: Basic Books.

Wacker, Grant. 2001. *Heaven Below: Early Pentecostals and American Culture*. Cambridge, MA: Harvard University Press.

Wagner, C. Peter. 1979. *Our Kind of People: The Ethical Dimensions of Church Growth in America*. Atlanta, GA: John Knox Press.

Warner, R. Stephen. 1988. *New Wine in Old Wineskins: Evangelicals and Liberals in a Small-Town Church*. Berkeley: University of California Press.

———. 1994. "The Place of the Congregation in the American Religious Configuration." In *American Congregations*, Vol. 2, edited by James Wind and James Lewis. Chicago: University of Chicago Press.

———. 1997. "Religion, Boundaries, and Bridges." *Sociology of Religion* 58: 217–38.

———. 2004. "Coming to America: Immigrants and the Faith They Bring." *Christian Century* (Feb. 10):20–23.

Washington, Booker T., and W.E.B. Du Bois. 1907. *The Negro in the South: His Economic Progress in Relation to His Moral and Religious Development*. Philadelphia: George W. Jacobs and Company.

Wellman, David. 1993. *Portraits of White Racism*. New York: Cambridge University Press.

Wentzel, Fred D. 1948. *Epistle to White Christians*. Philadelphia and St. Louis: The Christian Education Press.

White, Willie. 1974. "Separate unto God." *Christian Century*, February 13.

Wilder, D. A. 1981. "Perceiving Persons as a Group: Categorization and Intergroup Relations." In *Cognitive Processes in Stereotyping and Intergroup Behavior*, edited by D. L. Hamilton. Hillsdale, NJ: Erlbaum.

Woodley, Randy. 2001. *Living in Color*. Grand Rapids, MI: Chosen Books.

Wrong, Dennis. 1979. *Power: Its Forms, Bases and Uses*. New York: Harper and Row.

Wuthnow, Robert. 1988. *The Restructuring of American Religion: Society and Faith since World War II*. Princeton, NJ: Princeton University Press.

___. 1995. *Learning to Care: Elementary Kindness in an Age of Indifference*. New York: Oxford University Press.

Wuthnow, Robert, and John H. Evans. 2002. *The Quiet Hand of God: Faith-Based Activism and the Public Role of Mainline Protestantism*. Berkeley: University of California Press.

Yancey, George. 1999. "An Examination of Effects of Residential and Church Integration upon Racial Attitudes of Whites." *Sociological Perspectives* 42:279–304.

___. 2003a. *One Body, One Spirit: Principles of Successful Multiracial Churches*. Downers Grove, IL: InterVarsity Press.

___. 2003b. *Who Is White? Latinos, Asians, and the New Black/Nonblack Divide*. Boulder, CO: Lynne Reinner.

Yancey, George, and Michael O. Emerson. 2003. "Intracongregational Church Conflict: A Comparison of Monoracial and Multiracial Churches." *Research in the Social Scientific Study of Religion* 14:113–28.

Zangwill, Israel. 1910. *The Melting Pot: Drama in Four Acts*. New York: The Macmillan Company.

Zhou, Min, and Carl L. Bankston III. 1998. *Growing Up American: The Adaptation of Vietnamese Adolescents in the United States*. New York: Russell Sage Foundation.

Index